KILLER IN THE KREMLIN

Also by John Sweeney

NON-FICTION

The Life and Evil Times of Nicolae Ceausescu
Trading with the Enemy: Britain's Arming of Iraq
Purple Homicide: Fear and Loathing on Knutsford Heath
Rooney's Gold
Big Daddy: Lukashenka – Tyrant of Belarus
The Church of Fear: Inside the Weird World of Scientology
North Korea Undercover: Inside the World's Most Secret State
Murder on the Malta Express: Who Killed Daphne Caruana Galizia? (with Carlo Bonini and Manuel Delia)

FICTION

Elephant Moon
Cold
Road
The Useful Idiot

KILLER IN THE KREMLIN

The Explosive Account of Putin's Reign of Terror

John Sweeney

PENGUIN BOOKS

TRANSWORLD PUBLISHERS
Penguin Random House, One Embassy Gardens,
8 Viaduct Gardens, London SW11 7BW
www.penguin.co.uk

Transworld is part of the Penguin Random House group of companies
whose addresses can be found at global.penguinrandomhouse.com

First published in Great Britain in 2022 by Bantam Press
an imprint of Transworld Publishers
Penguin paperback edition published 2023

A CIP catalogue record for this book
is available from the British Library.

ISBN
9781804991206

Typeset in Bembo Std by Jouve (UK), Milton Keynes.
Printed and bound in Great Britain by Clays Ltd, Elcograf S.p.A.

The authorized representative in the EEA is Penguin Random House Ireland,
Morrison Chambers, 32 Nassau Street, Dublin D02 YH68.

Penguin Random House is committed to a sustainable future
for our business, our readers and our planet. This book is made
from Forest Stewardship Council® certified paper.

To Liza Kozlenko, Vlad Demchenko and Semyon Gluzman

CONTENTS

Chapter One

The Killing Machine

Some idiot is moving heavy furniture around in the flat above and I wake up with a start. I'm about to give Lambeth Council a ring to get them to sort him out when I remember I am in Kyiv and it's four o'clock in the morning, and it's not tables and chairs that are going bang but Russian artillery.

The idiot is Vladimir Putin and his idiot war is two days old.

I grunt, fall asleep again, get up and go out, try to buy some loo roll, fail. In front of me in the shop are an old geezer and a housewife. The old guy buys ten packets of the same cigarettes and nothing else, his unique vice on vulgar display to the world. The housewife snaps up every saveloy in the shop, anxiety buying on a comic scale. It is funny but it's not amusing.

The walk from my Airbnb near the Olympic stadium to the centre of town takes half an hour. Khreshchatyk, the great street of the Ukrainian capital, has the flavour of a neo-Stalinist take on Bath's great Georgian Crescent with extra vodka shots. It's so wide you could drive three tanks abreast down it. This is Putin's plan. Halfway along I start chuntering into my phone camera when a tough-looking dude with a very pukkah British accent points out that I am walking past the town hall and that is not a good place to be today. I explain to my fellow Brit that the Russians are not going to hit the town hall today – that's for later – and move on smartly. By the time I get to the Post Office building a great curl of sound walls up in front of me like a monster wave at sea. It's the air-raid siren, going off big time, warning of incoming Russian artillery or missile fire. The noise is obscene.

They call it Putin's lullaby.

I record a little piece to camera into my phone and tweet it as the sirens wail: 'I'm worried about Roman Abramovich's yacht. I do hope it's ok.'

Someone on Twitter replies: 'Sink the yacht.'

Up through Maidan Square to the rented flat of my pal, Oz Katerji, a British-Lebanese reporter who is half my age. Oz offers me a cuppa of Earl Grey. We sip our tea like the English milords we might be in some parallel universe and through the window we hear a big crump of artillery. It's not close but this is never a good sound.

Crump. Vladimir Putin takes me back to revising for A-level English in 1976 and Wilfred Owen's great poem, 'Anthem for Doomed Youth': 'Only the monstrous anger of the guns . . .'

Both Oz and I are freelance, hoping to scratch a living by doing two-way interviews with radio stations BBC Northern Ireland, Scotland, LBC and RTE in Dublin. Each hit doesn't earn much but after a run you can buy a kebab or two.

We faff about for a bit trying and failing to get a cab or someone to drive us towards the war. Nothing doing. Anyone with a vehicle is driving their loved ones to the train station, to get them out. We take the Metro. You see anxiety scribbled on people's faces, a mum slapping her kid doing no wrong, an old lady mystified while her daughter barks into her phone, tough men in combat uniform surging in and out of the tube carriages as if there is a war on. Which, of course, there is.

We get out at the Arsenal stop, the deepest underground station in the world. It is built into the side of the cliff that makes Kyiv a natural citadel, one where the Rus civilization was founded a thousand years ago. Moscow was, is and always will be the branch office. Out of the carriage, we are hit by a tide of human misery. It feels like walking along a tube platform during the London Blitz in 1940. Hiding from Russian bombs in February 2022 are an old couple, fast asleep; an old woman, surrounded by shopping bags full of stuff, the muscles on her face twitching uncontrollably; two sweet kids transfixed by a film on their phone, a silly dog at their feet.

Damn you, Vladimir Putin.

We ride the escalator out, walk to the west bank of the River Dnipro, edging north. The Russian Army is rumoured to be up ahead. I have to stop to talk to Jeremy Vine for his BBC Radio Two show – he's middle England but a vital conveyor to ordinary people – and Oz moves on. That's the last I see of him, this day. As I walk along I film myself and in the distance capture a couple of Ukrainian soldiers hovering near the Triumphal Arch to the Friendship Between the Russian and Ukrainian Peoples – no irony here, folks. A soldier shouts at me to stop filming. I put my camera down, walk on another hundred yards and start filming some more.

Fool, Sweeney, fool.

A young Ukrainian with a rifle starts shouting at me in Russian. Kyiv is a majority Russian-speaking city. He is not dressed in full camo but sports plain green trousers. Other guys wave guns in my general direction.

Mr Green Trews wants my phone, to see the videos I have taken.

'Do I look like a Russian spy?' I'm wearing an orange beanie, a camel-coloured duffle coat as first worn by Trevor Howard playing Major Calloway in *The Third Man*, and a brown corduroy jacket with elbow patches. I look like an unemployed geography teacher from Dorking.

He demands my phone.

It's bonkers. 'Do I look like a Russian spy?' I'm yelling at him, and I can holler. If you doubt that, ask a member of the Church of Scientology.

The guns are no longer waving in my general direction. They are pointing at me.

I hand over my phone, passport and NUJ press card and, with my hands in the air, they walk me to their base. A steel door closes behind me. No one has seen me enter it; no one has seen my arrest. I am in trouble.

We're in a pumping station that keeps half of Kyiv supplied with fresh water. It smells of old ironmongery, properly oiled.

Someone makes a phone call to Ukrainian intelligence, the SBU, the Sluzhba Bezpeky Ukrayiny. I keep on saying, look at my Twitter banner.

Green Trews whistles up his commander and his second-in-command, who are the real thing, fully attired in Ukrainian Army uniform. The boss is a big man, bigger than me and I'm no petit four. The deputy is smaller but sharp. He eyes me up with amused irony. I suspect that he knows I'm no threat. The two men remind me of Captain Mainwaring and Sergeant Wilson from *Dad's Army*. But the boss scowls at me and says 'Russkiy shpion'. I did Russian at school and have forgotten nigh on all of it but I can work out 'Russian spy'. At this, I sit down and start laughing uncontrollably.

The Russian spy does not seem suitably afraid. The mood changes. Green Trews googles me and, about bloody time, sees the photo on my Twitter banner, of me challenging Putin to his face. In July 2014 a Russian BUK missile fired from pro-Kremlin eastern Ukraine killed everyone on board Malaysia Airlines flight MH17. I got to doorstep the President of Russia in Siberia and ask him about the killings in Ukraine.

Green Trews finds the photo in which Donald Trump is standing over me, seeking to shake my hand to signal the end of our 2013 interview, but I remain seated, with palm upheld. My question was: 'Mr Trump, why did you buy your concrete from Fat Tony Salerno?'

Of the two of us in the photo, one may be a Russian spy but it's not me.

An old grannie appears with a cup of tea for the prisoner. Green Trews then becomes my champion. He introduces himself as Vlad Demchenko, a sweet and bright film-maker who tells me he made a documentary about the Battle for Donetsk airport in 2014. In a previous existence, before the war, he went travelling. Like you do. His English is pretty good and we are getting on well, but the call has been made to the SBU so I am locked inside military bureaucracy, trying to prove my innocence of the worst charge possible. It's like fighting a charge of treason in a foreign language with people armed with guns. We get into a big brown pick-up truck, the commander at the wheel, his 2IC riding shotgun and Vlad and I in the back. Checkpoints are going up across town, soldiers with guns running to and fro, the sirens wailing continuously. The crumps are getting closer. We park on a side road next to the SBU HQ and sit there. And sit. And sit.

Vlad whispers to me: 'I think they're getting a bit paranoid.'

Welcome to my world, I say to myself, but not out loud.

It strikes me that the headquarters of Ukrainian intelligence is the second-best Russian cruise missile target in town, after the Presidency.

Eventually, a window blind shuffles open and something is said.

Three Ukrainian soldiers appear and take custody of me. I say my goodbyes to the commander, the deputy and Vlad, and we march up the street, around the top of the SBU HQ and down a bigger street up to the main entrance.

And then we wait. There is a heavy turnstile with an electronic control. But no one can move until the lead soldier makes a phone call. And he can't get through. I become aware that there are a number of machine guns pointed in our specific direction.

Finally, the other party picks up and I am shuffled through the turnstile into the lobby. There are sandbags everywhere; soldiers with automatic rifles, red-eyed, as if they haven't had a good night's sleep for a week – which would go for most people in Ukraine. A tall, stern man takes my passport and press card off a soldier and leads me up a staircase, past soldiers half-dead with sleep sitting on the steps like some Pre-Raphaelite painting of a scene from Tennyson's 'Morte d'Arthur'.

The stern guy takes me to his office, the windows criss-crossed with thick yellow tape to reduce glass splintering should the SBU get shelled. If it gets hit by a cruise missile, we're all fried. There are three or four more soldiers, sitting in office chairs, exhausted. He studies my passport and press card; then looks through the images on my phone. I've been in Kyiv since 14 February. Some Valentine's Day.

'These videos of Ukrainian soldiers. They must be deleted.'

I do so and apologize for wasting his time. Then I add: 'But I am not a Russian spy.'

'You are free to go. Don't film the Ukrainian Army again.'

Roger that.

Outside the SBU, dusk is gathering. I march swiftly along and there's the pick-up that brought me here, parked by the side of the road, the only person inside the commander at the wheel, on the phone. I tap on the window and give him the thumbs-up, to show that I had been freed. He looks up, scowls at me, and I hurry on.

More than a month later Vlad texts me: 'I didn't tell you before but of the people who were in the car that took you to SBU the day when I arrested you, only me and you are still alive, John. The other two disappeared after an operation here on a front line.'

Vlad goes out looking for the commander and the deputy, so that they can be properly buried. He texts me with an update: 'We didn't find their bodies. So they are captured alive or they are buried at unknown place. I don't know which option is better.'

And he sends me a photo of the burnt-out pick-up, a charred metal skeleton sitting in a wood somewhere in the Badlands, north of Kyiv.

Back in my flat, I record a film on Twitter from my Airbnb, telling people about my rough old day, taking a stiff slug of gin with borderline tonic as I talk about being arrested, then freed. I end by pointing out the electricity and the internet are still on, and that makes me think that the man in serious trouble is not President Zelenskiy or even me but Vladimir Putin.

That Twitter film gets one million views.

The days blur. Chou-Chou the clown is good, better than anyone could expect as her audience is twenty or so kids and their mums and dads who can never go far from their current home. It's the basement of the dialysis unit at Kyiv's Children's Hospital. If they leave the machines, they may die. If they stay, thanks to Vladimir Putin's war, they may die.

Chou-Chou, which means 'Crazy-Crazy', is a young woman in classic clown red nose, plaits, silly blouse and skirt. Her real name is Anastasia Kalyuha, and she is, of course, a refugee herself from Donetsk, where Putin first invaded Ukraine in 2014. One girl, aged twelve or thirteen, sits on a stretcher, her face, like all the other children in the basement, a sour yellow colour because of her kidney problems. But she is enough of a teenager to know that clowns are for the younger kids and the clown's patter is obviously silly. I tell Chou-Chou and the kid that I am from London. Chou-Chou offers me a bun, breakfast and tea in English.

The kid on the stretcher starts to smirk.

'What is your name?' I ask her.

'Elon,' she says or something like it.

'Elon Musk,' snaps Chou-Chou and at this, the idea that Mr Tesla might be here, both the yellow-faced kid and I start to snort with laughter. Chou-Chou is on a roll. I turn to her and say, on reflection rather too patronizingly like John Cleese to Manuel in *Fawlty Towers*: 'actually you're rather good'. Chou-Chou is, in fact, bloody amazing.

Next stretcher along lies Angelica, aged fourteen, who chats to me in her excellent schoolgirl English while two nurses plug her veins with medicine; a machine nearby beep-beeps; kids laugh. I tell Angelica that when she gets out of this, she will come to London, meet my granddaughter, and we will go see where the Queen lives. She gives me the thumbs-up. Courage under fire, grace under pressure: it's the Ukrainian way and behind my mask I am starting to tear up.

Chou-Chou has wriggled past me and is doing a routine involving a phone that is driving a small yellow-faced boy weak with laughter. His mates, yellow-faced girls and boys, snigger and even a mum, sitting on a stretcher, smiles along and waves to my phone camera.

I am a sixty-three-year-old war reporter. I have covered wars and madness in Rwanda, Burundi, apartheid South Africa, the Romanian revolution, former Yugoslavia, Iraq, Syria, Albania, Chechnya, Afghanistan and Zimbabwe. I have seen babies with hacked limbs and an old man with his eyes blown in by an artillery shell and people with their lungs sucked inside out and a man with his brain sliced with a machete – and there is nothing worse than watching kids smile in war, watching the aristocracy of the human soul. It makes me cry – and cry I do.

I get back to my rented flat in the centre of Kyiv and start grazing TikTok and Twitter, and I see a video of three Ukrainian farm boys towing an abandoned Russian gun by their motorbike side-car. I find myself laughing hysterically at these lads, the best warriors on earth.

Are they good enough to stop Putin's military machine from killing the dialysis kids in the basement? I don't know the answer to that, but I do know one thing and that is what makes me conquer my wholly rational fear, that keeps me staying on until my courage runs out, that keeps me reporting from Kyiv.

The Ukrainian fighters: can they stop Putin? I don't know. But, boy, they are going to try. And seeing that, and knowing the innocent lives they are trying to defend, they too are part of the aristocracy of the human soul that Vladimir Putin wants to destroy.

For the moment, evil is doing well.

The next morning I hitch-hike a ride to the TV Tower – remember I am freelance – and another bloke called Vlad picks me up in his wheezy little red Skoda. I appoint him my driver on the spot. We sail through the checkpoints, no big shots stop us as the screwed-up ball-bearings in one wheel howl in pain, and I get to the TV Tower complex before any other reporter. A fighter called Rost, sinister in hoodie and gun, shows me the blitzed TV Tower and transmitter control building and a huge hole in the masonry caused by a direct hit. Nearby, staining a light dusting of snow is a puddle of bright red blood where one of the workers has been killed.

'Fuck Putin,' says Rost.

'Fuck Putin,' I reply.

'What did you do before the war?' I ask.

'I was a hot-air balloon pilot,' says Rost and we both burst out laughing at the otherness of war.

Nearby, one Russian cruise missile has undershot, slicing through some trees at the Babi Yar shrine, a monument to the worst single mass murder by shooting of the Holocaust in which nearly 34,000 Jews from Kyiv were executed by the Nazis and Ukrainian collaborators. Putin says that the government of Ukraine is neo-Nazi. The president is Jewish; the Russians attacked Babi Yar. For the avoidance of any doubt, it's not the Ukrainians who are behaving like the Nazis in this war.

Rost leads me outside the complex and across the street, where one of the missiles has overshot its target and hit a row of shops, smoke still billowing out from the fires within. Bodies lie on the ground. The men from the morgue arrive and take blankets out of a dark green van. They drape them over the dead: an old man, a mother and her child. When the Kremlin says it is not targeting civilians, it's a lie. I know. I've seen the civilian victims of Russia's war with my own eyes. And I tweet as much.

Perhaps that's why in the middle of the night I get a report from Microsoft saying that I have been hacked and the hacker is based near or in the Kremlin. It's not exactly clear what's happened, it's also possible (and better) that it is a failed phishing attempt. But you know that just being here and making films for Twitter, and writing articles for whichever news outlet will run them, makes you a target of the Kremlin.

The Russian Army is not burying its dead. That causes low morale.

Low morale stems from the second big reason for failure, that Russia's high command does not give a tuppenny damn for its people. It only cares about money. It is corrupt.

Let's move on to the dog food. Russian soldiers eat the best possible nutritious rations of any military, so long as it's dog food. You can get a flavour of what's going wrong on the ground in Ukraine from a story Reuters ran a decade ago. The news agency reported ex-Major Igor Matveyev saying: 'It's embarrassing to say but soldiers here were fed dog food. It was fed to them as stew.' The tins of dog food were covered up with labels reading 'premium quality beef'.

The Ukrainians have found abandoned Russian Army vehicles with food rations listing 'eat by' dates from seven years ago. What is so gloriously funny about this scamming is that the man responsible is one of the Kremlin's favourite gangster cronies, Yevgeny Prigozhin, known as 'Putin's Chef'. Thick with Russian military intelligence, the GRU, Prigozhin, an ex-con in Soviet times, is suspected of funding troll farms and the murderous mercenary unit, the Wagner Group, named after Hitler's favourite composer. His empire has taken over 90 per cent of the business of supplying food to the Russian Army. The Ukrainians have released several videos of starving Russian soldiers scavenging for food. And that's down to Prigozhin and his boss.

The brilliant Russia watcher Christo Grozev is a sleuth for Bellingcat, investigative journalism that specializes in open-source intelligence. He has tweeted: 'While Russian soldiers are starving and breaking into Ukrainians' homes begging for bread, Prigozhin's "not for sale" military food rations have flooded Russia's Ebay-like sites at $3 a can.'

Corruption is killing Russia's killing machine.

And then there is bad leadership. Vladimir Putin launched a war without intelligence. He didn't look over on the other side of the wall and he didn't ask somebody what's on the other side. Or if he did, that person was afraid to tell him the truth, that Ukraine was going to fight. Bad leadership is the focus of Norman F. Dixon's classic, *On the Psychology of Military Incompetence.* Putin is a military incompetent, big time. That's because he is a weak authoritarian personality, because he is afraid of his own death – hence the long table for the sit-down with President Macron and even for senior Russian officials – because he is supremely paranoid.

Paranoia is destroying the Russian Army from within. Vladimir Putin is a prisoner in his own high castle, just like Stalin. His terror of revealing his hand too early, and it being leaked to the Americans, was so great that he kept back his true invasion plans for and from the army until the day before the invasion. So the Russian general staff have had to make up the war as they go along – and the result has been disastrous. Generals have been appointed on the basis of their fealty to the Kremlin, not their courage, not their competence. Servility is fine when an army is not fighting a difficult opponent. But General Uriah Heep isn't much cop against the Ukrainian Army.

Irina Borogan and Andrei Soldatov, two of the best watchers of the Russian psychodrama, suggest that Putin's paranoia is corroding trust inside the holy of holies, the Russian secret state (the FSB, formerly the KGB). They report that the head of the FSB's foreign intelligence service and its deputy are 'being held after allegations of misusing operational funds earmarked for subversive activities and for providing poor intelligence ahead of Russia's now-stuttering invasion'.

All three go straight back to the boss. Morale is poor because Putin doesn't care about his people or his soldiers; corruption is rife in his army because, as Alexei Navalny told me once, 'he is the tsar of corruption'; paranoia is what ex-KGB spies do instead of playing golf. His war is not going well and there is only one person to blame. No wonder the gossip in Moscow is that the FSB chiefs are selling their dachas in Crimea.

A few miles on from the roadside shrine to the Ukrainians killed in Stalin's Great Terror of 1937 – bleak metal crosses, a slab of granite, birch trees sliding into a dark past – lies the last Ukrainian Army checkpoint.

The last, at least, for us.

It's mid-March. As we get close, we are ordered back towards Brovary. Beyond the checkpoint, a week before, Russian tanks huddling towards Kyiv were blasted by the defenders to kingdom come. The site of the tank ambush lay ahead but a Ukrainian soldier is firm: 'Go back.'

To enforce his argument, a big crump sounds, outgoing, coming from the forest to our right. It is not close but it's not so far away. You learn to tell the difference between outgoing and incoming. Outgoing, there is one bang and the air pressure doesn't change. Incoming, there can be two bangs and you can feel it through your boots.

We get in the car, drive back a little bit, hang around in a picnic lay-by, listen to more crumps, see black smoke scribbling lazily against the cold blue sky. Every now and then an ambulance screams down the four-lane highway, heading for Kyiv.

A couple walk towards us, towards the war, and we have a brief chat. Vanya and Natasha are middle-aged, composed, purposeful. Before the war he traded in seafood, she grew cucumbers and salad.

'I'll have a smoked salmon sandwich with cucumber,' I venture.

Another crump from the woods to our right.

'I'm sorry, that's not available right now,' she says.

The Ukrainian sense of humour is a wonder to behold. Natasha is still stern.

'I'm going to give you a poor review,' I say.

She laughs too and, for a moment, the war is forgotten while we enjoy our joke, enjoy life. I'm working with Vlad the driver, who picked me up when I hitch-hiked to the TV Tower missile attack in Kyiv in the early days of the war, and Eugene, the world's worst translator. That is, of course, entirely untrue. Eugene is a star. Coming along for the laughs is Emile Ghessen, a film-maker from London who, in another life, was a sergeant in the Royal Marines. Iraq, Afghanistan.

Where are Vanya and Natasha going? 'Home, the next village along, a mile and a half away.'

'Is it in Russian hands?'

'No, ours.'

'And the next village, under Russian or Ukrainian control?'

'No one is sure.'

The Russians are close, maybe ten miles away, maybe less.

We drive back some more and stop at a gas station for a coffee on the east side of Brovary.

Denis, a thickset taxi driver, is helping a couple shift their stuff out of their war-damaged car into his vehicle. Most of the front of the car has gone – and how it got to the petrol station is one of those miracles of war. The man is grim-faced, silent; the woman wretched, crying. A phone rings and the woman starts a long phone conversation. While this happens Denis takes a drag on his cigarette and talks to us. (I didn't ask for his surname. If the Russian Army is in earshot it's bad manners to pester people for that kind of stuff.)

I'd heard reports that the Russian Army was not just stalled but here, on this, the eastern claw of its pincer attack on Kyiv, it was going backwards.

'Have the Russians moved?'

'No,' says Denis. 'They are staying in the same place, neither moving forwards or back.'

'How are they?'

'The villagers say that they are begging for food. They're so hungry, they come to the villagers and ask for something to eat. The villagers say they are not aggressive. Their commanders want them to fight, to be harsh, but they are too busy asking for scraps to eat.'

There's always a bar. In Kyiv, in March 2022, it's the Buena Vista Social Club, bang next to a Ukrainian police checkpoint, which is both funny ha-ha and funny peculiar because there is a nationwide ban on the sale of alcohol. Sssh. It's a joyful shebeen, Cuban-themed, run by Maks, and you never quite know what's available to drink and who's going to be there. All the women have a past; all the men have no future. You get the vibe.

Early on in the war, a fellow regular was a big bloke with a thick moustache and a mane of bubbly, curly hair, often seen with his female fixer, a Ukrainian freelancer. I never spoke to him but I clocked him as someone who had presence, who was an interesting character, who I had probably seen in Sarajevo or somewhere like that. In fact, he was a legendary cameraman, Pierre 'Zak' Zakrzewski, and she was Oleksandra 'Sasha' Kuvshynova. They were both killed on 14 March 2022 when their vehicle came under fire in Bucha – pronounced Butcher – twenty miles north-west of Kyiv. British journalist Ben Hall was wounded in the same attack. They were working for Fox News, something about which Zak, aged fifty-five, who had been brought up in Ireland, reportedly had mixed feelings. But he knew the risks of war too well and had made a decision that working for a big corporation was better risk-management than being freelance. His co-workers at Fox loved him, voting him an award as 'Unsung Hero' after he helped get Afghan freelancers out of Kabul.

Sasha was twenty-four, beautiful, bold and fiercely smart. After her death, her dad said that she learnt to read at the age of three and picked up English from reading restaurant menus while on family holidays. She was a fanatical photographer with five stills cameras, had founded a music festival for up-and-coming jazz musicians, worked as a DJ and wrote poetry. She wanted to make movies.

If you don't like free expression in a democracy, you blow up the TV Tower. The Kremlin's first journalist victim was Yevhenii Sakun, aged forty-nine, a camera operator for Ukraine's LIVE station. The Russian Army sent in two cruise missiles on the evening of 1 March, killing Sakun in the TV Tower complex along with four civilians. I saw with my own eyes the people from the morgue take away the bodies of a middle-aged man and a mother and her child.

The most dangerous area of Kyiv is the north-west suburbs, where the Russian Army's offensive, driving down through Chernobyl, has come closest to the capital. Reporters seeking human stories, of refugees fleeing with their dogs on a lead or their cat in a box, went repeatedly to Irpin nineteen miles north-west of the capital. Fearing a further Russian advance, the Ukrainian Army flooded the river plains near the suburb and blew up the most southerly bridge, leaving people to pick their way across the skeletal remains. Once beyond that crossing, there is a second bridge. That's where American film-maker Brent Renaud, aged fifty, originally from Little Rock, Arkansas, and formerly of *The New York Times*, found himself, filming refugees running for their lives. Brent knew what he was doing, having filmed and reported man's cruelty to man in Iraq, Afghanistan, Libya: all the nice places.

At Irpin, at the second bridge, some Russian soldiers shot him in the neck on 13 March. He died of his wounds.

Oksana Baulina was one of those intensely brave Russians who were on Team Navalny before their champion was arrested on fake charges in January 2021 and the organization broken up. Oksana, forty-three, was declared a 'terrorist' by the Kremlin and had to flee Russia. She set up as a reporter and film-maker in Poland and reported on the war. On 23 March, when Russian artillery smashed into a shopping centre in the north-west of the city of Podil, two miles from Kyiv, Oksana was killed.

A beautiful woman with russet hair and a courage that takes the breath away, when I think of her, Keats' line seems right: 'Beauty is truth, truth beauty – that is all / Ye know on earth, and all ye need to know.'

This is grim. But the good people in the Buena Vista are buoyed by the thought that we are in Ukraine exactly because Vladimir Putin does not want us to be here.

And the rum is good. My friend Oz Katerji once saw a great line of graffiti in Beirut that can work for every war reporter in every war: 'I don't believe in anything. I am just here for the violence.' That's one way of looking at it. The counter-argument is that the drinking, the dancing on the tables – the ceiling is pretty low and I have to crouch – is driven by love of life, not its negation.

There is, also, the line from Tom Stoppard's great play, *Night and Day*, which I quoted on Twitter while hurrying back from the bar just before – well, actually, just after – curfew had fallen. This, from memory, is how it goes: how the lover of the dead young journalist, played by Diana Rigg, killed on the front line, denounces the false romance of journalism, 'it's not worth the heartbreak beauty queen or the crossword and it's definitely not worth the leader'.

And the old hack, played by John Thaw, replies: 'Yes, you're right. But also the other thing. People do awful things to each other. But it's worse in places where everybody is kept in the dark. Information is light. Information, in itself, about anything, is light.'

RIP Zak, Sasha, Yevhenii, Brent and Oksana.

As the war drags on, I get digs in an attic overlooking the heart of the city, the Maidan, about six inches from the air-raid sirens on the roof of Kyiv's main post office. Every day the sirens go off pretty much inside my head. It's a hideous sound but in my new digs it is impossible to ignore. One day I pop up through the attic window, wearing my lucky orange beanie as flecks of snow sting my face, listen to Putin's lullaby droning out its horrible message of death to come, and record a simple message on my Android to my followers on Twitter: 'Vladimir Putin: Do Fuck Off.'

I sit down, pour myself a slug of Jameson whiskey – it's half past eight in the morning but to hell with it – and remember a half-forgotten line from the London Blitz in 1940. Harold Nicolson was a posh nob with common decency who wrote a diary, oftentimes depressed and miserable about Britain's prospects, but sometimes heroic. For too long, the British authorities did not want to fire their anti-aircraft guns lest our 'ack-ack' – the lovely slang for anti-aircraft gunnery – end up killing more Londoners on their way down, a grim fact of war, but eventually the risk management changed and the British guns opened fire. Nicolson recorded in his diary: 'We are conscious all the time that this is a moment in history. But it is very like falling down a mountain. One is aware of death and fate, but thinks mainly of catching hold of some jutting piece of rock. I have a sense of strain and unhappiness, but none of fear. One feels so proud.'

London, 1940. Kyiv, 2022. Same old, same old.

Four days before Putin starts his war of the body and the mind, I meet my old pal Semyon Gluzman who, at seventy-five, is still a crack-shot for the other side. In 1971 he was the first psychiatrist to open fire on the Soviet Union's weaponization of his branch of medicine to suppress dissent and he paid a heavy price for his courage. He did ten years in the Gulag in the Ural Mountains, near the city of Perm. He and his fellow zeks were pitifully clothed for the intense cold, which on one occasion dropped to 50 below zero. Semyon was a regular in the punishment cell, where it was cold to the bone: 'I didn't follow the rules of how we're supposed to behave. I didn't want to change my ways. I didn't want to fall in love with the KGB.'

The officers who ruled over them said ruefully: 'You have created a university for yourselves here', to which Semyon replied: 'But we didn't buy the tickets.'

I would like to thank the Church of Scientology for bringing us together. In 2016 I was invited to Lviv in western Ukraine by my favourite organization, whole planet, the Ukrainian Psychiatric Association, which Semyon heads, to talk to the country's shrinks about the dark nonsense spread by that space alien cult. Semyon and I hit it off. This time we talk for three hours straight in his book-lined flat off the Heroes of Stalingrad Street, in Obolon, in the north-west of Kyiv, one of a series of concrete boxes designed by the rulers of the Communist Party of the Soviet Union for others, but not of course themselves, to live in. But the mind within the concrete box soars, a thing of beauty.

The first hour is filmed by Oz Katerji. Then Semyon cracks open a bottle of cognac. With classic self-deprecation Semyon says he speaks 'pidgin English', so every now and then an interpreter steps in to convey complex nuance. If anyone claims to understand the mindset of a KGB officer like Putin better than Semyon 'Ten Years' Gluzman, I don't believe them.

Vladimir Putin is threatening war against Ukraine. Is he mad? The wrinkled face opposite me clouds. A stupid question. Still, he gives me an answer: 'No, he is not mad. He is very bad. I am certain he is totally healthy. He has a very peculiar personality. Not that of a KGB officer. He's different, sadistic, not thinking about other people, not even the Russian people, only himself. He has these predecessors like Hitler and Stalin. We can say they did bad things but that they didn't do them because a voice told them to do it. They were evildoers. They were sadistic people. But they weren't insane.'

Is there a problem with people like me thinking he's mad? 'As a psychiatrist I strongly dislike this question,' Semyon replies. 'I get asked it also by Ukrainian journalists. If we say that a person is insane, by doing that, we also distance this person from liability for their actions. This person is no longer responsible for what they do. They're just sick and they committed incredible evil because of voices inside their head or hallucinations. In this case, this person is evil, not because of voices inside his head, but because of his own actions.'

Angela Merkel's reflections on what goes on inside Putin's head interest Semyon: 'She said that the arguments she used did not resonate with Putin. He could understand them but he didn't let them in to his mind. It's easy to explain away Putin's specific personality from his experience, that he used to serve with the KGB. But, in fact, he wasn't a typical KGB officer, the kind who used to work with dissidents.' Semyon knew their type all too well. But also, while he was in the Gulag, he got to know three ex-KGB officers who had been locked up for political crimes too. Semyon studied the psychology of the KGB prisoners and the KGB guards, and when he was freed and returned to Kyiv, he got to know ex-KGB officers too. All this KGB face-time makes him conclude that, like everyone else, different KGB officers have different personalities. But Putin is a one-off.

Comparing Putin with Hitler makes me shudder a little because Hitler is in his own circle of hell, but my old friend is right, I think, with one qualification. Putin is a rational actor inside a bunker, so deep, so deprived of light and information, that he is pulling levers without understanding how the modern world is responding, without understanding that some of his levers at least are no longer working, without understanding that invading countries at peace is what the Nazis did.

So many dogs. Dozens of them, milling around under the feet of the Ukrainian soldiers, the few elderly civilians still left, the international press staring at the bare trees, the houses, charred black, the line of Russian tanks, burnt orange.

Sniffing around the fried tanks blocking Station Street (Vokzalna) in Bucha is a big daft Alsatian with a good, healthy coat. He starts following us around. I'm working with two Maltese and two Ukrainian journalists, Giuseppe Attard, Neil Camilleri, Alex Zakletsky and Liza Kozlenko. We film the broken Russian ironmongery. On the pavement, a Russian boot lies with a foot still inside it.

Liza kneels down and cuddles the Alsatian and I try to give him some water, but he backs off, terrified of men. Liza starts chatting with some Ukrainian soldiers, who tell us where to look. Halfway down Station Street we find the house, strangely intact, and go around the back, followed by the Alsatian and a little scruffy white terrier.

The first man in civilian clothes was shot in the back of the head. You can see an inky puddle of blood by his head. His skin is a greeny-blue. The second man, also in civilian clothes, also greeny-blue, was shot in the face at point-blank range. The hole where his forehead should be is the single most obscene thing I have ever seen with my own eyes.

The two men have been executed.

Then the most logical explanation for the fact that the Alsatian and the other dogs are running wild dawns on me. Their owners are dead.

Two locals arrive holding white plastic body bags with a zip-up front. They load each corpse into its body bag and zip them up. The sound of the zip kept on cutting into my sleep that night, like a buzz saw in a horror movie.

The line of dead Russian tanks on Station Street is proof that Vladimir Putin's war is going catastrophically to the bad. Fighting war from inside the last century, the Russian armoured assault on Kyiv was slowed down here in Bucha by drones, so very twenty-first century, and then stopped dead in Irpin, the next town along towards the capital. When the Kremlin decided that it was foolish to keep sending yet more of its boys to die here, the Russian Army hit reverse gear. And as they did so, they expressed their dismay at their wretched performance against proper soldiers by butchering innocent civilians in the hundreds. By the way, satellite imagery taken during the Russian occupation shows bodies on the streets before the Ukrainians recaptured Bucha. The Russian Army carried out these killings. Full stop.

At the centre of Bucha was a scene that we have been told would never happen again. But 'Never Again' feels a bitter, dark joke when you look at what lies in the death pit opposite the main Orthodox Church. There's a hand pointing upwards with flesh on it but the flesh has gone greeny-blue; here the body bags are black plastic.

Please note that this one is not a classic mass grave like Babi Yar, where the Nazi killers dug a hole in the ground, shot people next to it and then covered it up. This is a mass grave where under Russian Army occupation the dead were buried: a trickle of Ukrainian soldiers, at the start of the war; then a flood of innocent civilians, shot or shelled or otherwise killed by Vladimir Putin's war machine. It is said there are around 280 corpses in this mass grave; another forty dead, like the two we've just seen, littering the streets and backyards of Bucha.

Russia denies everything. Russia's ambassador to the United Nations, Vassily Nebenzia, has said that while Bucha was under Russian control, 'not a single local person has suffered from any violent action', adding that video footage of bodies in the streets was 'a crude forgery' staged by the Ukrainians. Russia's parliamentary Speaker, Vyacheslav Volodin, said Bucha was 'a provocation, with Washington and Brussels the screenwriters and directors, and Kyiv the actors'.

Overlooking the mass grave stood the local Orthodox priest, Father Andrii. You could read the shadow cast by the war in his pale, gaunt face: 'They dug the first pit on March 10th.'

'What do you say to the Kremlin line that you did this?'

His eyes look blankly at me. Don't talk rubbish.

At the crossroads at the start of Station Street I meet Rabbi Moshe Azman of the Central Synagogue in Kyiv. I've interviewed him before at his synagogue for one of the newspapers I'm freelancing for: the *Jewish Chronicle*. (I'm lapsed Catholic but no one seems to mind.) The rabbi tells me: 'First of all I knew what happened here before because I was here at the start of the war. We have a Jewish community here at Anatevka. We heard what happened here. But to see the war, the cars crushed by tanks, people shot by Russian soldiers. And many bodies. It's terrible and it's a war crime. The whole world just needs to stop at least Russian aggression. It's like World War II but different. What is the difference? Because the Wehrmacht came, after them, the SS. And SS, they killed people. But here, the regular Russian Army, they make war and they kill people. They murder people. The world has to stop the war. It's not only a Ukrainian problem. It's a problem for the whole of Europe. For the whole world.'

Down the road six members of the same family, the youngest a woman of twenty, all burnt. The photos my Ukrainian colleague Alex Zakletsky takes are too horrific to share.

Not far away a line of corpses was discovered with their arms tied behind their back. Survivors have explained what happened to *Vot Tak*, a Ukrainian website. The Russians arrived in Bucha on 2 March, said Vladislav Kozlovsky, an eyewitness to some of the executions. He explained that he was in Bucha, looking after his mum and granny, when shelling came down. He and his friends, all unarmed, took shelter in a basement. The Russians blasted the first door, so the people in the basement opened the second one to try and save themselves: 'the first days they treated us well, helped with food. But they were brainwashed by propaganda. Normal people do not come to a foreign land.'

As the war turned darker for the Russians, the early conduct went by the board: 'They would not let us out.

We were sitting in complete darkness. There was no light, water, or heat.' On 7 March the Russians made a selection, freeing the women and children but not the men: 'They made us kneel and started to "search" us. They took my watch and money. They tortured me and beat me over the head with the stock of a rifle. If anyone had fought for the Ukrainian Army in the war in the east of the country, in Donetsk and Luhansk, or were a soldier, they were shot. They shot them either in the back of the head or in the heart.'

'How many people in all were killed in your presence?'

'Eight, I think. I saw photos of their bodies yesterday behind a stone building.'

'How many of your acquaintances were killed during this time?'

'I don't divide people like that anymore, I feel sorry for everyone. An acquaintance of mine named Sergey Semyonov, who is about forty years old, decided to go with a friend through the glass factory to the city of Irpin. Their bodies were found a few days later. Sergey was killed with a shot to the back of the head. The other man was tortured. His face was cut, they finished him off with a shot to the heart. We buried them in the factory grounds.'

The prime suspects for many of the war crimes are Chechen fighters loyal to Putin's satrap, Ramzan Kadyrov. They're called the Kadyrovites, they sport long beards, wear black uniforms. The locals in Bucha could identify them by their accents. Please note: there are Chechens fighting on the Ukrainian side, too. Collective guilt is always wrong, and besides, I first saw evidence of Russian Army war crimes in Chechnya in 2000: the wanton killing of civilians; torture;

contempt for the rules of war. Bucha is Kremlin inhumanity on repeat.

Among the Russian Army were men from far-off Buratyia, in Siberia, Mongol soldiers who are mostly Buddhist. This is Vladimir Putin's war but a lot of his drone fodder don't come from swish apartments in Moscow.

The dark irony here is that Putin is accused of having used Chechen killers to do his dirty business for the past two decades. The assassinations of his critics, people like Anna Politkovskaya, Natasha Estemirova and Boris Nemtsov, may well have been the work of Kadyrovites. Now the Kremlin is faltering, stepping backwards as it faces mounting outrage from the West because its tame killers over-achieved in Bucha.

Ukraine's President, Volodymyr Zelenskiy, told the UN from Kyiv: 'There is not a single crime that they would not commit there. The Russians searched for and purposely killed anyone who served our country. They shot and killed women outside their houses. They killed entire families – adults and children – and they tried to burn the bodies . . . Civilians shot and killed in the back of the head after being tortured. Some of them were shot on the streets; others were thrown into the wells. So they died there in agony.'

What the Russians did in Bucha was no different, he said, from the conduct of Islamic State in Iraq and Syria. The difference is that the savagery was perpetrated by Russia, a member of the UN Security Council. He urged the Council to live up to its name. 'It is obvious that the key institution of the world which must ensure the coercion of any aggressor to peace simply cannot work effectively.'

Zelenskiy is right about that. Russia – the greater part of the Soviet Union – had a true claim to be at the top table at the UN in 1945. Vladimir Putin has now lost the right to that table.

And Zelenskiy called for a new Nuremberg tribunal: 'The Russian military and those who gave them orders must be brought to justice immediately for war crimes in Ukraine. Anyone who has given criminal orders and carried them out by killing our people will be brought before the tribunal, which should be similar to the Nuremberg tribunal.'

The evidence at Nuremberg Two of Russian war crimes will be overwhelming. Satellite images, drone footage, eyewitness accounts, Bellingcat open-source material. A cyclist on a green bike in Bucha. His execution in early March by a Russian Army tank as he turns a corner, filmed by a drone. His body next to the wrecked bike filmed by reporters when the Ukrainian Army returned to the city. Once again: Kremlin inhumanity on repeat.

The Russians have lost soldiers too, of course, but – how to put this? – they started this monstrous war. By a single railway track lie two Russian corpses, burnt beyond recognition, their skins waxy in death. In another street, we pick our way through a charred house. When people say that everything is destroyed that's not quite right. I see the burnt remains of a child's bike, the inner tubes of a fridge. Weirdly, a gas meter remains intact while the rest of the house is charred wood and blackened bricks. Out the back, you can see the herb garden that the people who used to live there cherished. It is a reminder of normality amidst all the chaos of war and somewhat all the more haunting for that.

On the way out of town we come to yet another line of Russian tanks, fried to cinders. One of the soldiers, a Burat from Siberia, managed to struggle out of his tank but was burnt to death in its shadow.

I take a photo of his scarlet sock, his bare leg tattooed.

Having seen what his fellow Russian soldiers have done in

Bucha, I realize that I feel nothing for this corpse. But that would be another dark victory for Vladimir Putin's war, for Kremlin inhumanity on repeat. I force myself to think of this young man going for a walk by Lake Baikal in the spring, of drinking with his pals, of falling in love.

And now his mother getting a telephone call: 'We are very sorry to announce . . .'

I still don't understand why Vladimir Putin started his idiot war. So the best way of answering that question is to write a book about him. He won't like it – but I don't care.

Chapter Two

Rat Boy

Let's start at the very beginning with Baby Vladimir. He was born on 7 October 1952 in Leningrad, what is now St Petersburg. Stalin had another year to go in the Kremlin, one more victim of his own murderous paranoia. Towards the end of his life, Stalin wrote: 'I trust no one. Not even myself.' The same could also be said of one of his successors.

Putin's grandfather Spiridon had been one of Stalin's under-chefs, a lowly member of the household of the red tsar. But the connection to the Kremlin was not a high-powered one and Putin was brought up dirt-poor on the wrong side of the tracks in Leningrad, the only surviving child of an elderly couple. Putin's mother, Maria, was a factory worker, and his father, Vladimir Spiridonovich Putin, a submariner in the Soviet Navy. (In Russian naming practice, a man's second name comes from his father; the 'ovich' means 'son of'.) After the Nazis invaded Russia in the summer of 1941, Vladimir senior fought in a military battalion of the NKVD, the secret police which, down the track, was renamed the KGB and then the FSB. Old dog, same tricks. The old man was badly wounded by shrapnel to both legs in 1942 but survived with a lifelong limp. Putin's grandma and her brothers on his mother's side, who lived in the western city of Tver, were murdered by the Nazis.

The couple had had two sons before Vladimir. The first, Albert, died in infancy, sometime during the 1930s. Viktor was born in 1940 but then in the autumn of 1941 came the Nazi siege of Leningrad which lasted 900 days. The Germans encircled the city apart from one supply route, across an ice-bound lake. Leningrad was pounded by heavy artillery and bombing raids every day. Soon people started to starve. Everything was made worse by the coldest winter in living memory when the temperature fell to -40 degrees Fahrenheit.

To keep warm, people burned books. All the animals in the zoo were eaten; then people's cats and dogs. Wallpaper was scraped off the wall so people could eat the paste; leather boiled to make jelly; grass, weeds, pine needles and tobacco dust were eaten. Humans too: the Leningrad cops formed a special unit to counter cannibalism. At the end of the siege, one million citizens had died, including Viktor Putin, of starvation.

When Maria had her third boy, Vladimir, at the age of forty-one, it was a kind of miracle.

Or was it?

The alternative version is that Vladimir Putin is a bastard. There is an old woman, Vera Putina, an ethnic Russian living in Georgia, who has claimed since 1999 that Putin is her long-lost bastard son. The story goes that after she had Vladimir his birth father vanished. Vera found another man but her new fella hated the bastard. Poor Vladimir was beaten and brutalized by his stepfather. Vera told reporters of her new man's dislike of 'Vova' – the common Russian short-form nickname for Vladimir – 'My husband didn't want Vova to live with us any more . . . Who wants someone else's child?'

There are other witnesses. Retired teacher Nora Gogolashvili confirmed Vera's story and recalled Vova as 'a quiet, sad, introverted child ... whenever anyone hurt him, I defended him. I pitied him so much ... I felt so sorry for him. He stuck to me like a cat.'

The story goes that Vera decided to send her boy away to be adopted by relatives in Leningrad – but that to do so she tricked her son. Yuri Felshtinsky is a Russian historian, now living in exile in the United States, and the author of *The Age of Assassins: The Rise and Rise of Vladimir Putin*, which is savagely critical of its subject. Felshtinsky told me: 'They sent him off to a distant cousin, who took the boy to the old woman in Leningrad. She told him that she would pick him up in two weeks, but she never did.'

What is striking is that Vera Putina looks very much like Vladimir Putin, astonishingly so; while his official mother, Maria, looks nothing like him. A photograph of Maria and son, taken when he was five and a half in July 1958, shows him looking like Gollum, staring mournfully at the camera; his official mother seems distant, unattached.

There is a world of hurt in this bastard story that could explain much about him.

Is it true?

Felshtinsky says it is. 'There is one more piece of information recorded by the American director Oliver Stone. He interviewed Putin and believe it or not, Putin doesn't remember when his parents died. He also doesn't remember who died first, mother or father.'

Donald Rayfield says the bastard story isn't true. Rayfield is a friend of mine, Emeritus Professor of Russian at Queen Mary University of London and the author of *Stalin and His Hangmen*, the great book about that monster's monsters.

Rayfield set out his logic: 'Vera Putina became convinced years later when Putin became President that this was her Putin. The fact that her Putin was not Vladimir Vladimirovich' – son of Vladimir – 'but Vladimir Platonovich' – son of Platon – 'didn't seem to matter. The fact that her Putin was born two years earlier didn't. She is perfectly convinced that she is the mother of Putin.'

I moaned that, as a storyteller, I love the story of Vova Putin the bastard so much I want it to be true.

Rayfield: 'I'm sorry to spoil the story. There's sufficient proof that he was born in wedlock. The third son, but the only one who survived. There's enough evidence of his youth from the old men who grew up with him as boys in the yard where he played.'

The non-bastard version continues that Vera's real son, Vladimir Platonovich Putin, became an oil worker in Siberia and is thought to have died some years ago.

Rayfield knows his Russia. And in my forty years as a reporter, more, the perfect story never quite rings true. That said, there is something unexplained about Putin's origins before he was five years old. The truth remains murky and that comes as standard throughout the whole story, because he is a man who starts in the shadows as an infant and he never leaves them.

Vova the boy is nasty, brutish and short. His mother is traumatized by the loss of her first two sons; his father by his war wounds and the state's failure to properly look after him or his family. Putin 'was born into this atmosphere of hunger, disability and profound grief' is how psychotherapist Joseph Burgo put it in *The Atlantic*.

He grows up in Soviet Leningrad in the 1960s; few streets, in those bleak days, meaner in the whole world. They lived in a fifth-floor apartment with two other families in grim conditions. Vera Dmitrievna Gurevich was Putin's schoolteacher: 'They had a horrid apartment. It was communal, without any conveniences. And it was so cold, just awful, and the stairway had a freezing metal handrail. The stairs weren't safe either, there were gaps everywhere.' And the facilities? 'There was no hot water, no bathtub. The toilet was horrendous.'

Decades on, the democracy activist Alexei Navalny releases an extraordinary video, *Putin's Palace*, which has had 123 million views on YouTube and counting. The film is about a billion-dollar palace that Putin's cronies built for him on the shores of the Black Sea. One of the most extraordinary revelations by Team Navalny is that the palace has gold toilet brushes each worth €780. Any normal human being would be revolted by such pitiful extravagance, but not perhaps if you were brought up using a toilet that gave your schoolteacher the shivers.

Putin tells a story about rat-hunting in *First Person*, his ghosted autobiography released in 2000 to give some flesh to the grey character who had suddenly emerged from the gloom of the secret state. All ghosted autobiographies are unsatisfactory, but they often disclose more about the subject than they might realize. His block of flats was infested with rats, some of which even turned on their tormentors. Putin's ghost writes: 'There, on that stair landing, I got a quick and lasting lesson in the meaning of the word "cornered". There were hordes of rats in the front entryway. My friends and I used to chase them around with sticks. Once I spotted a huge rat and pursued it down the hall until I drove it into a corner. It had nowhere to run. Suddenly it lashed around and threw itself at me. I was surprised and frightened. Now the rat was chasing me. It jumped across the landing and down the stairs.

Luckily, I was a little faster and I managed to slam the door on its nose.'

Killing rats with a stick is inefficient. The best way of killing them is to use rat poison. Perhaps this is the moment when Putin became seduced by the power of venom. Leastways, it is striking that so many of his enemies end up being poisoned and as his grip on power becomes stronger, the rat poison becomes more and more expensive, the chemistry more fiendishly complicated. But the method remains the same.

His mother did various poorly paid jobs: caretaking, delivering bread at night, washing laboratory test tubes by hand; his dad made train carriages in a factory, his earning capacity limited by his disability. Putin the boy was small, even for those ill-nourished days, slight, and left to fend for himself for much of the time. But pretty soon he earned a reputation for punching – or kicking or biting – above his weight. In 2015 he gave an interview in which he said: 'If a fight is inevitable you have to throw the first punch.'

Did Young Vova get mixed up with gangsters by any chance?

Zarina Zabrisky is a Russian novelist, now living in exile in the United States after the Russian authorities deemed her a terrorist. Her hobby is researching Vladimir Putin's gangster past. 'Around the age of twelve or thirteen, he gets deeply into martial arts in Leningrad (St Petersburg). He learns judo and sambo.'

Sambo is a Russian combination word meaning 'self-defence without weapons', originally developed by the Soviet secret police and the Red Army in the 1930s. One of its founders spent years in Japan but died in the Gulag during Stalin's Great Terror, suspected, falsely, of being a Japanese spy.

Putin's coach at the Leningrad martial arts club was a gangster, says Zabrisky: 'he trained under Leonid "The Sportsman" Usvyatsov, who was a professional wrestler, a stuntman and an organized crime group boss. He had two convictions for currency fraud and group rape and spent almost twenty years in prison.' On his gravestone, his epitaph reads: 'I'm dead but the mafiya is immortal.'

Many of the friends Putin made in the martial arts club are still part of his gang now and, guess what, some of them are billionaires. There is one more aspect to young Putin which requires some study, his sexuality, but we shall look at that down the track.

So many of Putin's preoccupations as master of the Kremlin are, or appear to have been, stamped by his childhood: the old gangster as role model; the habit of staying in the shadows; and a passion for killing things.

This, then, is the childhood story of the man who would become the tsar of all the rats.

Chapter Three

Once and Future Spy

Leo 'The Sportsman' Usvyatsov used his connections to get Putin, a student from a poor family, into university on an athletics scholarship. Putin mastered German and some English, studying law at Leningrad State University, graduating in 1975. There, one of his professors was Anatoly Sobchak, who would re-emerge in 1991 as the mayor of St Petersburg and Putin's democratic mentor. His thesis at university was on 'The Most Favoured Nation Trading Principle in International Law', ditchwater-dull stuff but noteworthy because of the subject.

In 1975 Putin joined the KGB, training at the 401st KGB school in Okhta, Leningrad. For many young Russians, getting into 'The Organs', the heart of the Soviet secret state, was a ticket out of poverty. The KGB training programme was as brutal as it was intense, a mixture of brainwashing and tuition in the dark arts of killing and psychological manipulation. Chris Donnelly, the senior adviser on Russia to four Secretaries General of NATO, now retired, told me a grim story he believes is true. It's hard to verify but it goes like this: 'KGB trainees were given an Alsatian puppy at the start of their training. At the end, to graduate, the trainees were required to strangle their own dogs with their bare hands.'

Top-flight graduates got postings in New York, Paris or Rome. Putin was clearly not rated very highly by the bosses because his first proper job was monitoring foreigners and consular officials in Leningrad. That is, the man who wanted to spy on the world was posted to his home town.

He wasn't very good. The psychiatrist Semyon Gluzman explained that he has a woman friend whom Putin tried to recruit as a KGB informer back in the day when he was a runt working in Leningrad. His approach was dogged, unsubtle and maladroit, so much so that the woman ended up despising him, not just because he was KGB, but so clumsily KGB. The officers Semyon tangled with during his time in the Gulag were of higher grade.

The feeling you get from his later chit-chat was that he was too boring, too small-minded to become a top-flight spook. Putin once said he could not read a book by a Soviet defector because 'I don't read books by people who have betrayed the Motherland.'

That would rule out, say, Alexander Solzhenitsyn, author of the definitive books about the Gulag, *One Day in the Life of Ivan Denisovich* and *The Gulag Archipelago*. The author was a brave artillery officer in the Soviet Army fighting in East Prussia in 1945 when he wrote a private letter to a friend criticizing Stalin. The letter got intercepted by the secret police. From his cell in the Lubyanka, Solzhenitsyn recalled Victory Day in 1945: 'Above the muzzle of our window, and from all the other cells of the Lubyanka, and from all the windows of the Moscow prisons, we too, former prisoners of war and former front-line soldiers, watched the Moscow heavens, patterned with fireworks and criss-crossed with beams of searchlights. There was no rejoicing in our cells and no hugs and no kisses for us. That victory was not ours.' He was expelled from the Soviet Union in 1974 and lived in exile in Vermont in the United States.

More than any other pieces of writing, *One Day in the Life of Ivan Denisovich* and *The Gulag Archipelago* nail the inhumanity of the Soviet project. To take pride in rejecting great works of literature and documentary history because of their lack of political loyalty to the state shows that, however street-wise and gangster-savvy Putin may be, he has a small mind and that a great intelligence officer does not make.

Nothing about this stage of Putin's life suggests that he was ever cut out for the Kremlin, not even the woman who became his first wife. Putin's ghosted book, *First Person*, records the story of his first date with Lyudmila, an Aeroflot hostess. It's not exactly love at first sight. In her words, 'Volodya was standing on the steps of the ticket office. He was very ... poorly dressed. He looked very unprepossessing. I wouldn't have paid any attention to him on the street.'

They were married in 1983, a good career move for him. The KGB liked its officers to marry early. It meant that they had another set of eyes on the officer and some kind of leverage, through family, if he was ever tempted to defect.

A slow developer, Putin learnt to hide his frustration at his early lack of success skilfully. His first posting outside of Russia was a second disappointment. He was sent to Dresden in Communist East Germany, working from a grey villa on Angelikastrasse, in a fancy part of town overlooking the River Elbe, directly opposite the local HQ of the Stasi, the East German secret police. The film *The Lives of Others* is the best single take on the Stasi, how it graded and degraded the human soul. In Dresden, its files on the local population would, if laid end to end, have stretched seven miles.

In their coruscating 2012 biography of Putin, Russian-American journalist Masha Gessen wrote: 'Putin and his colleagues were reduced mainly to collecting press clippings, thus contributing to the mountains of useless information produced by the KGB.'

Catherine Belton is a brilliant British journalist, originally from Rainhill, Liverpool. She and her publisher HarperCollins were variously sued by Roman Abramovich, other Russian oligarchs and the energy company Rosneft for her 2020 book, *Putin's People.* After expensive battles in and out of the London law courts for her and her publisher, Belton corrected some piffling errors whereupon Abramovich and the other litigants ran away, very much like the knights run away in the last scene of *Monty Python and the Holy Grail*. Belton sets out the evidence that the press-clipping story was a cunning cover to mask Putin's serious job of funding terrorism against West Germany by supporting the Red Army Faction, a far-left group responsible for multiple murders, kidnappings and bomb outrages. The RAF, also known as the Baader-Meinhof gang, was a death cult in love with a gibberish unreality, that West Germany was Nazi, while neo-Stalinist East Germany was a place of virtue. Belton's evidence for her story that Putin helped run the RAF is based on subtle deduction and testimony from anonymous sources. They say that the Baader-Meinhof people presented Putin with a shopping list of weapons which were then delivered to them in West Germany, that Putin tried to recruit an author of a study on poisons, that he ran a neo-Nazi agent. None of this is 100 per cent proven fact, but Belton is a journalistic rock star and her work is darkly fascinating.

Putin's collaboration with the Stasi won him a bronze medal in 1987 from the East German security service. Not silver, not gold: the next level up, said one source, from the lowest award of all.

He made some useful friends in the East German secret police, one of whom might be Matthias Warnig, a former Stasi agent who had spied on his fellow Germans, his cover names being 'Arthur', 'Economist' and 'Hans-Detlef'. Warnig and Putin deny knowing each other at this time, but a Stasi snap shows the two men on a joint visit to the 1st Guards Tank Army in Dresden in 1989. After the fall of the Berlin Wall that November, Warnig stops being a neo-Stalinist secret policeman and becomes a banker, pops up in Russia and befriends – or renews his friendship – with Putin. Years later Warnig becomes the German front man for the Nord Stream project, gas pipelines running from Russia underneath the Baltic Sea to Germany. It's a pipeline and it's a cosh, both at the same time. Nord Stream pipelines sidestep the previous supply routes which benefited the transit countries in Eastern Europe. If the Kremlin was minded, it could cut off gas to those countries until they showed their fealty to the Russian President. No wonder Putin is content with Warnig running the show. The German has pooh-poohed such talk: 'I'm not a Kremlin mouthpiece. And I don't report to the Kremlin, either, or have cozy chats about what goes on there.' The former Stasi man of course denies any wrongdoing.

While Putin was in Dresden – either compiling piles of paper or running a terrorist group by proxy – the Soviet Empire was falling to pieces around his ears. Come the fall of the Berlin Wall, Putin found himself feeding file after KGB file into the boiler in the basement of his office building until it cracked, broken by too much heat.

There were three big reasons for the death of the Soviet Union. The first was the fall-out from the Soviet invasion of Afghanistan in 1979. Soviet generals knew that war in Afghanistan would be a terrible mistake, but the defence minister dared not say so to then leader, Leonid Brezhnev. So the tanks rolled – shades, once again, of 2022. Perhaps as many as two million Afghans were killed and 15,000 Russian soldiers died, to be returned home in zinc-lined coffins, so called Zincy Boys, or, following the Soviet Army signal code, 'Cargo 200'.

The war drained the Soviet Union of blood, of treasure, of moral purpose – until it was a bleached-white corpse.

The second great catastrophe exploded on 26 April 1986 at Chernobyl in Soviet Ukraine. The engineers at Number 4 RBMK reactor were ordered to carry out a test-shutdown. Instead of shutting down, the reactor blew up, showering Europe with radiation. The engineers were tried for the failure. But there was something critically wrong with the reactor design, something that had been hushed up after a near-tragic accident in Russia. The engineers at the station were blamed for a fault in the entire Soviet system. Readers who want to know more should check out the brilliant HBO drama series, *Chernobyl*, and the beautifully written book by the Nobel Prize winner Svetlana Alexievich, *Voices from Chernobyl*.

The third failure happened over decades but came to a head in the 1990s. The Communist command economy could not compete with the West's free markets.. The late American satirist, P.J. O'Rourke, put it pithily when he said: 'Ronald Reagan may have been a bit ga-ga, but he understood that a country which bans the Xerox photocopier and the fax machine cannot win over a country that creates them.'

The Soviet Union could not afford to feed or house or care for its people, so it started to implode. Putin, the secret policeman in Dresden, never properly grasped the power of these three failures. His tragedy – our tragedy – was that he had no first-hand knowledge of the three catastrophes. He was too high up in the secret police food chain to be sent to Chernobyl; too pathetically low to be sent to the fag-end of the failing war in Afghanistan; let alone to the fleshpots of the West where he would have seen the stark evidence of how ordinary people in New Jersey or New Brighton in the Wirral lived so much better than in Moscow, let alone Omsk or Tomsk. He never saw the comparative evidence of Soviet economic failure with his own eyes or, if he did, he was too brainwashed to understand what he was looking at.

Instead, from the bowels of Stasiland, he came to internalize a dark nonsense, that his country's collapse was due to Western trickery and domestic betrayal, rather than the simple facts that the Soviet Union had run out of cash and self-belief and purpose. It was a failed state, just like the Kaiser's Germany became a failed state after it launched its own stupid war in 1914. Like Hitler in 1923, Putin from 1991 onwards breathed a poisonous fiction, that his country had been wronged, that it 'had been stabbed in the back'. In truth, it fell apart because it had been wrong, it had stabbed itself in the front, three times over.

Vladimir Putin is not, I believe, mad, for the reasons my friend the psychiatrist Semyon Gluzman set out to me four days before the 2022 invasion. But Putin's understanding of the world is maddeningly narrow, reduced to a gloomy tunnel vision, locked into a false narrative of betrayal. He once declared the fall of the Soviet Union 'the greatest geopolitical catastrophe of the twentieth century'.

What?

Worse than the First and Second World Wars? Worse than the Holocaust? The Soviet Union was, in reality, a dark totalitarian dictatorship under Stalin that slowly morphed into a gloomy senility.

With his tail between his legs, Putin in 1991 headed back from Dresden to St Petersburg – the old, new name for Leningrad – doing bits and bobs for the Russian secret state, spying on students, recruiting new candidates for the KGB, running errands, marking time.

President Mikhail Gorbachev was struggling hard to make sense of the Soviet Union's catastrophic internal contradictions when in August 1991, while on holiday, he fell victim to a coup. A gang of sclerotic KGB officers and army generals set out to kill off the democratic mood of *glasnost* and *perestroika*, locked up Gorby in his holiday villa and switched off Russian TV news to be replaced by a film of *Swan Lake*, on repeat.

Putin claims, without solid evidence, that he resigned from the KGB, his rank lieutenant colonel, on the second day: 'As soon as the coup began, I immediately decided which side I was on.'

Maybe. In truth, the coup plotters and Gorbachev were upstaged by Boris Yeltsin, a force of nature with too much love of the bottle, but, when it mattered, a brave and good man. He stepped onto a Russian Army tank, denounced the coup and halted the threat, but set in motion the end of the Soviet Union, which splintered into its component parts, the biggest of which being Russia itself.

Putin hooked up with his old law professor, Anatoly Sobchak, a rising star who soon became mayor of St Petersburg. The story goes that during the coup Sobchak, an outspoken democrat, flew back to the city from Moscow and was met at the airport by Putin, thus securing his safety when the coup plotters could have seized him. To return the favour, Sobchak made Putin one of his deputy mayors. There's a photo of him, moonfaced, in a very cheap suit, with sad, balding hair, carrying the mayor's bag, looking small, unimportant, very much the underling. The other deputies were more glamorous, more photogenic. Igor Artemyev, leader of the social-liberal Yabloko Party back then, said: 'In the Petersburg days, it was always other people in front of the television cameras. Almost all the other vice mayors lined up next to the boss. Putin was always in the farthest corner.'

He must have hated them so.

If you saw Vladimir Putin's address to the Russian National Security Council just before the invasion of Ukraine in February 2022 – hyperbolically aggressive, openly contemptuous of his foreign spymaster, SVR boss Sergey Naryshkin – this facet of his character is the most difficult to get your head around. Before Putin held serious power, he could be intensely submissive, unassuming, servile. He pulled off this trick with at least three big men, the first of whom was Sobchak, the second the oligarch Boris Berezovsky, the third Boris Yeltsin. They saw a good and faithful servant. Each one, in turn, got to realize their mistake.

The exact nature of the relationship between Sobchak, handsome, fluent, something of a narcissist, and the little spy remains opaque. It's worth pointing out that Sobchak had been a professor in a law school where many of the students were fledgling KGB officers. Ostensibly, Sobchak was a democrat but he may also have been under the wing of the Russian secret state. And the liaison officer between the men in the shadows and the flashy mayor? Well, that could only be

Putin. The relationship also appears to have been mutually beneficial.

Professor Donald Rayfield doesn't mince his words about the mayor and the man who carried his bags: 'Anatoly Sobchak was mayor and he had a reputation of being a democrat and a liberal. But, of course, it's possible to be a democrat and a liberal and a complete conman at the same time. Sobchak may not have ordered killings. But I think his bagman was probably a little more ruthless.'

Behind the scenes Vladimir Putin was reconnecting with friends of his old judo coach, Leo 'The Sportsman'; that is, the mafiya, the Russian mob, and they with him. The details are dense, the subject matter knotty, but in essence Putin the deputy mayor sold licences, permits, paperwork, to enable businessmen, often or in fact almost always connected to the mafiya, to make a killing getting around the draconian Soviet-style rules and regulations forbidding or restricting free trade. So at the exact same time that Sobchak was liberalizing St Petersburg, his deputy was making the mob and himself and Sobchak rich by undermining the rule of law. Putin became a past master at using administrative law to screw natural justice. He used his connections in the KGB – now broken up into two entities, the FSB, the internal secret police, and the SVR, the foreign intelligence service – to make sure that he always came out on top. Critical to Putin's masked gangsterism was the inverting of the police and the judiciary from their true function of safeguarding the rule of law to subverting it. Everything Putin did to Russia when master of the Kremlin from 2000, he did it first in St Petersburg: creating a corrupt system, turning the forces of law and order inside out, using the rebranded KGB to enforce his will. Donald Rayfield put it like this: 'the mafiya turned to the KGB people who had the money and the contacts. There was a merger of the secret police and the mafiya and it was disastrous for the Russian people.'

The Soviet Union collapsed because it could not provide enough food for people to eat, but its single biggest successor state, the Russian Federation, suffered from exactly the same problem. In St Petersburg, people were free to speak but they were starving. Sobchak appointed Putin to head the city's foreign relations efforts. More than anything, the city needed food. It had big stocks of precious metals, locked away in warehouses supplying arms and ammunition factories. Marine Salye, a ferociously brave local councillor on the city's food committee, told the *Washington Post*: 'There was no food in the city at all. There was no money. Barter was the only way – say, metals for potatoes and meat.'

Putin organized contracts to swap the precious metals for food. But when Salye investigated, she discovered that the metal was sold cheap, the food was booked at prices that were too high and it never arrived. The profits went to shell companies which then vanished, taking the money with them. Salye could not prove Putin's criminality definitively. But she believed he 'was manipulating these contracts and was directly involved'. When she confronted him, he brushed her off: 'You are just making up things.' The issue went up to an audit commission in Moscow but was quietly dropped.

Putin got close to the Tambov crime gang, the biggest and nastiest set of gangsters in St Petersburg. One big player connected to it was Roman Tsepov, a very bright gangster. Tsepov, a former captain in the armed wing of the Ministry of Internal Affairs, had founded Baltik-Eskort in 1992. The personal security firm provided protection to high-ranking St Petersburg officials, including Mayor Sobchak and his family and his deputy mayor, Putin. The word was that, in this role, Tsepov also played go-between for the deputy mayor and the mob, handling the 'black cash'. His firm also looked after senior gangsters, including several figures in the Tambov syndicate. Tsepov was arrested on a number of occasions but for some reason the charges never stuck. He also survived five unsuccessful attempts on his life. For a time, the gangsters and the deputy mayor got on like a house on fire. Tsepov reportedly got so thick with Putin that Putin gave his wife, Lyudmila, an emerald stolen from South Korea. The joke in the city was that Sobchak was mayor by day, and Putin mayor by night.

But then the wheels came off the bus. Sobchak was kicked out of office by the electors of St Petersburg in 1996 and Vladimir Putin was out of a job. But Sobchak still had some clout with Team Yeltsin and he helped Putin secure a new job, in the underbelly of the Kremlin, working for the property administration department in Moscow. It sounds deeply unglamorous but it turned out to be a very good career move. As the 1990s grew older, the whole world could see that Boris Yeltsin was running out of road. The question was: who would replace him?

To set the context, Yeltsin's raw courage during the coup in 1991 was his finest hour. What followed was a long and pathetic alcoholic wobble towards the grave. New Russia's dream of democracy and the rule of law gave way to a chaotic, vodka-raddled mess, a hiccoughing anarchy where rich gangsters got killed by richer oligarchs. I first went to Russia in the mid-1990s and I have a vivid memory of going to the John Donne pub in central Moscow and seeing a middle-aged businessman, watched over by an anxious and gloomy bodyguard, sobbing his heart out in the middle of the bar.

On reflection, he must have been under horrific duress – your money or your life, something like that – and he had made the decision that the hit would not happen in plain view in a British-themed pub. This scene, or something like it, was replayed across Russia as organized crime muscled in on anyone who made honest money.

Great fortunes were made as the oligarchy stole billions from the hapless Russian public. Boris Nemtsov, a gloriously funny and extraordinarily clever Russian nuclear physicist turned politician, was, for a time, Russia's deputy prime minister under Yeltsin. Telegenic, charismatic and open to the world and honest about it, Nemtsov was, for a time, Yeltsin's heir apparent. That that never happened is part of Russia's tragic decline and fall.

Nemtsov took the word 'oligarchy' – meaning rule by the few in Greek – and played with it, making it personal, coining the noun 'oligarch'. Figures like Roman Abramovich and his then mentor, Boris Berezovsky, made a killing out of a crooked system. The two men profited from a rigged auction for the Siberian oil giant Sibneft, both putting in $100 million each and buying a company worth untold billions. Abramovich later admitted in court that, to get the prize, he paid billions of dollars bribing government officials and gangsters. This was the biggest heist of the twentieth century. It made thefts such as Britain's Great Train Robbery of August 1963 like stealing sweets from a sweet shop. Oleg Deripaska did something similar with his aluminium mines and smelters in Siberia, before he established effective ownership. Bill Browder, the grandson of a former general secretary of the Communist Party of the United States, went to Russia as a venture capitalist to piss off his family and organized a deal to buy the Soviet Arctic fishing fleet, worth one billion dollars, for roughly one hundred million. What happened was that the immense wealth of the Soviet Union was directed into the bank accounts of a very few men and Russia became, overnight, one of the most unequal societies on earth. Schools, hospitals and the basic functions of the state teetered from crisis to crisis while the oligarchs spent their obscene wealth in the flashy parts of London and the South of France on mansions, super-yachts and football teams.

To be fair, Yeltsin's record was not wholly negative. The mental blinkers of the old order were ripped off and ordinary Russians were free to travel and see just how far behind the West they were. Parliament, the Duma, worked, kind of. Journalism was committed, in print and more impressively on radio and on TV. Killers and corruption were called to account in the papers, if not in the courts. But the whole was more miss than hit.

Many older Russians mourned the loss of the old certainties of the Soviet Union and the passing of the might of the Greater Russian Empire, masked as it was by the Soviet entity. The old servant nations had grown mutinous. The Balts, the Estonians, Latvians and Lithuanians, all filed for divorce and set up their own nations, as they were before the Nazi-Soviet pact of 1939, what George Orwell called the 'midnight of the century'. Ukraine, its capital Kyiv the founder of the Rus civilization, stumbled towards a future outside the fraternal Russian umbrella. To the south and east, the Chechens, a forever rebellious Muslim people in their mountain strongholds, rose up against Russian imperialism. Yeltsin launched a war and the Russian Army started to lose it, badly, until a peace of sorts was hammered out.

In 1996 Yeltsin's poll numbers tanked and the Russian oligarchs feared that he would be unseated from the Kremlin by the Communists. So they pitched in and bought the election for him. And, in return, Yeltsin, his family and his advisers were in hock to the oligarchs and their dirty money. The money started looking around for a new front man. Boris Berezovsky had spotted Putin as a possible contender very early on when he met him in St Petersburg in 1990. Berezovsky was a brilliant mathematician turned car-dealer. He was importing foreign cars but wanted to set up a unit where he could service and repair the Mercedes and BMWs he was bringing in to Russia, but he had to get a permit from the city council. That's how he met Putin. 'He was the first bureaucrat who did not take bribes,' Berezovsky told Masha Gessen. 'Seriously. It made a huge impression on me.'

That scenario was an act, a piece of theatre. The truth was that Putin was monstrously corrupt from the get-go, but what is fascinating is that he was subtle and discerning about it. Milking Berezovsky for a small bribe wasn't smart. Playing the long game was Putin's strategy – and it worked. He wasn't just Berezovsky's man. There were other players in the shadows.

Behind the Kremlin's curtains, the secret policemen had never given up on taking back power. They had, after all, secured Soviet power in 1917 by killing the far more numerous liberal democratic opposition to the tsar's autocracy. They stayed in power until 1990, failed to overthrow the lurch towards a more open Russia with the 1991 coup but as Yeltsin & Co destroyed democracy's good name they bided their time, gathered their forces and plotted. Vladimir Putin, the once and future spy, was their man.

His job in the Kremlin's property administration department was an important stepping stone. The word is that that department provided a pathway to the thing that mattered most to Boris Yeltsin's family: the alchemy of turning political power into money. Tenders for work on the Kremlin were put out to private contractors. The story goes that they would overcharge, big time, and the kickbacks wound up with the Yeltsin family and their facilitators.

But the bad news for the Yeltsin family was that the Russian government still had a system of checks and balances, of scrutiny, of law officers who did their job, more or less. In 1998 Prosecutor-General Yuri Skuratov, Russia's top law enforcement officer, started investigating the Mabatex Group, based in Switzerland but headed by the world's richest ethnic Albanian, Behgjet Pacolli. The investigation accused Mabatex of bribing the Yeltsin family. The company won a $1.5 billion contract for doing up the Kremlin and other presidential properties and in return it transferred $1 million into a Budapest bank account for Yeltsin's use. Pacolli later confirmed that he had guaranteed five credit cards for Yeltsin's wife, Naina, and two daughters, Tatyana and Yelena. Worse for the family, the Swiss Attorney General, Carla del Ponte, was also on the case.

Skuratov was dangerous. But his nemesis was at hand. In 1998 Putin emerged from the shadows with the very first serious job of his life, when Yeltsin made him head of the FSB, keeper of the Kremlin's secrets and king of kompromat. In the spring of 1999 Russian prime-time TV viewers were treated to a grainy black and white video of a fat middle-aged man with a Bobby Charlton comb-over in bed with two prostitutes half his age. It was a sad moment of sexual indignity for Mr Comb-over and his women, but this video is also a key event in modern Russian history. They call this kompromat, Russian short form for 'compromising material', and the video is a classic of that dark art.

A very young-looking Vladimir Putin wearing a cheap black leather jacket came on the telly to identify Mr Comb-over as Skuratov, Russia's prosecutor-general, the very same officer investigating corruption in the Kremlin's property administration department. Putin told Russian television: 'The man in the infamous video has been identified as the Prosecutor-General Skuratov ... My opinion regarding this case is well known. It corresponds to the opinion of the president and the prime minister – Yuri Ilyich [Skuratov] has to resign.'

Skuratov denied he was the man in the video, but the damage had been done. There is a story behind the story of the kompromat against Skuratov. There was a second party who lived in fear of – or was deeply troubled by – Skuratov's investigations in the late 1990s, and his name was Alexander Lebedev, a former colonel in the KGB. He was the father of Evgeny, the Russian oligarch and owner of *The Independent* and *Evening Standard*, whom British Prime Minister Boris Johnson made Baron Siberia. Johnson has been to a host of exotic parties at the Lebedev palazzo near Perugia. When Johnson celebrated his general election victory in December 2019, he did so at Alexander Lebedev's mansion near Regent's Park. The old KGB officer had his own cause to party: it was his sixtieth birthday.

Alexander Lebedev joined the KGB in the early 1980s and worked first in Switzerland before moving to London. He had diplomatic cover but in reality he was a spy, working out of the Russian Embassy in Kensington Palace Gardens from 1988 to 1992. With the dissolution of the Soviet Union, Lebedev senior then became a banker, a co-owner of the National Reserve Bank and, for a time, a multi-billionaire, one of the richest men in Russia. Lebedev stayed close to

Gorbachev and, with him, co-owned *Novaya Gazeta*, a ferociously brave newspaper whose gifted staff consequently kept on getting murdered.

But Russia is a murky place and the idea that Alexander Lebedev is a true liberal democrat because of his co-ownership of *Novaya Gazeta* is a nice fairy story. In 2021 Jacopo Iacoboni and Gianluca Paolucci, two Italian reporters working for *La Stampa*, published their book, *Oligarchi*, claiming that Lebedev senior may never have cut his ties with the Russian secret state. The authors quoted a secret report by the Italian External Intelligence and Security Agency to its parliamentary oversight committee, Copasir, suggesting that Lebedev's resignation from the KGB and/or its successor agencies might not have been all it appeared to be because he 'continued to participate in annual KGB meetings'. Moreover, 'he would have started his business activity while still in the service of the KGB and using the funds he had acquired as an agent'. The Italian report is based on top-secret intelligence that is not in the public domain, and therefore the full facts are not known.

In simple spy terms, the KGB/FSB is like Hotel California in the song by the Eagles: 'You can check out any time you like / But you can never leave.'

In 1997 Alexander Lebedev claimed his former business associate, Igor Fyodorov, had stolen $7 million from his bank. Fyodorov counter-claimed, filing a complaint to Prosecutor-General Skuratov, alleging Alexander Lebedev and others were up to criminal no-good. Lebedev and his associates denied this. The prosecutor's office opened multiple investigations against Lebedev and his NRB bank, accusing it of tax avoidance and fraud.

Funny business started. Skuratov realized he was being spied on and his prime suspect was Alexander Lebedev. His bank, NRB, had its own security service, known as SB KONUS (SB means Sluzhba Bezopasnosti or security service). Skuratov told the then independent Russian TV channel NTV in September 1999, 'the security service of Lebedev, Konus and others put me and my family under surveillance . . . What I can say for sure is that Mr Lebedev used significant resources to counteract the investigation. His acquaintance with work for the special services [KGB/FSB] let him use various methods.' Skuratov went on to claim that personal stuff about his life and family popped up on social media but, 'due to a glitch with the internet', the private-eye snooping was traced back to SB Konus.

And then the sex kompromat tape appeared showing a man looking very much like Skuratov with the two women prostitutes. Once again, Skuratov denies it was him.

Alexander Lebedev in his poorly written book, *Hunt the Banker*, dedicates a lot of words to denigrating Skuratov and his officers' investigation into his bank. He suggests that unknown 'puppet-masters' may have had a hold over Skuratov, threatening him with exposure of the kompromat tape. Lebedev writes: '"We wouldn't want any trouble," they doubtless told him, "only . . ." and so on.'

Strange words. Or, on the other hand, exactly what you might expect from someone who had been in the KGB. There is, of course, no suggestion that either of the former KGB officers, Colonel Vladimir Putin and Colonel Alexander Lebedev and their entities, had any involvement in the sex kompromat operation against the prosecutor-general. I wrote an article about all of this for *Byline Times* which was published in March 2022 and have asked Alexander Lebedev several times to comment on the Skuratov kompromat story, and I did so, once again, for this book. I have yet to receive a response.

The only other person on the front cover of Alexander Lebedev's book, *Hunt the Banker*, is Vladimir Putin. Both former KGB officers are smiling.

The Skuratov scandal rocked Russia and kompromat ended the career of the prosecutor-general and his investigation into the corruption of outgoing President Boris Yeltsin and family. The payback was large. In the summer of 1999 Yeltsin made Vladimir Putin acting prime minister. Kompromat gave Putin the keys to the Kremlin.

And then the serious killing started.

Chapter Four

A Bomb Made of Sugar

September 1999: two bombs in Moscow in four days, both placed in working-class blocks of flats. The first bomb exploded just after midnight at Guryanov Street, killing ninety-two people sleeping in their beds in the early morning of 9 September. Several bodies were blown into the surrounding streets. By daybreak people could see the pitiful detritus of the atrocity: children's clothes, a sofa hanging off a ledge in what had been someone's living room, open to the sky, books, pictures scattered far and wide. Broken glass crackled underfoot.

You could cut the fear with a knife.

Four days later a second bomb. This blew up another block of flats at Kashirskoye Highway, Moscow, at five in the morning. The wounded, painted in dust, as semi-naked as when they went to sleep, a night and a lifetime ago, were carried off in stretchers. The most haunting image was of a man blackened by soot, crawling on his hands and knees through the wreckage. He survived. One hundred and thirty other residents in the block of flats – men, women, children – did not.

Enter the secret policeman. He stood on the edge of a

field of rubble, looking like Central Casting's idea of a KGB/FSB operative, sporting a cowpat hairdo, a cheap black raincoat, black tie, lean, tall, clean shaven, saturnine. He walked up to the TV cameras and presented to the compound eye of lenses a black and white e-fit picture. The e-fit depicted a Chechen man, with a fleshy face, almost Buddha-like in its plumpness, swarthy skin and tinted spectacles. This was the Chechen terrorist the authorities were blaming for the bombs. He was using the name of Mukhit Laipanov, who had recently rented ground-floor space in the two apartment blocks devastated by the bombs. The real Laipanov had died in a car crash earlier in 1999. The authorities were very quick to pin the blame on a group of Chechen-trained terrorists. It was the Chechens who did it – that was the instant effect of the secret policeman's e-fit. It was posted up all around the bus stops of Moscow. Three days after the second bomb, the bulldozers moved in, obliterating the sites and also destroying evidence against the bombers.

On 13 September, the day of the second Moscow bomb, the Speaker to Russia's parliament, the Duma, Gennadiy Seleznyov, announced that a third bomb had gone off in the city of Volgodonsk in southern Russia. A bombing did indeed happen in Volgodonsk, but only three days later.

There was another bomb, four in total, together killing more than 300 people in Moscow and southern Russia in less than two weeks. The Chechens again were to blame.

There was a fifth bomb. This one didn't go off.

Just before the bomb outrages, Putin had been appointed prime minister by President Yeltsin. With no public track record, the former secret policeman was widely mocked as a political nobody, a cold, faceless Kremlin insider who had spent sixteen years in the KGB and had emerged as the chief of its successor agency, the FSB. His polling numbers were pitifully low, something like a two per cent approval rating.

Boris Kagarlitsky, a seasoned Kremlin watcher in Moscow, commented: 'You cannot turn a bureaucrat into a glamorous person. He is as grey as he used to be. There is a propaganda machine which works but that is exactly the weakness of Putin, because as a politician he is a nobody. To be a politician you need some kind of past.'

Matt Bivens, then editor of the *Moscow Times*, thought the same: 'Yeltsin had been through a couple of prime ministers and each time he dropped them he made it clear that it had something to do with elections. By the end he's picking Vladimir Putin. No one has ever heard of Putin, except very careful watchers of politics or people from St Petersburg. He's announcing "this is my successor, this is a man who can run the country" and there is widespread ridicule. All the newspapers in town including ours said, there's no way this guy could win an election, unless something really extraordinary is going to happen.'

The Moscow apartment bombings were the something really extraordinary.

In the immediate aftermath of the bombs, Putin struck out on national TV: 'The people who have done this don't deserve to be called animals. They are worse . . . they are mad beasts and they should be treated as such.' His poll ratings soared and he struck again: 'We will waste them. Even when they are in the boghouse.'

This was pure gangsterese but it went down a treat with the Russian public. Putin was working with the grain of Russian racism. For centuries the Muslim renegades from the savage rocks of the Caucasus have been the folk devils of

Russia. The nineteenth-century poet Lermontov wrote a lullaby which has stuck in the Russian mind:

The Terek streams over boulders,
The murky waves splash;
A wicked Chechen crawls on to the bank
and sharpens his kinzhal;

But your father is an old warrior
forged in battle;
Sleep my darling, be calm,
Listen to the lullaby.

The Chechens had humiliated the might of Russia in the First Chechen War (1994–6), which Yeltsin had started in a drunken rage. The Russian Army had fought the war with great brutality and greater incompetence. The Chechens fought them to a kind of stalemate, partly because Yeltsin, when he had sobered up, realized that he had been stupid and cruel.

Putin used the Moscow apartment bombings as a *casus belli* to prosecute the Second Chechen War in the autumn of 1999. It was waged with pitiless savagery. At the same time Russian TV showed footage of Chechen guerrillas purportedly torturing and killing Russian soldiers. The worst clip shows a knife being put to the neck of a shaven-headed white man. Then his carotid artery is severed and one can see his blood drain from his face in close-up. The next shot is of the man lying prone on the ground, to all intents and purposes a corpse. There is no way of telling whether the victim was a Russian soldier and the killers Chechen, no supporting evidence. Nevertheless, this and other clips were shown on

Russian TV repeatedly – as if someone in authority was minded to harden Russian public opinion against the enemy, the other.

The Chechens lost everything they had gained from the first war. One Chechen view was: 'If we had wanted to bomb Moscow, we would have blown up the Kremlin or a nuclear power station. Why should we blow up a couple of blocks of flats?'

The Russian government's case that Chechen terrorists or Chechen-backed terrorists had bombed Moscow and the two towns in southern Russia was spelt out by Vladimir Kozlov, head of the FSB's anti-terrorism department, in a Moscow press conference a year after the outrages. Kozlov said that the terrorists were members of a radical Islamic sect, led by Achemez Gochiyayev, who was paid $500,000 by the Chechen warlord Khattab. He recruited Yusuf Krymshamkhalov and Denis Saitakov to blow up the Moscow apartment blocks. The official version, according to the FSB, continues that the terrorists were trained in Chechnya, then dispatched to neighbouring North Caucasian republics, such as Karachayevo-Cherkassia, with tons of explosives. There, they rented trucks and smuggled the explosives to Moscow, usually camouflaged as sugar, potatoes or some other produce. Most of the bombs were made of a mixture of potassium nitrate and aluminium powder, with Casio watches used as timers, according to Kozlov. FSB detectives say they also found 500 kilograms of this mixture near the Chechen city of Urus-Martan in December 1999, citing this as proof that those responsible for the attacks were not only trained in Khattab's camps in Chechnya, but also obtained explosives there.

Common sense says it would be madness for a group of

Chechens to smuggle explosives all the way from Urus-Martan to Moscow. Since the First Chechen War, Chechens are routinely singled out for harassment by Russian police, vehicles are stopped and searched, identity papers demanded. Besides, there has long been a strong Chechen mafia in Moscow, very capable of getting its hands on arms or explosives in the city. In Russia, in the 1990s, you could bribe your way into a nuclear rocket silo. The 'Chechen terrorists' would have been risking a great deal by hauling their explosives roughly 1,000 miles to Moscow when they could have bought them at the back of a local flea market.

Six of the suspects, including those for the bombs in southern Russia, were killed in fighting with federal forces down there. Dead men don't tell tales. Much of the evidence presented at the FSB news conference was circumstantial.

But the FSB's official version of the bomb outrages starts to fall apart when you examine the case of the fifth bomb. The story of its discovery, defusing and denial casts huge doubts on the Kremlin's line.

Around 9 p.m. on 22 September in the provincial city of Ryazan, 100 miles south-east of Moscow, Vladimir Vasiliev, an engineer returning home for the night, noticed three strangers acting suspiciously by the basement of his block of flats at 14/16 Novosyolovo – literally New Settlers – Street. Vasiliev said: 'A white car was parked outside the entrance, with the boot towards the entrance. In the car were two men, young men, about twenty or twenty-five years old.'

Vasiliev noticed that the last two digits of the front number plate had been stuck on with paper, showing 62, the Ryazan regional code. At the back of the car was the true plate number, giving a Moscow code. Vasiliev, puzzled, decided to call the police. 'As we were waiting for the lift and it was empty, one of the young guys got out of the car and a woman appeared and asked: "Have you done everything?" "Yes." "OK, let's go." And they got into the car and quite quickly left.'

Vasiliev observed the three in the car with the mismatched plates. 'I remember the driver sat at the wheel, quite thin, with a moustache, and the other man was heavier. The girl had blonde hair, cut short, wearing sports clothes and a leather jacket. They were Russian, absolutely, not Asiatic' – meaning not Chechen.

The Ryazan police officers arrived. Inspector Andrei Chernyshev was the first to enter the basement. He later explained: 'We had a signal from a man on duty. It was about 10 p.m. in the evening. There were some strangers who were seen leaving the basement from the Building 14/16 at Novosyolovo Street. We were met by a local girl who stood by the building. She told us about the men who came out from the basement and left with the car with a licence number which was covered with paper. I went down to the basement. This block of flats had a very deep basement which was completely covered with water. We could see sacks of sugar and amongst them an electronic device, a few wires and a clock. We were shocked. We ran out of the basement and I stayed on watch by the entrance and my officers went to evacuate the people.'

A grandmother, Clara Stepanovna, recalled that night: 'Neighbours began to knock at the door and said: "Get out fast, something's been planted in the basement." We quickly grabbed what we could and leapt out. My daughter leapt out without getting properly dressed, without stockings, without tights, not anything, just flung a jacket on. The kids also dashed out half-dressed. They held us away from the block of flats and started investigating. They didn't give us permission to get near.'

Vasiliev said: 'After we were standing in the square, my wife remembered that she hadn't switched off the stove so I went up to an MVD (Interior Ministry) officer to tell him. We went up in the lift. He told me they had found a device.'

Yuri Tkachenko, head of the local bomb squad, went down into the basement. 'For me it was a live bomb. I was in a combat situation,' he said. He tested the three sugar sacks in the basement with his MO-2 portable gas analyser and got a positive reading for hexogen, the explosive used in the Moscow bombs. The timer of the detonator was set for 5.30 a.m., which would have killed many of the 250 tenants of the thirteen-storey block of flats.

The sacks were taken out of the basement at around 1.30 a.m. and driven away by the FSB. But the secret police left the detonator in the hands of the bomb squad. They photographed it later that day.

As the residents were finally allowed back into their homes at seven in the morning, one of the policemen let Mrs Stepanovna see where the bombs had been planted. She said: 'There was a bit left, and the policeman said: "There, that's it. That's the stuff that was meant to blow you up."'

The local police arrested two men that night, according to Boris Kagarlitsky, a member of the Russian Institute of Comparative Politics. 'FSB officers were caught red-handed while planting the bomb. They were arrested by the police and they tried to save themselves by showing FSB identity cards.'

Then, FSB headquarters in Moscow intervened. The two men were quietly let go.

★

The next day, on 24 September, the FSB in Moscow announced that there had never been a bomb, only a training exercise. There was no hexogen, only sugar. Pro-Kremlin newspapers reported that the Ryazan bomb squad had made a mistake when they detected hexogen. One newspaper commented that perhaps they hadn't washed their tester, a remark to which Tkachenko, the bomb disposal expert, replied: 'It wasn't an enema. There are two sources of radiation in the tester. These people don't know what they are talking about.'

Alexander Sergeyev, head of the Ryazan regional FSB, said, when asked about the training exercise: 'The decision wasn't taken by our local FSB. If it was a training exercise, it was done for everyone to check the combat readiness of all the towns in Russia. Nobody told us it was a training exercise and we didn't receive a call that it was over. For two days and nights, we didn't receive any documents or order that it was finished.'

Officially, the Minister of the Interior has forbidden the police and the FSB from talking about the bomb that never was. But few believe the Kremlin's version that it was only a training exercise.

Vasiliev said: 'I heard the official version on the radio, when the press secretary of the FSB announced that it was a training exercise. It felt extremely unpleasant. A lot of neighbours started to call me and say: "Did you hear that?" I heard it, but I cannot believe it.'

A few months later I went to Ryazan for our Channel 4 Dispatches film, 'Dying for the President', and asked one of the residents if the strangers hanging about by the basement were Chechens. He told me: 'They were Russians. The girl and both men. The girl had blonde hair, cut short.'

For our documentary I got hold of a photograph of the detonator found by the Ryazan bomb squad.

What about the bomb made of sugar?

Novaya Gazeta reported the strange story of a paratrooper, Private Aleksei Pinyaev, who says he was guarding a military warehouse before the Ryazan sugar incident when he and a mate helped themselves to the stuff in the sacks marked 'sugar' for their tea. It tasted horrible so they threw it away. Fearing they had been poisoned, they had 'the sugar' tested and it was hexogen. Pinyaev later denied the story at a press conference, staged or perhaps stage-managed by the FSB, its then boss Nikolai Patrushev, now the head of the Russian National Security Council and Putin's stand-in if he has to have surgery.

Did anyone try to take the Russian authorities to court over the Moscow apartment bombings? Yes. What happened to the lawyer involved tells you all you need to know about the rule of law in Russia under Vladimir Putin. Mikhail Trepashkin was a former FSB officer, decorated for his work by his boss, Nikolai Patrushev. Having turned lawyer, he had been hired by two sisters whose mother was killed in one of the bombed Moscow apartment buildings. Trepashkin found an early suspect whose description matched someone seen delivering explosives. But his identity had conveniently vanished from the files. Nevertheless Trepashkin had evidence that the suspect was Vladimir Romanovich, an FSB agent who had been part of an extortion ring against the Moscow Soldi Bank in 1995.

Trepashkin discovered that Romanovich's description had been deliberately removed from the police investigation file into the Moscow apartment bombings, pointing to a black operation by the state. But Trepashkin never got his day in court. Or, rather, he did but not as a lawyer. In October 2003, just a week before a hearing in which he hoped to raise the issue of the FSB agent witnessed delivering explosives to one of the Moscow apartment buildings that were blown up, Trepashkin was arrested for possessing an illegal weapon. He was convicted by a military court – sitting behind closed doors – to four years for revealing state secrets. In prison, Trepashkin suffered from asthma, dermatosis and heartburn, but he was held in a freezing punishment cell and kept with prisoners suffering from tuberculosis.

I asked Donald Rayfield who was behind the Moscow apartment bombings: 'The KGB or the FSB, as it is now. There's absolutely no doubt about that. All the evidence of witnesses is that it couldn't possibly have been Chechens. And then, of course, they were caught attempting to do the same thing in the town of Ryazan and the local police, as often happens with secret services, caught them on the hop. A local plod comes along and says, "What are you doing?" And spoils it all. They say it was just sugar, just for practice. It wasn't sugar, it was high explosive.'

In Russia, they call TNT 'Ryazan sugar'. It's a joke but not a funny one.

The evidence is compelling that the very thing which galvanized Vladimir Putin's career in Russian politics – his fightback against Chechen bomb outrages – was, in fact, a black operation by the secret police.

That Vladimir Putin blew up Russia.

In his ghosted autobiography, Putin is challenged about this and he replies: 'Blowing up our own apartment buildings? You know, that is really . . . utter nonsense! It's totally insane. No one in the Russian special services would be capable of such a crime against his own people. The very supposition is amoral. It's nothing but part of the information war against Russia.'

September 1999 is the time, the way I see it, when Russia ceases to be a democracy. The Moscow apartment bombings were Vladimir Putin's original sin, and any Russian who dared to investigate them lived in mortal danger.

Chapter Five

War Without Pity

The Chechen woman was on her own at the border between Chechnya and Ingushetia when she spotted us, a Western TV crew starting to film. She came up to me and unpacked something in a blanket and then she started to scream, 'Thank you Mr Putin!', piercingly. The something was two charred skulls, the only remains of her sisters incinerated by the Russian Army. I was shocked, utterly so.

It is hard, virtually impossible, to convey just how cruel the Second Chechen War was, how pitiless the master of the Kremlin's killing machine. The hardest thing for me, as a reporter, as a human being, to bear was to witness the colossal mistake made by the West's leaders who cuddled up to Vladimir Putin while the evidence of his war crimes in Chechnya, and the crimes against humanity committed when the FSB blew up Moscow apartment buildings, was overwhelming. George W. Bush said after his first face-to-face meeting with Putin in 2001: 'I looked the man in the eye. I found him to be very straightforward and trustworthy. We had a very good dialogue. I was able to get a sense of his soul, a man deeply committed to his country and the best interests of his country.'

Tony Blair was the very first Western leader to celebrate the new leader of Russia, travelling to St Petersburg in the spring of 2000 to attend Prokofiev's opera, *War and Peace*, with the Putins. The British prime minister blessed Putin with a face-to-face meeting before the Russian electorate voted him into office. Blair told reporters: 'We have always made clear our concerns over Chechnya and any question of human rights abuses there, though it is important to realize that Chechnya isn't Kosovo. The Russians have been subjected to really severe terrorist attacks.'

They were not terrorist attacks but black operations by the FSB. And both the CIA and MI6 knew that. James Bond is a slick fantasy. Smiley, created by John le Carré, smacks of the real thing. Spies read newspapers. They would have read the stories in *Novaya Gazeta* that raised questions about who was really responsible for the Moscow apartment bombings. In March 2000 *The Observer* published my report on the Ryazan bomb made of sugar. In 2001 a brilliant and fearless Russian journalist and MP, Yuri Shchekochikhin, printed a special issue of *Novaya Gazeta* by a former KGB colonel, Alexander Litvinenko, and the Russian-American journalist Yuri Felshtinsky, on the scandal. This became the book *Blowing Up Russia: Terror from Within*, published in 2002. The title provides a clue that even Langley (HQ of the CIA) and Vauxhall Cross (HQ of MI6) would not have missed. To help the British and American spies get access to it, *Blowing Up Russia* was placed on Russia's Federal List of Extremist Materials. In plain English, it was banned because it divulged state secrets. And if you're an American or British spy, you read the books the Kremlin bans.

In 2005 I made a BBC documentary film about Craig Murray's failed attempt to bring down then Foreign

Secretary Jack Straw in the UK's general election. The former British ambassador to Uzbekistan told me that he had seen a MI6 report on the Moscow apartment bombings, setting out the evidence that it was an own goal by the FSB.

In his 2003 book *Darkness at Dawn* the American journalist David Satter set out the scandal, and he did so again in a second book in 2016, *The Less You Know, The Better You Sleep: Russia's Road to Terror and Dictatorship under Yeltsin and Putin.* That year Satter filed a Freedom of Information request with the State Department, the FBI and CIA to find out what they knew about the Moscow apartment bombings. He got zilch. The CIA refused even to acknowledge the existence of any relevant records because doing so would reveal 'very specific aspects of the Agency's intelligence interest, or lack thereof, in the Russian bombings'.

Satter, like a dog with a bone, even got hold of a cable on the Ryazan incident from the American Embassy in Moscow, sent on 24 March 2000, which he cited: 'A former Russian intelligence officer, apparently one of the embassy's principal informants, said that the real story about the Ryazan incident could never be known because it "would destroy the country".'

If Litvinenko, Felshtinsky, Satter and I could discover the truth about the Moscow apartment bombings, so could the CIA and MI6. What happened instead was a sick-think by the Western foreign-policy establishment. They wanted to believe that Putin was a democrat, a friend of the West, someone with whom they could do business. They set out to bury the evidence to the contrary.

Their calculus was wrong. At the end of the 1990s, Putin described communism as 'a blind alley, far away from the mainstream of civilization'. His contempt for communism is real. But that, of course, does not mean that Putin embraced democracy or its essential partners that must ride along: scrutiny by a free press, free speech, tolerance of mockery and humour. Rather, Putin cherry-picked a series of ideas that coalesced together and became his guiding star: ultra-nationalism; hatred of the other; contempt for a free press and free speech; intolerance of mockery and humour; profoundly conservative social values; an unfree market in hock to political power; a reverence for 'the organs', the KGB and its alphabetic spaghetti predecessors (Cheka, GPU, OGPU, NKGB, NKVD, MGB) and offshoots (SVR, FSB). Without articulating it, with no announcement, Putin was a Russian fascist.

Moreover, Putin's outlook fits snugly within the age-old tradition of Russian autocracy, sharply drawn by the Marquis Astolphe de Custine in his 1839 travel book on the land ruled by Nicholas I, *Empire of the Czar*: 'a government that lives by mystery, and whose strength lies in dissimulation, is afraid of everything'. Stalin was an heir to this strand of autocracy, from the late 1920s effectively projecting Russian imperialism over communism, albeit with fancy, newfangled and deeply dishonest rhetoric. Putinism flows with Nicholas I's tsarism and Stalinism – and this was bleeding obvious to anyone who was paying attention.

Listening to Blair and Bush talk about Vladimir Putin's soul, having seen what I had seen in Moscow and Ryazan and Chechnya, I felt I was going mad.

In 2000 I went to Chechnya, undercover, twice.

It was scary. Two years before, four British telephone engineers working on building a mobile phone-mast system independent of the Kremlin's control were kidnapped. Then their four severed heads were found by a road. As warnings go, this was not a subtle one. A brave Russian reporter, Andrei Babitsky, reacted to the Kremlin's absurd claim in January 2000 that there were no civilians left in the Chechen capital, Grozny, by going there and reporting that was not true. He risked death because the bombardment by Russian artillery was so intense. In mid-January he was captured by Russian proxies, tortured, and finally released into Russian custody by March. So my team and I went to Chechnya when the chances of getting your head chopped off or being kidnapped were on the high side.

In February 2000 I flew to Moscow, then Nazran in Ingushetia, which is the next-door republic to Chechnya, with cameraman James Miller and producer Carla Garapedian. James and I had made a Channel Four *Dispatches* documentary about a massacre in Little Krushe in Kosovo in 1999, when Serb police and paramilitaries slaughtered more than a hundred Kosovar men and boys in a haybarn. Our film had won a Royal Television Society gong and we were good pals. James taught my children, Sam and Molly, how to surf. Carla is a brilliant and fearless American-Armenian film producer. Together, the three of us went undercover to Chechnya to document Vladimir Putin's first war.

To start, we filmed interviews with Chechens who had made it across the border to Ingushetia. Both Chechnya and Ingushetia are autonomous republics inside the Russian Federation. Chechnya's long wars with the Russian tsars and then their successors have been fought because the people want to throw out the invaders. The Second Chechen War (1999–2009) was Vladimir Putin's answer. Russian artillery camped in the outskirts of Grozny and blew it to pieces.

When columns of refugees moved towards safety, white flags attached to their cars, they were bombed.

Her face burnt almost beyond recognition, a girl lay prone on her hospital bed attended by an aunt and told in a child's whispers of the day her mother, father, her two brothers, her sister and her cousin, among 363 people from the same village, were wiped out. At eight years old – let's call her Kamiisa – she was an eyewitness to a war crime. The village of Katyr Yurt, 'safe' in the Russian-occupied zone, far from the war's front line, and jam-packed with refugees, was untouched on the morning of 4 February 2000 before Russian aircraft, helicopters, fuel-air bombs and Grad missiles pulverized the village. They paused the bombing at 3 p.m., shipped buses in, and allowed a white-flag convoy to leave, including Kamiisa's family.

And then they bombed that as well, killing Kamiisa's family and many others.

Our brave Chechen fixer, Natasha, found a rogue FSB officer who for $2,500 in cash agreed to drive James, Carla and I to Katyr Yurt. We crouched behind the darkened windows of his Volga and sailed through multiple Russian Army checkpoints until we arrived at the village. We saw what was left: a landscape as if from the Somme, streets smashed to matchwood, trees shredded, bloodstained cellars, the survivors in a frenzy of fear. The village was littered with the remains of Russian 'vacuum' bombs – fuel-air explosives that can suck your lungs inside out, their use against civilians banned by the Geneva Convention.

Local witnesses, astonished by the first visit by Western outsiders to their village, ringed west and east by special troops from the Russian secret police, the FSB, said they had counted 363 corpses piled two or three high in the street – 'so many you couldn't get a car past them' – before the Russians took many of the bodies away and dumped them in a mass grave.

Kamiisa had a cruelly burnt face, both hands burnt and bandaged, a broken right leg swathed in plaster, a left knee pinioned by iron bolts and internal bruising, and yet she wanted to tell us what happened. Kamiisa's father, Mansour, forty-five, a builder; her mother, Hava, forty-five, a schoolteacher; her brothers, Magomed, fourteen, and Ruslan, twelve; her cousin, Hava, eight; and her sister, Madina, six – they were squashed into the family's black Volga saloon. She explained how the convoy left Katyr Yurt for what they hoped was safety. 'There was a white flag on our car, flying from a wooden stick,' she said. 'Then two planes came and they hit us. We were blown up. I fell to the mud in the ground.'

Kamiisa winced as her aunt swabbed the burnt skin around her eye. The aunt said: 'At night she is scared to close her eyes. She told me that she was afraid the whole picture would come back.'

The worst was that Kamiisa's aunt could not bring herself to tell the little girl she was the only survivor of the seven people in the family car: 'I don't know how to tell her. If we tell her now, she wouldn't be able to bear it. She's already afraid to close her eyes at night. Last night she woke ten times and we can't calm her down.'

Katyr Yurt, to the west of Grozny, was quiet, calm and untouched on the night of 3 February. But Grozny had fallen and Chechen fighters had fled Russian revenge. Some of them passed through Katyr Yurt. There was one story that two Russian soldiers were kidnapped or killed that night. On the morning of 4 February, all hell began.

In January the then British Foreign Secretary Robin

Cook – a good man in many other respects – met Putin in Moscow and went out of his way to praise the secret policeman who had given out hunting knives to his troops on New Year's Day. Cook said of Putin: 'I found his style refreshing and open, and his priorities for Russia are ones that we would share.'

For my old paper, *The Observer*, I set out the evidence of what the Russian Army forces did to the civilians of Katyr Yurt, evidence that called into question the Foreign Secretary's endorsement of Putin's priorities 'that we would share'.

Rumissa Medhidova was twenty-seven, but her face was so sick with grief and horror she looked thirty years older. She became a widow on 4 February. 'All the Russians left the village and at around 10 a.m. they started to bomb. They used everything. In the centre of the village, not one house is left standing. In one family there were three children around their dead mother. They had been shot in the legs by Kalashnikovs. The Russians said: "We will give you two hours." They sent buses in with white flags.'

People rushed around to find white sheets or anything at all white to mark their cars. There was even time for a joke: 'I saw a cow with white on its horns and people were laughing.'

The convoy set off, each car showing a white flag, some cars showing two or three, packed with mainly women and children – the men held back, to make more room for children, said Rumissa. It headed west towards the town of Achoi Martan and safety. 'When we were on the open road, they fired ground-to-air rockets at us. It was a big rocket, not as big as a car. It was strange. It didn't explode once, it exploded several times. Every car had flags, how many cars I don't know. It was a mess, lots of them. They hit us without stopping.'

This sounds like Grad missiles but, with the distance of time, it is impossible to tell.

Could the Russians have mistaken the white-flag convoy for fighters? 'No, they couldn't mistake us. They knew very well there were a lot of refugees: 16,000 refugees and 8,000 locals in the village. In front of us was a big car full of children, not grown-ups. They burnt before my eyes.'

Her husband stepped out of the car and was killed by shrapnel. With her children, she ran from the carnage and made it to Achoi Martan: 'I saw a lot of bodies but I don't know how many. There were a lot of people lying on the road. I didn't count them. I also saw different parts of burnt bodies collected in buckets.'

And then the cover-up began: 'The Russians wouldn't allow the people in the village to collect the bodies. They only allowed people on the fifth day to go and collect the bodies. When people arrived there, they asked: "Where are the bodies of our people?" The Russians said some had already been burnt. People say the Russians took the bodies and threw them in a mass grave.'

Another eyewitness, a wounded man of the killable age, said: 'They started bombing. Bombs, artillery. They were killing people. At our local school on the edge of the village there were Spetsnaz [Russian Special Forces] troops. They said: "We will give you a safe corridor." So everyone started to go towards Achoi Martan. Then they used rockets against us. Some say 350 refugees were killed, 170 from the village itself.'

Zara Aktimirova, aged fifty-nine, had been looking after her mother, Matusa Batalova, eighty-five, hit by shrapnel. 'The fear was so terrible I do not have the words . . . We were in a cellar. You could hear the vacuum bombs: "Whoosh,

whoosh". We just got into this cellar and the whole house next to us was completely destroyed. If someone ran to the apartment block entrance, snipers would fire and hit arms and legs.'

Later she and her mother passed along the road and saw the wreckage of the white-flag convoy: 'The cars were mangled up, like mincemeat. I didn't count the cars, I was carrying my mother. The convoy stretched maybe three kilometres. Every car was hit.'

Her mother was dying.

Our fifth witness, a doctor, was glassy-eyed and dead-tired after operating on hundreds of patients without anaesthetics, medicines or electricity during the bombardment. He said: 'First they hit the village, then they gave civilians a corridor and then they opened fire. They didn't bring the dead to us, only those in agony. They brought ten bodies, to check if they were alive or not: one baby among them, grown-ups, teenagers, some without both legs, burnt with traumas to the head, stomach. There were a lot of bodies in the village they didn't bring to us.'

Our sixth witness stood outside the ruin of his home in Katyr Yurt, leaning on two crutches. Rizvan Vakhaev, forty-seven, was contemptuous of the dangers of speaking out. When two vacuum bombs fell outside his house, the blasts killed eight people: six women, a man and an eleven-year-old boy outright; ten more died later. His wife was seriously injured, as were three of his children. His daughter-in-law died immediately.

He showed us where the children had been lying before the blast, and the remains of human intestines lying on the ground. The vacuum bomb was dropped by a parachute. As it falls to the ground, it releases a cloud of petrol vapour, which ignites, and the sky explodes. A US Defence Intelligence Agency study from 1993 reported: 'The kill mechanism against living targets is unique and unpleasant. What kills is the pressure wave, and more importantly, the subsequent rarefaction [vacuum], which ruptures the lungs.'

An old lady, our seventh witness, emerged from a hole in the ground, trembling. She put a piece of bread to her mouth: 'We didn't eat yesterday and today. It was like Doomsday. Helicopters, planes, three bombs fell when we were in the cellar. Three sons and one daughter died. Our fourth son is dying at the hospital.'

On our way out of the village, we stopped by the mosque. There we met our last eyewitness. He had made a tally of all the bodies before the Russians took them away, dragging some by chains from car bumpers. He had tried to wash the bodies and give them some decency in the Muslim tradition. And the number of the dead? '363,' he said.

As we left the ruins of Katyr Yurt, we saw wreckage from what was left of the white-flag convoy: broken cars, twisted, charred metal, a boot lying in the mud. And then we heard a burst of machine-gun fire, an echo of what Robin Cook had called 'the refreshing and open' language of Vladimir Putin.

For my podcast, 'Taking On Putin', released after the February 2022 invasion of Ukraine, I dug out a clip from our 2000 film. You could hear Kamiisa's words read by a little English girl: 'When we were going on the road, two planes hit our car, my Daddy, Mamet and Mummy were sitting in front. Rusik, me, Medina, Hava and Luisa were sitting in the back. Daddy and Hava were still in the car. Rusik, me, Medina and Louisa were thrown out onto the mud.'

I asked Kamiisa whether the car had been flying a white flag?

'It was tied on a wooden stick,' she said.

By the way, the voice of Kamiisa back then in 2000 was read by my daughter, Molly, who was also eight at the time.

In the summer of 2000 I left *The Observer* and joined the BBC. I popped into Chechnya again, this time my cover was that I was an accountant for the Salvation Army – no one asked, so it worked – and I made a documentary for BBC Radio Five, *Victims of the Torture Train*. Russian soldiers parked a long train on a branch line, handcuffed Chechen prisoners to the seats and slowly worked them over, going down the carriages. They also had a base where they tortured the high-priority prisoners. One procedure was known as the Slon or Elephant after the flexible trunk of the standard Russian Army issue gas mask. A prisoner would be handcuffed behind the back, the 'Slon' fixed to his face. The Russians would unscrew the filter and then squirt CS gas down the trunk. The prisoner would start to drown in his own tears and snot, a hideous enhancement of water-boarding.

There were other tortures I heard about, too horrible to tell anyone, let alone report. To deal with this, I deliberately brought with me six books by P.G. Wodehouse. I would interview Chechens who had been tortured all day, then return to my hotel and knock back a bottle of vodka and inhale *The Code of the Woosters*. By around two o'clock in the morning the combination of alcohol and Bertie getting back the cow-creamer for Aunt Dahlia would work its magic and I'd fall asleep. Some nights, I just could not.

Bombing a white-flag convoy is a war crime. So is using vacuum bombs against civilians. So is torture on an industrial scale. I saw damning evidence of all three in Putin's war on Chechnya and I came away struggling to understand how the West could let these Russian crimes against humanity go unchecked. The evidence that Vladimir Putin was a war criminal in 2000 was clear. All I can say is this: I bloody well told you so.

Why did Blair and Bush, the Foreign Office and the State Department, MI6 and the CIA read Putin so wrong?

Before the 2022 invasion of Ukraine, I chewed that fat with Professor Donald Rayfield, thinking about the West's love-in with Vladimir Putin, when he was the new secret policeman on the block. The professor reflected: 'He doesn't drink. That to them, after Yeltsin and Khrushchev, was a blessing. The most frightening Soviet leaders were the ones that drank because they could press a button at any time. Putin drinks a little, but not enough to be out of control. Secondly, he's pretty rational. He calculates the risk and profit and loss of every action he undertakes. He's rather like Stalin in that sense. He's very, very good with occasional mistakes about calculating risk and therefore pretty cautious in international adventures. When he rips off a bit of another country, he does it at a time when he's pretty sure there'll be no consequences or none worth worrying about. So I suppose dealing with a rational or apparently rational psychopath is better than dealing with an irrational drunk. And the fact that he had everything under control meant there was going to be no more trouble in Russia. They felt there wouldn't be territories trying to break away, there wouldn't be rioting. Russian oil, gas, nickel and whatever else they supplied to the West would be mined, sold and distributed without hitches. I think that this was the West's calculation. He may be a bastard but he was going to run things properly and we will be able to make a profit out of it.'

But what if Tony Blair & Co made a big mistake, that Putin wasn't a stable psychopath but an unstable one? What then? And the butcher's bill? Well, to begin with, that was paid by others. People like Kamiisa.

Twenty-one years after I first saw Kamiisa's horribly burnt face in hospital, I caught up with her, thanks to great digging by Jenny Klochko, a Ukrainian journalist based in London. Now Kamiisa is married with two girls and a third on the way. I asked her, when you see Vladimir Putin coming to London and meeting the Queen, talking to our prime ministers, what do you think?

'Can I really say it? Who is going to listen to it?' replied Kamiisa.

'You know what you think, and you don't want to say it,' I replied.

'Yes.'

'I understand,' I said. 'People in Russia are afraid to talk. That's true isn't it?'

'We are afraid to breathe.'

Chapter Six

The Poisonings Begin

Vladimir Putin's first election campaign running up to the poll in March 2000 for President of Russia went swimmingly. He was hugely popular with the Russian electorate and Western leaders because he was – or seemed to be – everything that Boris Yeltsin was not: sober, measured, coherent. His poll ratings soared on the back of his populist tough talk about the Chechen terror threat and soared again when Grozny was flattened and victory declared. But he couldn't be too careful. Yeltsin's legacy of free speech still lingered, more or less; a rough and ready journalism clung on. There were people who knew stuff about Putin, back in the day, back in St Petersburg when he got too close to the Tambov crime gang. The number one danger was his oldest friend in politics, Anatoly Sobchak.

One of Putin's first moves as prime minister in September 1999 was to kick a corruption investigation into Sobchak – which, of course, would also have reflected badly on his one-time deputy – into the long grass, enabling Sobchak to return to Russia from self-imposed exile in Paris. Sobchak's gratitude was effusive. The old narcissist wanted to get back into the big time and he dropped his old liberal values to pump up the coming man, comparing Putin to Stalin. What was needed, said Sobchak, was 'a new Stalin, not as bloodthirsty but no less brutal and firm because that is the only way to get Russians to do any work'.

Behind this gibberish, what was really going on inside the former law professor's head? Did he really think Russia needed a new Stalin? Or did he just want to get a desk at the Kremlin and, in reality, was faking his fealty to the man who used to carry his bags? If so, there was a Sobchak problem.

On 17 February 2000 Putin asked Sobchak to do some campaigning for him in Kaliningrad, a Russian enclave sandwiched between Poland and Lithuania on the ruins of what was, until 1946, Königsberg, the historic capital of Prussia. Sobchak duly went there, accompanied by two assistants-cum-bodyguards. Three days later he suffered a heart attack and died. He was a healthy man, sixty-two years old, with several books to his name and an international reputation as one of the most interesting figures of the New Russia. The odd thing was that his two bodyguards also reportedly suffered heart attacks. Cardiac infarctions are not infectious. That three men suffered heart attacks all at the same time points to a single cause: poisoning.

The late Russian journalist Arkady Vaksberg wrote a superb yet very grim book on the love affair between the Kremlin and poison from Lenin to Stalin to Putin. *Toxic Politics: The Secret History of the Kremlin's Poison Laboratory from the Special Cabinet to the Death of Litvinenko* touches on the Sobchak story. Vaksberg writes that the journalist Yuri Shchekochikhin told him that Sobchak was 'poisoned by a substance sprayed onto the reading lamp on his bedside table. The heat radiating from the light-bulb dispersed the poison into the air, attacking anyone in the vicinity and causing heart failure.'

Vaksberg goes on to suggest that only Putin would have the power to commission the poisoning. But, given that Sobchak helped him get a job in the Kremlin back in 1996, why? Vaksberg writes: 'What Sobchak had done should have made Putin even more grateful. But in politics gratitude is a double-edged sword. When it becomes a constraint and you are constantly reminded of the debt you owe, the situation can become intolerable.' Vaksberg cites an anonymous source, saying: 'Sobchak was the victim of his own folly in thinking he could return to power since that would have made Putin a hostage to Sobchak's personal ambitions. Putin had to pull this thorn out of his flesh as quickly as possible ... It was no fun being the boss of his former boss if only because Sobchak would have made a better president.'

Sobchak could not keep up the flattery of his old servant and new master. He announced that he was running for parliament. Just before his death, he gave an interview to a reporter from the Spanish newspaper, *El País*.

Question: 'Is it your hope that Putin will help you out?'

Sobchak: 'I don't need his help. I am a university lecturer and writer whose books have been published all over the world ... I am not interested in holding office. I prefer being independent.'

Vaksberg writes: 'It was not a totally honest answer and it showed that there had been a falling-out between the two men.'

At the funeral, a grieving, red-eyed Putin supported Sobchak's widow Lyudmila and her daughter, Ksenia. It is the only time that the Russian public have ever seen Putin cry.

Sobchak's widow had her own autopsy done on her husband's body. Gabriel Gatehouse, for the BBC, asked her if she thought her husband had been murdered. She paused long enough to say 'Yes' ten times over and then replied: 'I don't know.' She never made the autopsy results public but keeps the documents locked in a safe in a secret location outside Russia.

> Gatehouse: 'It sounds like you've got yourself some kind of insurance policy.'
> Lyudmila: 'You could see it that way.'
> Gatehouse: 'Are you afraid for your own safety or that of your daughter?'
> Lyudmila: 'You know to live in this country is scary. Especially for those who hold opposition views. So yes, I am afraid.'

You might take out this kind of insurance policy against a gangster who has a thing about poison.

Or a president.

Or someone who is both.

During that summer of 2000 something happened which showed Putin's true colours. A Russian submarine, the *Kursk*, on exercise in the Barents Sea, suffered an explosion and was crippled. Twenty-three sailors were still alive but entombed in the sub. NATO had the kit and the know-how to save the trapped submariners, but the Kremlin's response was to sit, in near silence, until every last one died from lack of oxygen. Putin stayed on holiday in the Black Sea. When he finally gave an interview about the tragedy, he stared impassively at the interviewer and said two words: 'It sank.'

A four-page summary of a secret report into the tragedy was damning, revealing: 'stunning breaches of discipline, shoddy, obsolete and poorly maintained equipment' and 'negligence, incompetence and mismanagement'. That could also be the epitaph for the Russian Army in the Battle of Kyiv.

The relatives of the dead submariners were outraged. Ten days after the tragedy Putin and the navy top brass met around 500 people who had lost family on the *Kursk*. The Russian state TV channel, RTR, was the only media granted official access but they had to up their satellite feed via a sat truck lent to RTR by the German TV company, RTL, which captured the whole thing. Putin assured the grieving relatives that the Russian Navy had accepted offers of Western help immediately. This was a dark lie and everyone knew it. In fact, British and Norwegian divers did finally open a hatch on the doomed sub but found no one alive. Had the Kremlin moved faster, it's not impossible that lives could have been saved. What is certain is that Putin came across as callous, cold and uncaring. Nadezhda Tylik, mother of submariner Lieutenant Sergei Tylik, turned on Putin and his deputy prime minister: 'You better shoot yourselves now! We won't let you live, you bastards!'

A nurse jabbed the bereft mother in the arm with a syringe, knocking her out cold. Her husband was quoted as saying that he had asked the nurse to give his wife the injection because 'she was prone to excessive emotions'. Later, his wife said that this was a lie: 'the injection was done to shut my mouth'.

In 2000 Russia's parliament, the Duma, still functioned as a body that called power to account. Yury Shchekochikhin MP, a tough liberal democrat from the Yabloko Party, originally an Azeri, with steel-grey hair, a boxer's nose and bright, mischievous eyes, accused the Kremlin of covering up the fact that Russia did not have the resources to attempt a rescue of the *Kursk*. Deputy Prime Minister Ilya Klebanov denied that the government had lied during and after the disaster, but amid hostile questions he conceded that statements were made 'in the heat of the moment without enough analysis'.

Everything about the loss of the *Kursk* in 2000 prefigures the 2022 invasion of Ukraine: the Kremlin's lack of interest in its own people; their shoddy and obsolete kit; the contempt for proper scrutiny; the silencing of honest criticism. The lesson Putin learnt from the sinking of the *Kursk* was entirely fascistic. He had suffered a lot of heat from Russia's free and independent media for his slow and heartless response. The solution was to switch it off. Russian TV had been a source of fearless news. Putin used his proxy oligarchs to take it over and remove its teeth. People could switch on and watch something that called itself news, but as time wore on it became a work of fiction. Boris Berezovsky, who had once been Putin's champion, was stripped of his assets including ORT, Russia's largest television channel. Elbowed out of the power ziggurat, he found himself in exile in London, breathing fire.

Putin was lucky twice over. His first great test in 2001, following the disaster of 9/11, was to react immediately by being the very first foreign leader to express his condolences to President George W. Bush, and to offer all practical support for the American mission to stamp out Al Qaeda. From that point onwards, Putin's acquiescence in the 'War on Terror', first in Afghanistan, then Iraq, meant that he was somehow baked in to the West's grand strategy, foolish as it was. It meant that, time and again, Washington DC and London gave the Kremlin the benefit of the doubt because Putin was on side in the war against Islamist extremism. That he was something of an Orthodox Russian extremist got missed.

His second source of luck was that the Iraq War in the Middle East drove up oil prices from a long low of around $25 a barrel up and up to peaks of $141 a barrel in 2008. During Putin's first eight years in office the Russian economy grew by 7 per cent a year and the price of oil and gas went up fivefold. Compared to anxieties in the Middle East, Russian oil and gas was cheap and stable and this meant that the Kremlin was sitting on a sump of black gold. Much of this money disappeared into sunny places for shady people, so that the oligarchs could buy their mansions and palazzos in Britain, France and Italy, sometimes for themselves, sometimes as proxies for Putin. But it is true that some of Russia's oil and gas boom did trickle down and Putin was the beneficiary. The deal between the Russian state and the oligarchs was pretty clear: keep your nosy beaks out of politics, out of power, and enjoy your money. But if you ask the wrong kind of questions, things will not go well for you. It was a recipe for the zombification of Russia.

There is something Nixonian about Vladimir Putin. In 1972 Nixon had every prospect of winning a landslide victory against his Democratic rival, George McGovern, without cheating. But Nixon had to cheat. Likewise, Putin had to kill.

In October 2002 more than fifty Chechen terrorists broke into the Dubrovka Theatre in Moscow and held 850 hostages, demanding that the Russian Army withdraw from their homeland. Instead of negotiating, Russian special forces gassed the theatre, killing at least 170 people. Instead of a proper inquiry into the tragedy, nearly all the Chechen terrorists were executed on the spot; the nature of the lethal gas was never properly investigated; nor who made the critical decision to pump a chemical poison into a restricted space packed with people. Questions remain about the siege. In simple terms they are: first, how was it possible for fifty-plus Chechens, armed to the teeth with machine guns and explosive vests, to travel across Moscow without being stopped by the police? For context, I have never once been to Moscow without being detained, at least for a short time, by the state. They go through your passport, check out your address, eat your time with a bone-numbing persistence. Second, why didn't the terrorists set off their explosive vests immediately when the gas was detected? It took some ten minutes to take full effect. Third, why were nearly all the terrorists executed? Fourth, why was there no antidote to the poison gas?

The Duma, the Russian parliament, dominated by the Kremlin, threw out a motion by the liberal democrats to set up a committee to investigate the theatre siege. So the good people set up one of their own. It was carried out in Russia by the veteran dissident Sergei Kovalev, MP, Sergei Yushenkov, MP, the lawyer and former FSB officer Mikhail Trepashkin, the journalist Anna Politkovskaya, with help from the rock-steady Yuri Shchekochikhin; and, from the United States, the Hoover Institute scholar John B. Dunlop, and the former FSB colonel Alexander Litvinenko in London.

When Sergei Yushenkov visited London in early 2003, Litvinenko handed him a file on one of the terrorists, Khanpasha Terkibayev, also known as Abu Bakar. (The formula is Arabic, Abu meaning 'father of'.) His name was published by the Russian media as one of the hostage-takers the day before the Russian special forces launched their poison-gas attack. Mysteriously, Terkibayev was still alive. How come? The Terkibayev file contained astonishing evidence, much of it from the former anti-Kremlin Chechen foreign minister and freedom fighter, Akhmed Zakayev, now based in London. Terkibayev was a Chechen who had switched sides and was suspecting of working for the Russian secret services. In April 2001 and March 2002 he was arrested by Russian forces in Chechnya and, twice, miraculously, released. This was when Chechen men suspected of fighting for the rebels were routinely tortured, then shot.

One month after the theatre siege, Terkibayev surfaced in Azerbaijan, alive and well. Of course he was. Incredibly, Anna Politkovskaya tracked him down and interviewed the terrorist who got away. She didn't trust him for a second but found him to be a vain and boastful fop, eager to tell her that he worked for Moscow. The objective facts were simple. Anna had got into the theatre in the early hours of the siege as a peacemaker. She had seen Terkibayev in the theatre and somehow he had been allowed to leave and was seen to be working in tandem with the Russian government. Terkibayev was, indeed, Moscow's man.

The independent investigation into the theatre siege concluded that Chechen terrorists did attack the theatre but they were directed and controlled by the FSB agent provocateur, Terkibayev. A few days after getting the file from Litvinenko in London, Yushenkov returned home to Moscow where he was shot dead outside his flat. Four men were convicted of his assassination, the most noteworthy being Mikhail Kodanev, a former chairman of Yushenkov's Liberal Russia party. Kodanev denied guilt at the trial. The evidence against him came from another convicted suspect, Alexander Vinnik, who made a series of nonsensical claims that contradicted each other.

Some months later, Terkibayev died in 'a car crash' in Chechnya. As the body count grew, the Kremlin and its patsies in parliament blocked any further inquiry. But the evidence of wrongdoing by the Russian secret state piled up.

One mystery was that the terrorists never exploded their bombs when the poison gas was detected. The reason? The detonators for the bombs in the theatre had no batteries; the bombs were, in fact, 'imitation plastic explosives' provided by the Russian Ministry of Defence, according to the Moscow City prosecutor's office.

One can only conclude that the Moscow theatre siege of 2002, like the Moscow apartment bombings of 1999, was a black operation by the FSB. The machinery of fear was in place and in power and anyone who stood up to it would suffer.

Yuri Shchekochikhin had courage which made him stand out, even in this select company. He had tremendous energy, a nose for a story and, I've been told, a fondness for Armenian brandy. In his book Vaksberg recalls meeting him in January 2003: 'I met Yuri quite by chance in Peredelkino near Moscow. He told me with his relaxed smile, "They [and, of course, there was no reason to specify whom he meant by they] would love to have me shot, but somehow can't bring themselves to do it."' Later, writes Vaksberg, he told a friend: 'For the first time in my life I feel frightened.'

In an interview in early 2003 Shchekochikhin set out Putin's Russia in a nutshell: 'The mafiya has put on uniform. The gangsters are boy scouts compared to our security services. Today it is precisely the people who are supposed to be fighting crime who are corrupt. This has not bypassed the secret police. The protection that they provide, the enormous amounts of money that they receive, the control that they exercise.'

Such a crystal spirit could not be allowed to exist.

Still on the case of the bomb made of sugar, the one that didn't go off in Ryazan, Shchekochikhin was planning a trip there, roughly 125 miles south-east of Moscow, and then he was going to New York to talk to the FBI. They were investigating the Moscow apartment bombings on behalf of a Russian-American woman whose mother had been killed in the flats. But then Shchekochikhin started feeling unwell. He went ahead anyway with his trip to Ryazan, grew feverish, felt as though his head was on fire. When he returned to Moscow, he became dizzy and his throat burned. His blood pressure dropped, his skin turned red. The next day his skin began to peel off and his hair started to fall out. He was rushed to the Central Clinical Hospital, known by its nickname 'the Kremlinka' because it looks after the power elite and, sometimes, those who cross them. The doctors diagnosed 'toxic agents of an unknown origin'.

Shchekochikhin's girlfriend Alyona Gromova described his condition to journalist Jenny Klochko for the 'Taking On Putin' podcast: 'On the day he was taken to hospital, he felt very weak. After he had a shower, his hair was a mess. I went to stroke it and great clumps of hair came out in my hand. The symptoms were confusing. First, it seemed like a cold but his face was very red, as if he had sunburn, then lumps of his skin started to flake off.'

Vaksberg writes about his dying friend: 'Yuri's condition worsened by the hour. His temperature rose continuously. His mucous membranes were swollen and his kidneys were failing . . . Then the worst began. His skin began to peel off as though he had suffered severe burns. Even a layman could see what was happening: it was either due to radiation or to some unknown poisons.'

The official verdict was Lyell's Syndrome or a severe allergic reaction. Shchekochikhin died on 3 July 2003. By then he had practically no skin left on his body. Vaksberg writes:

'The word poison was never pronounced, although everyone took it for granted. Fear kept people quiet.'

Shchekochikhin's friend, the poet Andrei Voznesensky, wrote some words mourning his loss. This is my attempt at translation:

Shards, a mirror cracked.
In pieces, then, a dread July sky,
Hats, velvet stumps,
A silence.
Yuri's restless soul
Could not be shamed.
So, for the last Russian saint:
Poison.

Alyona went to say goodbye to her lover in the morgue: 'It was a big place, a huge hall. There were bodies on slabs, due to be buried the next day. I looked around. There were about twenty people but I couldn't find Yuri. I went up to the supervisor and explained that I might be in the wrong place as I couldn't find him. Through the corner of my eye I saw a dear old lady who was lying on a slab. The strangest thing, she reminded me of my grandma who passed away a long time ago. The curious resemblance of the two old ladies hit me. In my worst nightmares, I could never, ever have imagined that the dear old lady was in fact Yuri.'

Her lover was so unrecognizable that Alyona could not find him in the morgue until the supervisor pointed out his name tag to her.

The poisonings had only just begun.

Chapter Seven

A Death of No Significance

The Second Chechen War ended to be replaced by a dark and cruel peace, the republic run by a Kremlin quisling, Akhmad Kadyrov, and when he was blown up by Islamist rebels, his son, Ramzan. Chechens loyal to the cause of national self-determination, or simply ordinary people who got in the way, were tortured and killed. The number of Russian journalists willing to call the Russian Army to account was vanishingly small. The best of Russia was Anna Politkovskaya, a slight, steely woman with ash-blonde hair, cut short, and wire-framed spectacles.

In 2001 Anna came to London, where I was asked by Amnesty International to interview her. My BBC radio documentary, *Victims of the Torture Train*, had won an Amnesty prize and they thought we would make a good fit. To be honest, it didn't work out very well. The public Anna was forbidding, steely, not impressed by my silly patter. When in this kind of slightly tricky situation, I go all Frankie Howerd – 'ooh, er, missus' – throwing bad jokes after bad. We didn't gel. It was only years later when I saw a brilliant documentary about Anna, *A Bitter Taste of Freedom*, that I recognized her as someone with a gorgeous sense of the absurd, helpless with laughter at times, bent double cackling at the black comedy of life.

She was ferociously brave. Early in 2001 she was in the mountain village of Khattuni where she had been investigating complaints by dozens of families about the brutal conduct of the Russian authorities. Rosita, a Chechen grandmother from the village of Tovzeni, told Anna she had been tortured for twelve days, enduring beatings, electric shocks and being held in a pit, open to the freezing air, by FSB officers. The torturers demanded and got a ransom. Another interviewee described the systematic rape and killing of Chechen men. Anna reported it all, describing a 'concentration camp with a business angle' run by the FSB, where torture was used to extort money.

On her way home, Anna was arrested, interrogated and beaten by the Russian FSB troops: 'The young officers tortured me, skilfully exploring my weak points. They went through photos of my kids, saying what they would like to do to them.'

Anna explains what happened next in her book, *A Small Corner of Hell*. Read it.

'A lieutenant colonel with a swarthy face and dull dark bulging eyes said in a matter-of-fact tone: "Let's go. I'm going to shoot you." He led me out of the tent into complete darkness. The nights here are impenetrable. After we walked for a while, he said, "Ready or not, here I come." Something exploded, fire, so close, screeching, roaring, growling. The lieutenant colonel was very happy when I slumped with fear.'

The officer had led Anna right under the barrels of a 'Grad' multiple rocket launcher the instant it opened fire. After the mock execution, the colonel told her to take off her clothes. She refused. They were afraid of her courage and, in some strange way, in awe of it too.

The evidence of the Russian secret state's black operation in the Moscow apartment bombings and the Kremlin's extreme brutality in Chechnya was plain and clear for all to see by spring 2001. That summer George W. Bush invited Putin to his ranch in Texas, looked into his soul and liked what he saw.

Bloody hell.

And, of course, there was the then German Chancellor, Gerhard Schröder. Don't worry: I shall deal with him later on in this narrative.

On the first day of the school term in September, the tradition in Russia is for all the kids to put on their very best uniforms and for the girls to wear ribbons in their hair. In 2004 the first day at school in Beslan, a town in the far south of Russia, led to a bloody massacre and yet more questions about the relationship between the Russian secret state and Islamist terrorists. The Chechens held a thousand staff and children hostage while an uneasy stand-off developed. Thanks to her fearless reporting of the brutality of the Russian authorities in Chechnya, Anna Politkovskaya was trusted, even by the most militant extremists. The moment news of the siege broke, she hurried to Moscow's Vnukovo airport. Flights south kept on being cancelled. She used her phone to contact a Chechen go-between, knowing that it would be tapped, and suddenly an airport executive introduced himself and got her on a flight to Rostov, still 430 miles north of Beslan but the closest hub.

Anna wrote up what happened next in her diary, published in *The Guardian:* 'In the minibus, the driver tells me that the Russian security services, the FSB, told him to put me on the Rostov flight. As I board, my eyes meet those of three passengers sitting in a group: malicious eyes, looking at an enemy. But I don't pay attention. This is the way most FSB people look at me. The plane takes off. I ask for a tea. It is many hours by road from Rostov to Beslan and war has taught me that it's better not to eat. At 21:50 I drink it. At 22:00 I realize that I have to call the air stewardess as I am rapidly losing consciousness. My other memories are scrappy: the stewardess weeps and shouts: "We're landing, hold on!"'

The peacemaker woke up in a hospital in Rostov. A nurse whispered to her: 'My dear, they tried to poison you.' All the medical tests taken at the airport were destroyed on orders 'from on high', the doctors told her. The poisoning had a lasting effect on Anna's health. At the time Lana Estemirova was a schoolgirl who looked on Anna – a close friend of her mother, Natalia Estemirova, a human rights worker and journalist in Chechnya – as an auntie. Lana told the 'Taking On Putin' podcast: 'After the poisoning, Anna would not eat my mum's cooking. To be honest, it was not the best but I was a little offended on my mum's behalf and, being a kid, I didn't properly understand what had happened. I remember Anna bringing some packets of oatmeal. She just used to make oatmeal for herself in a little cup. I asked my mum why she wouldn't eat our food. And my mom explained to me why. I'll never forget that conversation.'

With the peacemaker out of action, recovering in hospital from the poison, Putin ordered his troops to attack and 333 people were killed, thirty or so of them terrorists. Of the dead, 186 were children. As with the Moscow apartment bombings and the Moscow theatre siege, a series of questions about the Kremlin's conduct were raised but were never properly answered. The mothers and fathers of the dead children wanted to know why the Russian special forces attacked while some form of peace negotiations were still going on, why they used tanks and Shmel rocket flamethrowers, and why the Russian tactics showed such a complete lack of concern for the children?

The Russian journalist Pavel Felgenhauer accused the government of firing rockets from an Mi-24 attack helicopter, something the authorities denied. It is possible that 80 per cent of the dead, more than 250 adults and children, were not killed by the terrorists but by Russian forces. Felgenhauer wrote: 'It was not a hostage rescue operation but an army operation aimed at wiping out the terrorists.'

Yuri Savelyev, one of Russia's leading rocket scientists, wrote a coruscating 280-page report for parliament in 2006 which clearly blamed the massacre on Russian forces and the Kremlin. He concluded that the authorities decided to storm the school but falsely contrived to give the impression they were only responding to the actions of the terrorists. Savelyev, a weapons and explosives expert, said that special forces, ignoring active peace talks, fired rocket-propelled grenades without warning and then launched their attack.

When you look deeper into the siege of Beslan, the clock strikes thirteen.

David Satter wrote an extraordinary piece for the Hudson Institute in 2006, setting out the evidence that the attack on the school could have been prevented. Internal police documents obtained by *Novaya Gazeta* showed that the police knew four hours in advance that an attack on a school in Beslan was planned for 1 September 2004. The terrorists were allowed to train for weeks nearby, undisturbed. They were able to drive in convoy to the school down roads which are normally heavily policed. The majority of the terrorists were supposed to be in prison and had been freed recently. None of that could have happened without the say-so of the FSB.

Once again, the only credible explanation for the siege of Beslan is that the Russian secret state orchestrated an attack by terrorists and then used maximum force to destroy the evidence of its complicity. So not one black operation by the machinery of fear, but three: the Moscow apartment bombings of 1999; the Moscow theatre siege of 2002; the Beslan massacre of 2004. The goal was to create a state of terror; the victims the ordinary people of Russia in their hundreds; the only true beneficiary the master of the Kremlin.

Two months after the Beslan siege, human remains and passports were found in a local rubbish dump. A coda giving all you need to know about how much the Russian secret state values the lives of others.

Whenever I see TV footage of Putin pimp-rolling into the great hall of the Kremlin, doors the size of African bull elephants being swung aside by soldiers dressed to the nines in pseudo-tsarist schmutter, I am reminded of Anna Politkovskaya's withering contempt for the little spy. Anna called Putin 'this strutting Chekist' – the common nickname for the secret police, dating back to Lenin's time when the forerunners of the KGB were known as the Cheka, a short form for the Extraordinary Commission.

She focused her wrath into a book, *Putin's Russia*. She accused Putin and the FSB of killing civil society in order to bring back a Soviet-style dictatorship. But the complacency of ordinary Russians disgusted her too: 'Society has shown limitless apathy as the Chekists have become entrenched in power, we have let them see our fear, and thereby have only intensified their urge to treat us like cattle. The KGB respects only the strong. The weak it devours. We of all people ought to know that . . . We are hurtling back into a Soviet abyss, into an information vacuum that spells death from our own ignorance. All we have left is the internet, where information is still freely available. For the rest, if you want to go on working as a journalist, it's total servility to Putin. Otherwise, it can be death, the bullet, poison, or trial – whatever our special services, Putin's guard dogs, see fit.'

Re-reading just one of Anna's lines, 'We are hurtling back into a Soviet abyss, into an information vacuum that spells death from our own ignorance', while sitting in a flat in Kyiv, with tank-traps on Khreshchatyk, the capital's great street, and sandbags piled up outside City Hall, knowing that Putin is still polling well, that his 'special military operation' enjoys, more or less, public support in Russia, makes me weep for the loss of the power of her prophecy.

Some of the last lines she wrote were in an essay, *Am I Afraid?* 'People often tell me that I am a pessimist, that I don't believe in the strength of the Russian people, that I am obsessive in my opposition to Putin and see nothing beyond that ... If anybody thinks they can take comfort from the "optimistic" forecast, let them do so. It is certainly the easier way, but it is a death sentence for our grandchildren.'

In October 2006 Lana Estemirova, then a young teenager, and her mother Natalia were together on a bus in Chechnya, waiting for it to start moving, when her mum's mobile rang: 'I just remember her face turning white, actually seeing the blood leave her face. And she just said, "Anna's been killed in Moscow." We almost fell out of that bus, she said, "Stop. Don't, don't, don't drive off." And we just got off and I was really scared that she would cry because for me, just the scariest sight in the world was my mum crying because I'd only seen it maybe once before. But she didn't cry. She really composed herself in front of me. And we just walked home for about maybe three or four miles, in silence. Probably she was getting phone call after phone call after phone call but in my head, it was just this complete silence. That's what I remember. And she left, I think, the next day to Moscow, to the funeral. I stayed behind. And it was a very, very grim moment.'

Anna Politkovskaya was gunned down by a lone assassin as she stepped out of the lift in her apartment block in Moscow. The date? 7 October. Which just so happens to be Vladimir Putin's birthday.

A man who may have pulled the trigger was convicted, but who ordered the hit? We don't know. Afterwards, Putin said that Anna was a woman whose influence was 'extremely insignificant'. The truth was that she was extremely significant, very dangerous to his hold on power. No one else was asking the questions she was.

And then her voice was silenced.

Chapter Eight

One Lump or Two?

It's the summer of 2006 and Vladimir Putin gets out of his motorcade and walks towards the Kremlin. Every now and then he likes to play folksy leader, at one with and at ease with the 'narod', the Russian people. On his walkabout he spots a blonde Russian boy, who looks five years old, if that, and kneels before him. Putin lifts up the boy's shirt and kisses him on the stomach. You can watch a video on YouTube: just search for 'Putin kisses a boy on stomach.'

It is creepy, very.

I ask a Russian woman for her reaction, whether this was a Russian thing. She replies: 'I was shocked. It's not a Russian thing. It's totally wrong. It's absolutely not in Russian culture. OK, Russians, after maybe one bottle of vodka, they become more friendly, but not like this.'

The name of my Russian friend is Marina Litvinenko and her husband was Alexander 'Sasha' Litvinenko, a former colonel in the KGB-FSB. What he made of the video of Putin kneeling down and kissing the little boy on the stomach and the Kremlin's reaction to it created headlines around the world. But to work out what happened we need to understand the back history of the strange relationship between the two former KGB officers, Putin and Litvinenko.

A career officer in the secret service, Litvinenko, when the Soviet Union imploded, stayed with the renamed FSB, working in its branch dealing with organized crime. He came across repeated instances of his fellow FSB officers working for and being paid off by organized crime. Straight, moral, incorruptible, Litvinenko was disgusted by the sleaze and went out of his way to write detailed, lengthy reports on it and set them out on the desks of his bosses. Time and again, his efforts to clean up his own service came to naught: 'If your partner cheated you, or a creditor did not pay up, or a supplier did not deliver, where did you turn to complain? When force became a commodity, there was always demand for it. Protection rackets' – in Russian, *krysha*, literally, 'roof' – 'appeared, people who sheltered and protected your business. First it was provided by the mob, then by police, and soon even our own guys realized what was what, and then the rivalry began among gangsters, cops, and the agency' – the FSB – 'for market share. As the police and the FSB became more competitive, they squeezed the gangs out of the market. However, in many cases competition gave way to cooperation, and the security services became gangsters themselves.'

This is exactly what Yuri Shchekochikhin warned about before his skin started to peel off.

In 1994 Berezovsky, the Russian oligarch who later on invested heavily in Vladimir Putin as a potential successor to Yeltsin, was making a fortune by importing foreign cars, much to the dismay of Russian car-makers. The solution was to blow up his car. His driver died but the oligarch survived and Litvinenko investigated the assassination plot. Berezovsky was grateful for Litvinenko's honesty and tenacity and the two men hit it off. In 1998 Berezovsky, ever the power-broker, introduced Litvinenko to Vladimir Putin, whom he had just helped become the new boss of the FSB. Berezovsky said: 'Go see Putin. Make yourself known. See what a great guy we have installed, with your help.'

Litvinenko reported to Putin on the scale of corruption inside the FSB – his current investigation was into how FSB officers were providing 'roof' for Uzbek drug barons – but it was like pissing on marble. Litvinenko told his wife, Marina, after the meeting: 'I could see in his eyes that he hated me.'

In November 1998 Litvinenko and four other FSB officers in the organized crime branch held a press conference, denouncing corruption inside the service and saying that they had been ordered to kill and kidnap prominent Russians. It was the kind of thing that, early on in the Yeltsin years, would have been just part of the rough and tumble of a new and energetic democracy. But now the mood had soured and Putin sacked his troublesome agent. Later Putin said: 'I fired Litvinenko and disbanded his unit because FSB officers should not stage press conferences. This is not their job. And they should not make internal scandals public.'

The writing was on the wall, not just for Litvinenko, but also for his old mentor, Berezovsky. In 2000 Litvinenko got out to Turkey, tried to claim political asylum with the Americans, who turned him down, then flew to London where the British showed more nous. Effectively, Litvinenko defected to MI6. The British Secret Service spirited Marina and their son out, so by summer 2006 the Litvinenkos were living in Alexandra Palace – Ally Pally – in North London. In exile in London, too, was Berezovsky, who helped fund Litvinenko's research into corruption in the highest levels of the Russian secret state up to and, of course, including Putin himself.

There's a clip of Litvinenko talking about what it is like to be on the run from the FSB which appeared on our BBC Panorama in 2007: 'It's like a freefall parachute jump. It's only terrifying when you're jumping from the plane, when you look down. But after you jump there isn't much you can do. You're in freefall. You can't go back. You can only go down.'

Sasha Litvinenko was, in Putin's eyes, a traitor to the FSB, to the Fatherland, to everything the master of the Kremlin held dear. When Putin kissed the boy on the stomach, Litvinenko wrote in his blog, from the safety of Ally Pally, that Vladimir Putin is a paedophile.

Litvinenko's blog is set out in full in Sir Robert Owen's report into the affair. The former KGB colonel claimed that Putin has been secretly filmed in the same flat where Skuratov was kompromatted with two women prostitutes, but in Putin's case it was him with young boys. Litvinenko said the authorities at the KGB-run Andropov Institute hushed up the scandal but decided not to send Putin, a fluent German speaker, to the West. Years later, Litvinenko claimed, when Putin became the director of the FSB in 1998, he went hunting for the secret files on him. Litvinenko blogged: 'He began to seek and destroy any compromising materials collected against him by the secret services over earlier years. It was not difficult, provided he himself was the FSB director. Among other things, Putin found videotapes in the FSB Internal Security directorate, which showed him making sex with some underage boys.'

If you dare to say that about Vladimir Putin, nowhere is safe. Nowhere on earth.

For the record, the kissing of the boy on the stomach is

deeply unpleasant and extraordinarily peculiar. But aside from that incident, there is no clear, verifiable evidence that Putin is a paedophile. Litvinenko provided none in his blog. By this point Litvinenko, and his financial and moral backer Berezovsky, hated Putin. Hate is the enemy of good intelligence. You need to be able to step back, to assess what you have got and what you haven't, and call it. Journalism requires the same skill set. What gets a story over the line is multiple sources standing it up. Here, we have only Litvinenko's word for it that the FSB Internal Security directorate had kompromat tapes on Putin. That does not mean that his claim is inherently untrue. Putin's sexuality, like so much else about him, remains opaque. It's just that to stay credible in intelligence and journalism you have to be able to supply evidence to back up your story. If you don't, people start to cross the other side of the street, to ignore you. That's what happened to Litvinenko. His claim, without supporting evidence, got little traction in the West.

But the Kremlin took note.

Paul M. Joyal is an American expert on the Russian secret state and former director of security to the Senate Select Committee on Intelligence. He knows the Kremlin's secret corridors very well and was a good friend of Litvinenko and another former KGB officer, retired Major General Oleg Kalugin. The youngest major general in the history of the Soviet KGB, Kalugin was high up in the Foreign Counter-Intelligence section, responsible for penetrating foreign intelligence services worldwide. In July 2006 Litvinenko sent his draft blog calling Putin a paedophile by fax to Kalugin, who immediately shared it with Joyal, both of whom live in the Washington DC area.

Litvinenko's draft blog analysed Putin's faltering trajectory at the start of his KGB career. Joyal provided me with a succinct summary: 'Litvinenko said if you look closely at the blank spots, including Putin's biography, you can find an explanation for his stalled career early on. When he graduated from the Andropov Institute, which trains officers for the KGB, Putin was first sent to a junior position in the Leningrad directorate of the KGB. For a graduate of the Andropov Institute, fluent in German, this is a very unusual turn. Something happened shortly before he graduated, people who studied with him say, the authorities caught a piece of the real Vladimir Putin, that he was a paedophile. Rather than start a full investigation, which could, of course, have caused a scandal, it was easier to come up with an excuse not to send Putin abroad. Many years later, when Putin became head of the FSB, he began to seek out and destroy the evidence collected against him. So that's what the blog says.'

Litvinenko's draft fax referred to someone else on the trail of, in his words, 'Putin's sexual perversion', years before. Litvinenko wrote that the reporter Artyom Borovik published a story on Putin the paedophile and one week after publication he 'died in mysterious circumstances'.

Borovik died in early March 2000, a few weeks before Russia voted Putin into office as president. He was killed along with the passengers and crew, nine people in all, of a private jet taking off from Moscow's Sheremetyevo airport. The official explanation was that the jet had not been de-iced properly, but the weather was not fiercely cold. Many suspected he had been killed by the secret state, but that this was because he had been investigating the mystery surrounding Putin's birth, that he was a bastard, and not, as Litvinenko claimed in the draft fax, because he knew the paedophile angle. For some reason, Litvinenko dropped the claim about

Borovik knowing the paedophile allegation in the blog that he finally published.

Joyal recalls: 'Now, of course, Alexander Litvinenko and Boris Berezovsky were involved in a kind of war with Vladimir Putin. After seeing this document Alexander was about to publish, Oleg Kalugin and I expressly told him not to do it. We said that this is way too personal and there really isn't enough to warrant the accusation of paedophilia, as shocking as the incident was.' The thing that worried Joyal and Kalugin was the risk Litvinenko was taking if he ran the paedophile allegation: 'Litvinenko's blog was an extremely personal insult and a personal attack. And to make this attack on a head of state of a country like Russia was of course extremely dangerous. And, to tell you the truth, one that few people took seriously.'

That is true. The Western world ignored Litvinenko's blog. Moscow did not. That summer the Russian parliament, the Duma, passed a new law allowing the state to kill any extremist who defamed the president. Joyal said: 'It provided justification for extreme measures' – in plain English, assassination.

Joyal believes that control over people is the thing that rocks Putin's boat: 'This is in line, by the way, with lifting up a shirt and kissing a boy on the belly. I can do this, so I'm going to do it.' The intelligence analyst says that he's not a professional psychologist but a student of human behaviour.

Litvinenko did not listen to his friend's warning and pressed publish on his blog. That November 2006 he drank tea with two Russians in the Millennium Hotel in Mayfair. It was a case of one lump or two. He came home to Ally Pally and then a few hours later he told Marina: 'I feel sick.'

He started vomiting and once he started, he could not stop. Immediately, he told Marina: 'This is chemical poison.'

She could not believe that anyone would do this to him. They called an ambulance and the paramedics told him that it looked like seasonal flu. Marina takes up the story: 'The next day, it was the start of November, he became even worse, vomiting blood.'

Three days later, he was admitted to Barnet Hospital, but the doctors didn't realize what – or who – they were dealing with. 'When Sasha first asked them, would you check me for poison? They looked at him as if he was a crazy man. I remember I went to see him and he said, "Marina, they don't trust us."'

Litvinenko was moved to University College Hospital, where some of the best doctors in London remained baffled. Marina told me: 'I noticed his hair when I just touched his head. A great lump of hair would fall off in my hand. I said "Sasha, what is this?" He said: "I don't know." And I did it again, and again a great lump of his hair was in my hand.'

His skin started to blister, his white blood count was very low. But he was determined to help the police nail his killers, telling the detectives about his last movements, helping them investigate his own murder.

As he lay dying, Litvinenko issued a statement, his last testament: 'You may succeed in silencing one man but the howl of protest from around the world will reverberate, Mr Putin, in your ears for the rest of your life.'

On the last day he could speak, Marina, exhausted, was about to head home to look after their son when Sasha told her: 'Marina, I love you so much.' That night he lost consciousness and never recovered.

The last photograph of Alexander Litvinenko shows him entirely bald, in green hospital pyjamas, monitoring tabs on his bare chest, staring defiantly at the camera.

For the 'Taking On Putin' podcast, I set out to talk to someone who knows a thing or two about radioactive poisons. Ever the sceptical reporter, I probed my source:

Sweeney: 'Have you passed an O-level?'
Norman Dombey: 'One or two. I'm Professor Emeritus of Theoretical Physics at the University of Sussex.'
Sweeney: 'Before that, where did you get your degree?'
Dombey: 'I got my first degree at Oxford.'
Sweeney: 'They give them away.'
Dombey: 'I have a doctorate from Cal Tech.'
Sweeney: 'In theoretical physics?'
Dombey: 'Theoretical physics. And my supervisor was Murray Gell-Mann, who won the Nobel prize and invented Quarks.'

Then he cracked open a can of Spitfire beer.

Norman Dombey knows his stuff. The professor was an expert witness for Marina Litvinenko at the public inquiry into her husband's poisoning, which took place a full nine years after he was assassinated because the British government considered good relations with the Kremlin to be more important than investigating the killing of a British citizen with a weapon of mass destruction.

The biggest mystery was how come the doctors could not work out what had happened to Litvinenko. His hair falling out, skin falling off, a horrible way to die but common symptoms of radioactive poisoning. They tested his blood with a Geiger counter for radiation. I asked Professor Dombey what happened?

'Nothing.'

'There was no reading, so it wasn't radiation?'

'No, it was radiation, but it wasn't radiation which was detectable by a Geiger counter.'

Geiger counters detect the kinds of radiation that affect us nearly all the time: gamma and beta. But there is a third kind, alpha radiation. And that the Geiger counter cannot detect. The Russian poison factory had pulled off a fiendishly clever trick. It wasn't the kind of radiation that people normally think about.

And then someone smart worked it out. Britain is a bit rubbish in many ways: it rains too much, the food is grim, Brexit. But we do love a puzzle. Sherlock Holmes wore a silly hat and had superhuman powers of detection, but he was very, very British – and someone a bit like the resident of 221b Baker Street cracked the puzzle and by so doing fucked the Kremlin.

The person – or, more likely, the team – that solved the Litvinenko poison problem works at Aldermaston, Britain's nuclear bomb factory in Berkshire. Professor Dombey explained that the doctors at University College Hospital thought: 'This is strange, it looks like radiation, but we can't measure the radiation. And they sent the samples from Litvinenko's body fluids to Aldermaston. They did some tests, looking for particular nuclear decays, and they found two – alpha radiation of a particular energy and also gamma radiation, which was much weaker. The two results together led to only one finding. They identified the isotope as polonium-210.'

'Can you buy polonium-210 in a shop?' I ask the long-suffering prof?

'No.'

The thing about poison as a murder weapon is that it can tell you something about the poisoner, more than you might think. Polonium is a radioactive element which the brilliant physicist Marie Curie first discovered and named after her home country Poland. Radioactive elements have different isotopes, so there is polonium-186 and 201, and more. Think of isotopes like salad dressings: Thousand island, honey mustard, garlic. Polonium-210 is like garlic: it's very distinctive. Moreover, the dose used to kill Litvinenko was extraordinarily high. Dombey said he swallowed an astonishing 26.5 microgrammes.

Dombey did some of his own detective work. First, he said, scientists at the Mayak nuclear reactors in the Urals irradiated bismuth, a metal known to the ancients, a sister to lead and tin, producing radioactive bismuth and an extremely small amount of polonium. This was then transported to the Avangard laboratory in the closed city of Sarov, two hundred plus miles to the east of Moscow, where the polonium-210 was separated from the bismuth. By the way, if this is triggering Lord of the Rings flashbacks, I'm not making names like Avangard and Sarov up. Nowhere else refines the polonium-210 garlic flavour, if you like, by the necessary bucket-load with the exquisite purity.

Next, some kind of Russian state poison factory converted it from metal to soluble so it could end up in a cup of tea.

'How sure are you of this?' I asked Professor Dombey.

'Ninety-nine point nine nine per cent? More nines on this, if you like.'

The prof had earned his Spitfire beer. Diffident, softly spoken, Norman Dombey is a hero of our time.

The Russian secret state thought they had deployed the ultimate stealth poison. They were wrong about that. Once the British scientists worked out it was polonium-210, then following the trail of the poisoners was like following a burglar's footsteps in the snow. There were three prime suspects for the poisoning, all of whom met Litvinenko in the afternoon and early evening before he fell ill. They are Mario Scaramella, a rather loopy Italian intelligence analyst-cum-conspiracy theorist who goes to a sushi bar with Litvinenko on Piccadilly, and two Russians, Andrei Lugovoi and Dmitry Kovtun. They're in town for the game between Arsenal and CSKA Moscow. They're on the gin. Litvinenko has a cuppa.

For our BBC Panorama programme, 'How to Poison a Spy', I followed the polonium-210 trail in January 2007.

At lunchtime, 1 November 2006, Litvinenko catches the 134 bus into town. No trace of polonium on his ticket or the bus. He is still clean. The Itsu sushi bar, Piccadilly? Contaminated. But no polonium where Litvinenko and Scaramella sit. That's odd, an anomaly. Is Scaramella a red herring?

Then the trail goes backwards in time.

Two weeks before, on 16 October, Lugovoi, once a KGB officer, now a millionaire, and his friend Dimitri Kovtun, a porn star turned KGB agent, are staying at the Parkes Hotel in Knightsbridge. Two rooms at the hotel are tested for polonium. The result? Contaminated. The polonium trail begins for sure. Itsu sushi bar on Piccadilly is one of Litvinenko's haunts. During the October trip Lugovoi and Kovtun meet Litvinenko for lunch at Itsu sushi bar in Piccadilly. The restaurant is contaminated but not at the same seats which Scaramella and Litvinenko would use two weeks later. Scaramella is a red herring.

On 25 October Lugovoi returns to London and checks in at the Sheraton Park Lane Hotel. He meets Litvinenko two or three times during this trip. One room at the hotel is left a radioactive mess. In January 2007 not just one room but a whole section of the 8th floor corridor is still boarded up. On 28 October 2006 Lugovoi flies back to Russia on British Airways flight GBNWX. And you've guessed it, at least one seat on the plane, contaminated. On the same day Kovtun arrives in Hamburg and sees his children, a toddler and a baby who live with his ex-wife. They are contaminated. Lugovoi and Kovtun next meet with Litvinenko on the day he's poisoned, at 4:30 p.m. in the Pine Bar of the Millennium Hotel, just an hour after the sushi bar. This is when the polonium trail gets really hot. Lugovoi and Kovtun are drinking with a third Russian, Vyacheslav Sokolenko. Business was done for the day, and they were relaxing ahead of the game. Litvinenko doesn't touch alcohol, but he'll always have a cuppa.

Marina told me: 'In Millennium Hotel Sasha told me he met Lugovoi and during this meeting he drank tea, and he said the tea was already served on the table and he just took this cup of tea and didn't finish it all. Later he said, "the tea wasn't very tasty".'

The polonium trail across London proves that Litvinenko's tea had been laced with polonium-210. The dose was massive, we estimated four billion becquerels of radiation. The normal level in the body is just twenty becquerels. The contamination trail at the Pine Bar is astounding. The cup that contained the tea, contaminated. The seven bar staff at the hotel who took the cup away, washed it, wiped it, set it out for other guests, contaminated. The Pine Bar itself, contaminated and was still closed two and a half months on. Contamination isn't necessarily lethal because alpha particles don't jump about. They are lethal if you ingest them. But long-term risks are not known. Lugovoi and Kovtun go to the match. Seats at the Emirates stadium, contaminated.

Everything points to not one but multiple attempts to kill Litvinenko. The polonium trail makes Lugovoi and Kovtun prime suspects for the assassination. They deny it, blah, blah, blah.

You can make the argument that a rich man like Lugovoi could have got hold of polonium-210 under the counter, as it were. I asked Professor Donald Rayfield whether it could be an oligarch or another actor in the Russian secret state?

Rayfield replied: 'If you think that, you have to totally ignore the way the Russian state or any dictatorship works. Nothing important happens to anyone outside that might have international consequence without the direct orders and consent of the head of state, any more than it would in North Korea or in China. These loose cannons have been eliminated in Russia. It does not happen. One businessman might order another businessman to be killed, but it is more likely he will report him to the tax authorities and they will extort his wealth. But murder with a radioactive substance, which can only come from one source, would cost millions even for the state to isolate, to bring, to pack, to train the assassins? It's inconceivable that this wasn't done on Putin's direct orders.'

For our Panorama programme I went off to Moscow and St Petersburg, asking anyone who would talk to me about my favourite question, 'Can you buy polonium-210 in a shop?' My then girlfriend, Tomiko Newson, later my wife, later my ex, but we are still pals, popped in to Moscow to do some shopping if anyone was following her – she played the part beautifully – and secretly ship home our footage. One night we sang 'Land of Hope and Glory' in our room in the Hotel Ukraina, something I would never dream of doing in London.

Panorama bid for and I got to interview Putin's all-powerful press officer, Dmitry Peskov, in the Kremlin. BBC Current Affairs never has enough money to do things, so I recall I did this interview with a freelance camera operator but no staff producer. To be honest, when I rocked up to the Kremlin's mighty red walls, walked through a gate and the door closed quietly behind me, my heart did flutter a little. Peskov's got a suggestion of a mullet, boasts a centipede for a moustache and has a rather mournful air, suggesting a forlorn football manager of, say, a down-table Rotherham United. His English is fluent, softly spoken. He is stiletto, not sabre. He lies so beautifully. I put it to Peskov that Litvinenko had blogged that Putin was a paedophile and then he dies. Putin did kiss the boy on the stomach. Is Putin a paedophile, I asked?

'No,' said Peskov, flatly. You could tell from his eyes that he did not like the question one little bit. The BBC cut out that question. To be fair, I did not think that Litvinenko had proved his claim and I didn't have a big row with BBC management about that edit, then. Now, I would. I cited the book *Blowing Up Russia* by Litvinenko and Felshtinsky, in which Putin was accused outright of being behind the Moscow apartment bombings and then the co-author gets poisoned in London. Is that story true, I asked Peskov?

He replied: 'No, it is not true. What he wrote in that book blaming Putin, the FSB, for blowing up these apartments in Russia has nothing to do with reality. Actually, I mean, again in my personal opinion, this is, let's say, a product of an ill brain.'

Peskov laughed quietly: 'I don't know a proper English word for that.'

Sweeney: 'A sick brain.'

Peskov: 'Yes, sick brain. Sick brain. I mean it's . . .'

Sweeney: 'Mentally ill?'

Peskov: 'Well, in my understanding, only a mentally ill person can think about Russian government blowing up homes of its own people.'

Marina Litvinenko had told me: 'I can't say exactly that Putin killed Sasha, but I can say Putin is behind everything that happens in Russia.'

I put that to Peskov and he replied: 'And I answer directly, Russia has not done that. And it is absurd even to think about that.'

Sweeney: 'And she's a liar for saying so?'

Peskov: 'In these words, yes.'

Sweeney: 'She's a liar?'

Peskov: 'Yes. If she says that Russia has killed Sasha, she's a liar in these words.'

Sweeney: 'She's safe, is she? Nothing's going to happen to her? Because she is a critic.'

Peskov: 'I hope British police is effective. She's living in London. Why don't you ask British authorities about her being safe or unsafe? She's not living in Moscow.'

Our Panorama programme gave the last word to Litvinenko's widow: 'Something worse can happen again. Because list of these people not finished yet. It was second person who was killed from this list by polonium-210. OK, what they will use to kill another person? Atomic bomb? Could you tell me please, what is next?'

The answer to her question is a chemical weapon of mass destruction but I am getting ahead of the story.

The assassination of Litvinenko got Professor Norman Dombey thinking, that the Russian poison factory would not have first used polonium-210 against a target in Britain. They would have most likely tried it back in Russia first. He looked into the strange death of a Chechen fighter, Lecha Islamov, who was serving a nine-year sentence in prison in Moscow when, in April 2004, something horrible happened.

Akhmed Zakayev, the former Free Chechen foreign minister, told me: 'The night before Islamov was due to be transferred from his holding cell in Moscow to the prison where he would serve the rest of his sentence, he had two visitors, FSB officers. They tried to turn him but he refused to work for Russian intelligence. They drank tea together. Next day, he was in transit to the main prison and he started feeling very ill. They took him to the nearest hospital in Volgograd.'

Islamov's lawyer described his client's condition: 'He cannot speak or move, has become absolutely bald, lost his hair, his beard and his eyebrows, his skin is peeling off from his head and his hands.'

Zakayev said Islamov's symptoms were the same as Litvinkenko's but more acute: 'Lecha died in ten days. Sasha [Litvinenko] lasted twenty-three, twenty-four days because he was in hospital and the doctors were fighting for his life.'

The second poisoning that struck Professor Dombey was that of Roman Tsepov, the old St Petersburg gangster who, the story goes, once gave a stolen emerald to Lyudmila Putin back in the day. Tsepov had known all the deputy mayor's secrets, had, reputedly, taken the 'black cash' from the grateful mob and handed it over to Putin. US intelligence analyst Paul Joyal recalls that Tsepov and his partner Viktor Zolatov had a security company called Baltik-Escort. In the 1990s they got the city contract to provide personal protection services for Mayor Sobchak and his deputy, Putin. Zolatov followed Putin to Moscow as his bodyguard and has risen to the pinnacle of power as chief of Putin's Praetorian Guard, the Rosgvardiya or National Guard, and is a member of the Russian National Security Council. Tsepov was present for Putin's inaugural ceremony as president. But then in the autumn of 2004 something went wrong.

On 11 September 2004 Tsepov visits colleagues at a local FSB office where he has a cup of tea. He falls unwell, the symptoms being vomiting, diarrhoea, a sudden drop of white blood cells. His hair falls out. His skin blisters. And then he dies.

Professor Norman Dombey drew my attention to the following: 'The three Russians who seem to have died as a result of radiation poisoning are Yuri Shchekochikhin, Lecha Islamov and Roman Tsepov. And in all of the cases, it looked like radiation but no radiation was found. Just like, for much of the time, Litvinenko. So the official Russian verdicts were "cause unknown". And that was what Putin & Co wanted in the case of Litvinenko. They wanted to show that they could assassinate without leaving any trace. It had worked three times before. With the three Russians, we can't be 100 per cent sure that it was polonium-210, because nobody did the tests which Aldermaston did.'

But the professor's logic is good. The Russians would not use a weapon of this kind against such a high-profile target in London without having tested it beforehand.

One year after Litvinenko, who had got British citizenship by the time he was assassinated, died in agony, the British government responded by expelling four Russian diplomats. This was such a feeble slap on the wrist that – guess what? – this wasn't the last Kremlin-sponsored assassination using weapons of mass destruction on British soil.

I asked Professor Norman Dombey, did he think that the British state had been too slow to join the dots? Dombey replied: 'Absolutely they didn't. There were so many Russian millionaires spending money in London. I don't think there is anything else.'

The US intelligence analyst Paul Joyal believes that Litvinenko calling Putin a paedophile 'was the tipping point. There were many people that wanted to get rid of Litvinenko. But if you look at the way they killed him, it was absolutely horrible. Basically, his insides melted from the polonium. And it was something that was meant not to be discovered.'

And they almost got away with it.

Joyal's working hypothesis is that Litvinenko had sources inside the KGB who knew that when Putin was waiting for assignment overseas there was some issue about his sex life hanging over him. Litvinenko believed the issue was that Putin was a paedophile. Joyal has another theory: 'I think that the evidence was that Putin had some type of sexual experience, not with children, but with young men. He's not necessarily gay. Maybe that is to put it too forcefully. With him, I suspect it's a power thing. The KGB knew this, so rather than put him overseas, in the West, they decided to ship him to East Germany. I find it hard to believe if it was confirmed that he was a paedophile. If Putin was a paedophile, he would not have been posted to East Germany.'

Joyal believes that to state categorically that Putin is gay would be wrong, an overstatement. Even to say that he is bisexual may be too strong: 'I don't know whether it is a real attraction which bisexuality implies or it is motivation to exercise power over a weaker individual. There are indications that Putin when he was young may have experienced this abuse himself. Maybe this behaviour is in part revenge. I have heard of instances that indicate to me that he's more motivated by power and control than of an orientation.' Everyone – including Vladimir Putin – is entitled to determine their own sexual orientation. The problem arises in a country where the president, who some sources suggest is bisexual, has essentially criminalized homosexuality.

What happens next in the narrative of people who dare to make public what they knew about Vladimir Putin's private life makes one's blood run cold. Joyal set it out for me: 'I had heard about the death of Alexander Litvinenko at a dinner party I was having at my home on Thanksgiving. We received the call. And in my home for the Thanksgiving meal was General Kalugin and his wife, a former foreign minister of a former Soviet Republic, and a prominent Russian critic. When we found out about Alexander's death we discussed what was to be done. And that's when I decided to work on a story that could illustrate our firm belief that the Russian government murdered him by the most horrible means possible. That's what brought me to *NBC Dateline*.'

Both Joyal and General Kalugin took part in the NBC documentary, broadcast in early 2007 when lots of conspiracy theories were still doing the rounds about how Litvinenko had died. Joyal told me: 'The Russians were putting out a lot of disinformation related to his death, that it was Berezovsky who had killed him, that MI5 was sick and tired of him and they killed him. So there was a lot of confusion about who was responsible. There was even a version from the Russians that he killed himself inadvertently with polonium.'

I know this to be true because I had reported our BBC

Panorama programme. Our conclusion was crystal-clear, that Litvinenko had been murdered by the Russian secret state with a nuclear poison. But many in London and Washington DC were sceptical, afraid or too alarmed to join the black dots. Having been to Ryazan and Chechnya in 2000, having known Anna Politkovskaya before she was murdered on Putin's birthday, I no longer gave the Kremlin any benefit of the doubt whatsoever.

The *NBC Dateline* took the same line, that Litvinenko had been murdered by the Russian secret state. Someone else who took part in the *NBC Dateline* show was the *Times* reporter Daniel McGrory. I knew Danny from my time on the road for *The Observer* as a war reporter. He was a brave and good journalist, nicknamed 'McGrory the Story'. He had given *NBC Dateline* an interview in which he had said Litvinenko had been killed in a 'state-sponsored assassination'. Five days after he recorded that interview, he was found dead. Joyal told me: 'When I mentioned that Danny had died before the airing of the programme in the United States, one particular friend said "You had better be very careful." I said: "Look, nothing's gonna happen to me."'

A British inquest found that McGrory had died of natural causes, a brain haemorrhage, a verdict his family agreed with. The McGrory family said that they were 'completely satisfied by the coroner's assessment that he died of natural causes' and that their 'beloved husband and father was not the victim of murder. The allegation that an experienced journalist was executed by a hostile foreign power in his own country is extraordinarily serious. If it were true it would have profound implications not just for our family but for investigative journalism in this country and international diplomatic relations. No one would be more concerned by this than Daniel

McGrory's family and friends. However, we do not believe the allegation that Daniel McGrory was assassinated by Russian agents has any basis in fact. People in the media, politics and the wider world should think very carefully before repeating these allegations as fact or launching inquiries on the basis of evidence that is flimsy at best.'

I asked Paul Joyal whether Danny McGrory was killed or died of natural causes. He told me: 'Well, I don't know. It's certainly an open question. I don't think it was pursued in a vigorous way to determine that question definitively. The Russian intelligence services, with their laboratories, may have perfected a number of poisons that could have caused a brain haemorrhage. If you don't start from that perspective, you will never find a subtle answer to the question: Could he have been poisoned?'

My personal experience of the quality of investigation by British coroners is not great. Too often I have found them to be too under-resourced or too Establishment-minded to place much confidence in their findings. But I cannot provide specific evidence that gainsays the coroner's verdict or the family's belief in it. They are good people and they are bright. There is always a danger in ascribing an event to a cause without sound evidence. In philosophy, they call this a corollary, not a consequence.

What really happened to Danny McGrory? To be honest, I don't know.

Paul Joyal, in his extended interview with *NBC Dateline*, before the edit, gave them his belief that 'the tipping point was Alexander's allegation that Putin was a paedophile in the Kremlin'. That line was cut out of the broadcast.

Joyal thinks that the Russians got hold of a transcript of his extended interview. He cannot explain to me exactly how he believes that is the case but he has a solid and informed theory. He continued: 'Four days after the broadcast, when I pulled into the driveway, in the darkness, in the rain, I was ambushed by two men waiting in the bushes for me. I confronted the first one but I was attacked from behind. I managed to neutralize the first one, after he hit me in the head from behind. I immediately turned around, faced him and counter-attacked. I took him to the ground. And he said to the other guy I did not see, "Shoot him."'

Joyal was shot by a nine-millimetre round which went through his colon and bladder. They tried another shot to the head but the gun jammed. Then his dog, all 200 lbs of him, went for the attackers and they fled. Joyal was on a breathing tube for thirty days and had seven operations over three and a half years.

The men who tried to kill him have never been caught.

Chapter Nine

Russia's Greatest Love Machine

Investigate Vladimir Putin's private life and things may not go well for you. In 2021 I arranged a Zoom call with one of the bravest living Russian journalists, Roman Badanin. He is part of the Proekt website – Russian for 'Project'. I wanted to talk to Badanin about a scoop he had just pulled off about Putin, a mistress and a secret daughter. But he never answered the Zoom. I started browsing Twitter to see what was up and there was a tweet saying that Moscow police were currently raiding Badanin's home. That would explain why he wasn't picking up. The next tweet said that he was being taken for questioning in a Moscow police station. That might explain why I might never, ever get to talk to him.

And that made me sick with fear.

Nataliya Pelevina is a Russian woman, a serious figure in the opposition and a known critic of Vladimir Putin. She told me: 'There were days when I didn't know how things could possibly progress in any normal way after what happened. It was just so grim. The pain, the shame, all of it seemed endless.'

Nataliya's courage in taking on Putin came at such a cost to her dignity, she thought about killing herself. In 2016 she and Putin's first prime minister, Mikhail Kasyanov – a serious rival to the president – were secretly filmed in bed. The kompromat sex tape led national TV news that night and is still plastered all over the internet and on YouTube. Nataliya said: 'I was completely and utterly destroyed. My world collapsed around me and there was nothing left and I didn't want to live. And I'm not exaggerating because obviously they didn't just show me as a horrible individual. They also showed me naked. They showed me in just an unimaginable way for a woman. After that I got messages from people around the world saying that their friend killed themselves after a similar video. So people even take their own lives after something like that is exposed. For a while, I didn't want to live.'

In Russia, Putin's enemies are not allowed to have a private life. We know all about what they do in the bedroom. But no one knows simple facts about Vladimir Putin. How many kids has he got? With whom? And are they by any chance extraordinarily rich?

Sweeney: 'Nataliya, you've been sex shamed by the Russian secret state, almost certainly on the orders of Vladimir Putin. Can you tell me about Vladimir Putin's love life?'

Nataliya: 'Oh, I'd love to.'

She is a playwright, born in Russia, but she moved to Britain when she was young and she studied at university in London. In 2012 she returned home. She wrote a play about the Moscow theatre siege which, when it played in Russia, got banned after its first night. And people think West End critics are bad. She is such an eloquent voice against the regime that the police have raided her home twice, seizing her computer and phones.

But the kompromat tape was far, far worse: 'The film on Russian propaganda channel, NTV, showed Kasyanov and I in the bedroom of the apartment that we shared at the time. The camera was planted in the wall. It showed us very graphically. We had no idea it would come to this. Back in 2012 when I arrived in Russia to fight against the regime, we didn't know Vladimir Putin would become so monstrous that I would end up being shown on television naked, having sex.'

Who did this, not the technicians, but who, at the top of Russian politics, gave the order for this to appear on prime-time Russian TV?

'Well, Mr Kasyanov and I think that Putin agreed to this because he had to have had a say in it because Mr Kasyanov is not only a former prime minister, but he was Putin's first prime minister. They worked together. So for the FSB to go and do this without his OK would have been impossible. So, in all likelihood, he didn't come up with the idea. But when this idea was offered, he agreed to it. And then the FSB did the work.'

I told Nataliya that I felt sorry for them as a couple and for her as a human being, and that the people who did this are disgusting. She replied: 'Thank you. I appreciate that. Yes, I agree with the sentiment that they are disgusting and they really don't care for human life, let alone human relationships and human dignity. They have none themselves. I didn't want to give them the pleasure of killing me off completely, so I had to fight through this awful, horrible reality of mine and hope that there is some light at the end of it.'

The master of the Kremlin denies all of this, but his critics insist he uses shame to destroy the lives of others. But his own private life is hidden behind a wall of secrecy. The contrast and, yes, the brazen hypocrisy would be comic, if what happens to his victims was not so dark.

Putin shapes his public image to the nth degree. Never mind the fake sun shining from behind North Korea's fatty-fat despot, Kim Jong-un, or the Hollywood stars worshipping the leader of the Church of Scientology, Vladimir Putin's cult of personality is the richest, the most well-funded in the whole world. But like all great lies, some of it is true.

The audience matters. I have looked again and again at the pictures that the Kremlin's propaganda factory puts out, of Putin riding topless on a horse; going fishing, topless; sinking beneath the waves in a submersible, looking very much the Bond villain popping into his undersea lair; going picnicking with his pal, Defence Minister Sergei Shoigu; doing the butterfly in a freezing Siberian lake. None of this floats my boat. To me, it looks as though this is a man who had an unexceptionally unhappy and unloved childhood, who fears mockery and being laughed at, who wants to show to the world that he is the master of all he surveys, but comes across as a small boy, out for revenge. But then I'm not the target audience.

Every now and then, the image-makers slip up and something of the real Putin is revealed behind the mask. In 2013 he was snapped shaking hands with a walrus and feeding dolphins: very much on message. Then he went to a junior school in Kurgan in the Urals and in front of the schoolchildren he drew something on the whiteboard. One of the kids asked what it was and he replied: 'It's a cat. The rear view.' It was a cat's arsehole. For me, this is the most accurate representation of Vladimir Putin's immortal soul.

The image factory even put out a pop song, singing Putin's praises, from the mid-noughties. Imagine a sub-optimal Abba riff after you have taken bad acid and you get the flavour of the harmony. The words are worse:

I want a man like Vladimir Putin who is full of fire.
I want a man like Vladimir Putin who doesn't drink.
I want a man like Vladimir Putin who doesn't upset me,
I want a man like Vladimir Putin who will stand and fight.

Charlie Walker, a sociologist at Southampton University, knows his Russian man on the street and he suggests that my take, let's call him Vlad the Yuckety-Yuck-Yuckski, might be missing the point for how many Russians see him: 'It's intended for a very traditionalist market. These hyper-masculine displays that Putin engages in goes back to the beginning of his period as president. The cult of Putin began with him flying aeroplanes and helicopters during the Second Chechen War. As he became president, the Kremlin put out a fresh narrative. Putin was this man of action that Russia "desperately needed" after this long period of being led by Boris Yeltsin, who came across as a buffoon, who had sold out to the West. The country was out of control. Yeltsin was physically, personally out of control. And then Putin comes along and his popularity ratings surged very quickly, partly on the back of this kind of man of action cult, which his PR team were promoting. And when we see him on horseback and out fishing, this is a deliberate attempt to appeal to the man and woman in the street, as it were, because this sort of outward-bound masculinity that he's projecting is something that most ordinary Russians can relate to, particularly working-class men who've been in the army, people who were brought up during the Soviet period mostly would have served in the army. And so: going fishing with friends, cooking a kebab or cooking fish on a campfire next to a lake. In interviews, Putin says when he's out and about in nature, "I feel very close to Russian people.. I feel very close to ordinary people. I've never seen myself as part of an elite." And this physical display, the shirtless horse riding, the fishing, the masculinity is something that people can connect with quite easily.'

How did the Putin cult begin?

Charlie Walker explained: 'Gleb Pavlovsky was his first PR guy when he emerged as a presidential candidate and then when he won the presidential election. Pavlovsky was actively promoting what he himself calls this cult of Putin. It's not elites or intellectuals that he's appealing to.'

Zarina Zabrisky is a USSR-born American novelist now living in the US. She can't go back under the Putin regime because they have declared her a terrorist. Her response to that? 'I am absolutely not a terrorist, but I am a writer and writers are dangerous.' Zarina has made a study of Vladimir Putin's private life. Let's start with his ex-wife Lyudmila Putin and their two daughters. They are extraordinarily rich and there appears to be no legitimate explanation for their wealth. Lyudmila allegedly controls a famous Moscow mansion once owned by the Tolstoy family which rakes in millions of dollars a year in rent. She's said to have businesses and properties across Russia, including a house in Kaliningrad that she rents out.

Before the 2022 invasion, very little was known about Putin's daughters, Maria Vorontsova and Katerina Tikhonova. Zarina told me in 2021: 'First of all, we only hear about alleged daughters because he doesn't officially recognize them and they live by different names. Only very recently, they appeared at the St Petersburg Economic Forum, under their different names, but being treated as celebrities of the first rank, as if they were daughters of the tsar.'

Which, in a manner of speaking, they are.

The anomaly – and in investigative journalism, anomalies are always the thing you go for – is that here are two young women who have no commercial history, no evidence how they've made lots of money, who are treated like royalty. And that is because they're Putin's daughters. All three women are, by any standards, obscenely rich, closer to billionaires than millionaires. Holidays in Biarritz, weddings in Italy, palaces in Russia. But money does not guarantee happiness.

Putin is ferociously protective of his daughters. The oldest, Maria, married a Dutch businessman, Jorrit Faassen. In 2010 Faassen and Maria fell into a road-rage incident with Russian banker Matvey Urin. The banker's four bodyguards blocked their car and beat up the Dutchman with baseball bats while Maria looked on helplessly. Urin was the co-owner of Trado-Bank, a former head of Breeze Bank and connected to four other Moscow banks. Thirty minutes after the road-rage attack, Urin was locked up, spent eight years in the slammer, lost all his wealth and holdings, and all six banks he had connections with went bust.

Nataliya Pelevina, the victim of Kremlin kompromat, has some sympathy for Lyudmila. Putin divorced Lyudmila after thirty years of marriage: 'She never looked like a very happy, content woman. But I guess we now know why. Information that he's had multiple lovers has come out. There have been new revelations recently with regards to supposedly his first mistress during his presidency, Svetlana Krivonogikh.'

What does Svetlana's surname mean in English, I ask Nataliya: 'Crooked Legs.'

I explain I'm very bad at pronouncing Russian names, so I'm just going to call her Lady Crooked Legs, at which

Nataliya starts to laugh. I upbraid her, saying, 'You're enjoying this too much, Nataliya. Shame on you.'

To which she replies: 'I'm allowed to.'

Moscow police let Roman Badanin go and I finally managed to Zoom him. He got into trouble because he and his colleagues at the Proekt investigative journalism website had done a story about Putin's love affair with Svetlana 'Lady Crooked Legs' Krivonogikh. Badanin explained: 'To write a story on the personal life of Mr Putin or about his personal wealth is really dangerous in Russia. It doesn't mean that just after the article, for example, the police come for you. It can work out in a different way. We don't know how, but trust me it's a dangerous topic.'

Badanin stumbled on his scoop about Lady Crooked Legs' affair with Putin when he was working on another, far less interesting story. Then he met a Kremlin insider who talked too much: 'And at one particular moment, the source said, "Hey, guys, Ms X is not the most important part of the story. As far as I know, she has a close friend and that young lady had an affair with Mr Putin and they had a baby." And just after saying these words, he stopped. He realized that he said something dangerous and he stopped talking.'

For Badanin and his team, the hunt for Putin's secret mistress and their love child was on. They did not have a name but they found more clues. The Proekt team picked up a story that Putin's mistress owned 5 per cent of Bank Rossiya, styled by US intelligence as Putin's piggybank – a stake worth scores of millions of dollars. They went through the bank's books and found the name of a woman, Svetlana Krivonogikh, who had a 5 per cent stake. But there was no link to Putin: 'It was not easy. But we managed to organize a conversation with two really top-rank allies of Putin from the early 2000s. Of course, they spoke anonymously. And it was sensational. I remember the first meeting when we talked a lot about non-dangerous things, banks, money, something like that. And then I asked, "Do you know about a stakeholder in Rossiya Bank, she has 5 per cent, a Miss Krivonogikh." And he said: "Of course I know but I will never tell you."'

Bang, bang.

Badanin chuckled: 'Our final breakthrough was that we found the birth certificate for Miss Krivonogikh's daughter. She had a baby girl in the early 2000s, the name of her daughter is Elizaveta or Liza Krivonogikh. The first name of the father of the baby was Vladimir but on the birth certificate, no full name of her father, just blank. And we started to search for the daughter, Liza Krivonogikh, on social media. It was not easy because she used a different surname in social media, Luisa Rozova. And after a long search, we finally managed to find pictures of her. The daughter looks just like Vladimir Putin. And it was a bombshell.'

The Proekt team got in touch with a facial-recognition expert at Bradford University, Hassan Ugail, who concluded Liza 'bears a phenomenal resemblance to the Russian president'. Svetlana Krivonogikh, who was a cleaner in the late 1990s, was later revealed by the Pandora Papers to own a $4 million flat in Monaco. Proekt pulled off a brilliant piece of investigative journalism in one of the world's most difficult places to do investigative journalism. The wealth of Svetlana and her daughter is entirely unexplained. The evidence is compelling that the President of Russia, Vladimir Putin, had an affair with Svetlana, that she was his mistress, that they had a child, and that mother and child now have unimaginable riches. The only logical explanation for their wealth is Vladimir Putin's corruption.

Roman Badanin was following the money, not Putin's personal life: 'We focused, first of all, on his unlawful wealth, obtained by dubious ways. At one particular moment in the 1990s, Svetlana was a cleaning lady. And then she became one of the richest women in St. Petersburg.'

Badanin and his team run a terrible risk to tell this story of Putin's gross abuse of power. I told Badanin about my run-in with the Church of Scientology in 2007, how cult critic Rick Ross warned me about 'noisy investigations, they want you to be afraid. They want you to know that they are onto you.' Is this the same with the Russian secret state?

Badanin: 'Of course. It's a basic rule for them to make you afraid.'

Sweeney: 'Why aren't you afraid, because this story, you say yourself is dangerous. Why do you carry on doing what you're doing?'

Badanin: 'I really strongly believe that journalism, investigative journalism, the work we do, can really make different Russian society for everybody who lives here. So I believe in journalism and I like it.'

Sweeney: 'So what is strange is that you can look at people who might have caused trouble for Vladimir Putin, starting with the Prosecutor-General, Yuri Skuratov, and then Mikhail Kasyanov. We've seen them in bed. With Skuratov, there was video kompromat of him, the story goes, in bed with two prostitutes, Mikhail Kasyanov in bed with his lover. So we know about the sex lives of his enemies, but nothing about his own sex life.'

Badanin: 'Ha ha ha. Yeah, that's the point.'

There is a second mistress.

Nataliya Pelevina explained: 'Vladimir Putin's most famous alleged mistress is Alina Kabaeva. She is a successful gymnast and an Olympic champion. And they've been linked for many, many years now. Supposedly they have quite a few children. We have lost track of how many at this point. We heard about a son that was born around 2007 because at that time pictures appeared on the internet. Somebody snapped a picture of Alina Kabaeva, the mistress, pregnant. Then she disappeared out of spotlight. She just disappeared. She was nowhere to be seen.'

So Vladimir Putin has a son, allegedly. But there's more.

Nataliya continued: 'Then supposedly, she had another child a couple of years later, another son. And then very recently she had twins. The article came out that she had twins in Moscow in one of the hospitals, but the whole hospital was pretty much emptied out of all the patients when she was there so that she won't be seen by ordinary mortals.'

What we do know for sure is that in April 2008 the *Moskovsky Korrespondent* newspaper, owned by Alexander Lebedev, the former KGB colonel whose son, Evgeny, Boris Johnson made Baron Siberia, reported that Kabaeva was engaged to Putin. The spice in the gossip was that, officially, Putin was still married to Lyudmila; the couple only got divorced in 2013. The engagement story was denied, the newspaper was shut down, and for several years things did not go well for Alexander Lebedev. His bank was investigated by the tax authorities, its ownership was under threat of being hollowed out, and the former KGB man's fortune dropped like a stone from some billions to some hundreds of millions of dollars.

When he punched a fellow guest in a Russian TV studio, the state took an unusual interest in the scrap, so that Lebedev senior had to serve a community service sentence. Was this all because the master of the Kremlin was displeased with a rare Russian media intrusion into his private life? I suspect it was.

After the story broke, Putin said: 'I have always disliked those who, with their snotty noses and erotic fantasies, break into other people's private affairs.'

Dear Pot, Yours The Kremlin's Kettle.

In March 2015 Kabaeva was reported to have given birth to a daughter at St Ann's Hospital, an exclusive clinic for the very, very rich in Ticino, Switzerland. Then in 2019 she reportedly gave birth to twin sons at the Kulakov maternity clinic in Moscow.

So the best count of Putin's children is two daughters by Lyudmila, one daughter by Lady Crooked Legs, and three or four kids by Alina, the gymnast, seven or eight in all. Nobody knows for sure. For the record, Svetlana Krivonogikh and Alina Kabaeva have neither confirmed nor denied the rumours about having a relationship with Vladimir Putin, neither confirmed nor denied having children with him, neither confirmed nor denied having unexplained wealth. Furthermore, the gymnast Kabaeva was found guilty of taking performance-enhancing drugs, so she has a track record of dishonesty. In April 2022 the *Wall Street Journal* reported that the US Treasury Department had put her name on a list of Putin cronies to face economic sanctions – only for the US National Security Council to take it off, reportedly for fear of Putin 'responding in an aggressive way'. It's part of my job as a reporter to try and understand what makes people do the things that they do, to try and get inside their skin. When bureaucrats feather sanctions so as not to upset a serial killer like Vladimir Putin, I find myself wanting to bang my head against the wall.

Many ordinary Russians don't access the internet much, still less dangerous sites like Proekt. The throttling of a free and independent mass-market media has been one of Putin's great successes in the zombification of Russia. Almost no one dares ask questions about Putin and his women and, maybe, his men, and those few who do have to walk through walls of fear.

Last word to Natalia Pelevina, sex-shamed by the Kremlin but who found the courage to pull through. She knows a bleak truth, that most people in Russia are keeping their heads down, for fear of upsetting the current tsar: 'People are afraid to say anything about Putin, even on the internet. They think somebody will come after them. They read about opposition figures being jailed, poisoned, killed. They don't want to share that fate. They do realize that the government cracks down on anyone who speaks out against them or speaks the truth about them. And they want to stay alive and they want to not go to prison. And that's understandable.'

The problem is that for far too many Russians – living in Russia or in exile abroad – staying on the right side of Vladimir Putin is coming at too high a price.

Chapter Ten

Mr Pleonexia

The Church of Putinology's holy script is that the President of Russia is a monk, who has no time for a private life so busy is he attending to the nation's needs. He's merely an ordinary man who cracks down on the fat cats who betray ordinary Russians.

Woe betide anyone who challenges that dark fantasy to his face, who dares to say he presides over a system that is robbing the ordinary people of Russia blind. Mikhail Khodorkovsky was, once, the richest man in Russia, thanks to him setting up a bank, Menatep, ahead of the game and then buying up a huge chunk of Siberia's oil fields and oil firm Yukos at knock-down prices in the 1990s. Once Khodorkovsky had acquired his treasure, he got religion about honest capitalism. As Putin's grip on power tightened, in February 2003 Khodorkovsky let the master of the Kremlin have it with both barrels, or rather, via a PowerPoint demonstration. The writer Masha Gessen, who was brilliant on Putin and his greed long before it became fashionable, wrote a piece for *Vanity Fair* on the PowerPoint that cost its speaker the best part of $15 billion – a good estimate of Khodorkovsky's fortune at its peak.

Slide Six, Gessen reported, was titled 'Corruption Costs the Russian Economy over $30 Billion a Year'. Slide Eight showed that bright students competed to enter the Russian oil industry at a ratio of two applicants to one place; the tax office, four to one; the civil service, eleven to one. Khodorkovsky explained that in the civil service you could milk the system.

Putin simpered a fake smile, which is never a good sign. Yukos was rolled up, its assets stolen, its staff hounded, some dying in mysterious accidents, and Khodorkovsky spent the next ten years in a slammer in Siberia. It was not just ordinary porridge but a labour camp that served a uranium mine. The man who had once been Russia's richest often spent his days in a freezing solitary cell for 'violating' nonsensical rules. To rub it in, the secret police were on his case. In 2006 prison inmate Alexander Kuchma slashed his face while he was asleep. Down the track, Kuchma confessed that he was told to attack Khodorkovsky by shadowy operatives who were free to enter the penal colony and had beaten and threatened him. Kuchma had originally said that he had slashed Khodorkovsky because he had made homosexual advances to him. You wonder who wrote that script.

Mikhail Kasyanov, Putin's first prime minister who later got kompromatted, said that the breaking up of Yukos was a pivot: 'The business community were on one side, the president on the other. It was a very clear dividing line. That day was a watershed.'

From the moment Khodorkovsky took on Putin directly, working for Yukos upped your insurance policy, big time. Stephen Curtis was a British lawyer who was trying to salvage as much money as possible as the Russian state started to hollow out the company. Curtis was managing director of the Menatep Group, which had a controlling stake in Yukos, and he commuted from London to his nineteenth-century castle on the Isle of Portland, Dorset, by Agusta helicopter, one of the safest choppers in the sky. One day he told an old friend: 'If anything happens to me in the next few weeks, it will not be an accident.'

It was an accident. At least, that was the verdict of the British authorities when the helicopter carrying Curtis, flown by pilot Max Radford, fell out of the sky on the approach to Bournemouth airport in March 2004. Not everyone was convinced. One of Radford's friends, fellow pilot John Hackney, told the *Daily Mail*: 'I saw Max the morning of the accident. He had got this lovely new helicopter, it was a very nice piece of kit with all the latest navigational aids. He said he was going to pick up a guy in London and I set off on my day and then on the way back in the evening I heard about the accident.'

The Agusta was brand new; the weather was not dreadful; Max Radford was an experienced and sound pilot. Hackney expressed his doubts: 'We suspected foul play. The day of the funeral we were all still talking about it and all of us said exactly the same thing – "this is not an accident". We all said to his dad, "as long as we live we shall never ever believe this story".'

The other oligarchs got the message.

When the boss snaps his fingers, you bow and you bow low. There's a video of Putin upbraiding bosses of a big cement plant for closing it down and putting thousands out of work. The fattest cat in the room is billionaire Oleg Deripaska who is a bit of a gangster. He has a history of brushes with organized crime, something the US Treasury brought up when they banned him from entering the US in 2018. He is in a suit and tie; Putin is the man of the people in jeans and bomber jacket. He calls out the bosses for their 'ambition, incompetence and pure greed' which is 'completely unacceptable'. Every moment of this very public humiliation is being captured by the Kremlin's patsy TV cameras. Putin conjures up a new contract and he orders the bosses to re-open the plant.

'Has everyone signed?' Putin snaps.

The fat cats murmur yes.

'Have you signed, Deripaska?'

The billionaire grunts an affirmative. Putin says he can't see the signature, so Deripaska is called to the front of the class to sign. Putin flings his pen at him. Deripaska duly signs and hurries back to his desk, but Putin has one last scene for his play. 'Give me back my pen.' The humbling of the rich man is complete.

All of this is, of course, a dark pantomime, as nakedly dishonest as the lie that Putin lives a monkish existence. The Kremlin's Theatre of Cruelty has put on a show to entertain the masses. Set aside the mouldy bread and the moth-eaten circus. The truth is that the richest fat cat in the room, by far, is the man in jeans and bomber jacket. Vladimir Putin is, probably, the richest man in the world. Or at least he was until he launched his stupid war in February 2022. He's Mr Pleonexia.

By the way I'm not smart enough to dig up a word like pleonexia. I had to look it up like everyone else. I found it in Masha Gessen's great biography of Putin, *The Man Without a Face.* Gessen discards the idea that Putin's psychological condition can be described as him suffering from kleptomania – the pathological desire to possess things for which one has little use – and plumps for 'the more exotic pleonexia, the insatiable desire to have what rightfully belongs to others. If Putin suffers this irrepressible urge, this helps explain his apparent split personality: he compensates for his compulsion by creating the identity of an honest and incorruptible civil servant.'

Gessen, in their book, cites three weird examples of Putin taking things that rightfully belonged to others. In 2000, while talking the good talk about cleaning up the economy and ending corruption, Putin signed a decree creating a company that controlled 70 per cent of Russia's alcohol manufacturing and gave control to a crony from St Petersburg. Back then, when the oil price was low, booze was the biggest market in the Russian economy and Putin took more than two-thirds of it, albeit through a proxy. There's always a proxy.

Five years on, Gessen tells the story of Putin nicking a 124-carat diamond Super Bowl ring from US billionaire Robert Kraft. Word is the president asked to see it, tried it on, said something like, 'I could kill someone with this', then put it in his pocket and walked. Kraft later said it had been a gift. Also in 2005, Putin clocked a glass replica of a Kalashnikov filled with vodka in New York's Guggenheim Museum. He gestured to one of his security team, who nicked it. Neither the Russian public nor the American billionaire nor the museum worthies dared call the cops. So he got away with it. Perhaps that's the rush: it's not the stealing of a thing that excites him but the submission of others in the bald face of the theft: 'I can rob you blind and I am so frightening and hyper-aggressive you will accept it.'

If that's the case, then we can widen our frame of reference to take in other incidents where Putin hasn't stolen an object but someone else's peace of mind, which, of course, rightfully belongs to another. He has a long history of being late for meetings with his fellow heads of state. If punctuality is the politeness of kings, then Putin is deliberately, provocatively late, time and again. In 2017 *The Independent* generated a chart of how long he had kept VIPs waiting. The Queen did well: Putin kept Her Majesty waiting only fourteen minutes in 2003. By the way, in the time-chess world of British royalty, where every move, diagonal or straight, is planned and plotted months beforehand, fourteen minutes is an ocean of hours. Putin was twenty minutes late for the King of Spain, forty minutes late for Barack Obama, fifty minutes late for Pope Francis, one hour twenty minutes late for the UN General Assembly, three hours late for Shinzo Abe, the Prime Minister of Japan, four hours late for Viktor Yanukovych, when he was President of Ukraine, and four hours twenty minutes late for the winner/loser, Angela Merkel, when she was German Chancellor.

Merkel, the daughter of a Protestant German pastor who moved his family from West to East Germany when she was a baby, to keep the flame of Christianity alive, is fluent in Russian and, probably, understood Putin's mindset best of all the world leaders who met him. Was that why he kept her waiting the longest? Agonized by Germany's Nazi past, and her country's terrible invasion of the Soviet Union, she worked incredibly hard to do her best by Putin. Far from being grateful, he set out to humiliate her. And he was cruel to her, too. At some media access point in Putin's home at Sochi on the Black Sea in 2007, Merkel and Putin were talking in front of the cameras when someone – obviously, on purpose – let in the president's black Labrador, Koni. *The New Yorker* told the story that as the dog approached, Merkel froze, visibly frightened. She is afraid of dogs. Putin, legs akimbo, sensed her fear and said: 'I'm sure it will behave itself.' Merkel replied in Russian: 'It doesn't eat journalists, after all.'

Putin judged he could get away with taunting Merkel over her fear of dogs and, it seems, he was right.

He wanted to see her fear, in the same way he wanted the booze business, the diamond ring, the vodka AK. He wanted to be late for the Queen, the King of Spain, the Pope and all. He wanted to kiss the little boy on the stomach. He wanted Litvinenko dead, hideously so. His call: 'I can do whatever I want and no one dares challenge me.' You can lose touch with reality that way. The idea that you can appease someone like Vladimir Putin is – how can I put this plainly – just bonkers.

Putin's honeymoon with Lyudmila was in Ukraine. They visited Lviv, Kyiv, Crimea. He wanted Ukraine like he had wanted all the other things that rightfully did not belong to him, and no one, he thought, would stop him. Time and again, he had probed the West's steel and found jelly. But this time, Ukraine, its president, its people and its army had other ideas. This time Mr Pleonexia found people who said, 'No, that's not yours. It's ours. Give it back.' No wonder he seems so surprised that Ukraine played hardball. That was not supposed to happen.

On the stealing alone, what's striking about Putin is the lengths he goes to conceal his sickness, to hide his pathology behind proxies. The Russian proxies, in turn, hire their own foreign proxies: a British milord, an American populist, a French fascist, they're all available at the right price. The Russian proxies do the stealing. The foreign proxies are the smoke engine. And Vladimir Putin? He just looks the other way, then looks back and smirks.

In the early weeks of the war, there were not that many British freelance reporters in Kyiv. I got an email from the *Jewish*

Chronicle asking me if I could be their stringer. I pointed out that I was a lapsed Catholic, to which the *Chronicle*'s deputy editor, Ben Felsenburg, giggled. They never changed a word I wrote and every time I reported for the *JC* I found a Muslim who was also defending Ukrainian democracy against Russian fascism: one week a fighting imam, the next the pro-Ukrainian Chechen commander who started fighting the Russian Army back in 1991. But, being a good stringer, every week I popped into Kyiv's Central Synagogue to catch up with the rabbi and pick up some gossip. That's how I got to know a source, Chaim, who was originally from St Petersburg. As a young entrepreneur in the 1990s, he built a finance company that found foreign investors for new Russian businesses. It was doing so well the mob paid him a call. He was made an offer he couldn't refuse. Give the company to a friend of the mafiya and get out of Russia. Or you die. He handed over his company and fled to Israel where he met the young gymnast, Alina Kabaeva: 'a beautiful sweet woman'.

He knew Roman Tsepov a little, a 'clever gangster'. And Putin, what was the word about him? Chaim recalled that there was an old Soviet show with a character in it who, from the sound of him, was a little like Godot, someone who was there and not there at the same time, a grey ghost. You get the picture. But everyone knew he was stealing himself a great, dark fortune while playing to movers and shakers like Boris Berezovsky, the earnest and incorruptible official.

The received story of Putin's two decades plus in power was of his tolerance of a monstrously corrupt system. The trade-off with the oligarchs was they were allowed to keep much of their fortunes so long as they paid the master of the Kremlin homage and tithes. And they had to keep their snouts out of power. Or else. But that description masks what's really going on. Putin is stealing Russia's wealth, big time, personally, but he cannot be seen to be doing so – psychologically, he hates the idea of being caught out – so he employs proxies to do the stealing for him. True, the oligarchs emerged from the road-crash of the Soviet Union's implosion and Boris Yeltsin's alcoholic incompetence. But with Yeltsin out of the way, a new president had an opportunity to strip the oligarchs of their ill-gotten and obscene wealth and start afresh. Instead, Putin cemented the oligarch system because it best suited his secret urge to take things that rightfully belonged to others.

Oleg Deripaska was a theoretical physicist of great promise, but in New Russia's great crash in the early 1990s he gave up quarks to eat. Like many other oligarchs, he got in early on a closed, rigged market, bought assets worth billions of dollars at comically low prices, with the effect of cheating the Russian taxpayer, and then spirited big fat envelopes out of the country. Deripaska bought up grand properties in the fancy parts of London and fancy yachts which he parked where the rich riff-raff, their enablers and the dross of Europe and America hang out. We will get to Peter, Lord Mandelson, David Cameron and George Osborne shortly.

The mafiya were on Deripaska's case from the start and he was, to some extent, open about the necessity of paying them off. He was into metal, big time, and his rise to great riches came on the back of what they called The Great Patriotic Aluminium Wars. This was a dark joke fusing the immense loss of life during the Second World War with the battle of control over the world's biggest aluminium smelter in Krasnoyarsk, Siberia, in the 1990s. Around one hundred managers, factory bosses and gangsters were killed as rival firms or, in reality, organized crime syndicates fought for control of the smelter.

Deripaska's RUSAL group came out on top. RUSAL became EN+, but you still can't hide the bloody history.

Deripaska told the BBC that he had to pay off organized crime: 'It was very difficult but I believe that whatever I did, I can't say that I'm proud, but I believe I did the right thing.' He served up the same nonsense to the High Court in London in 2012, telling the judge that he had been forced to pay protection money to someone his lawyer suggested was a figure in Russian organized crime. In 2018 the US Treasury banned him from entering the States, saying 'Deripaska has been investigated for money laundering, and has been accused of threatening the lives of business rivals, illegally wiretapping a government official, and taking part in extortion and racketeering. There are also allegations that Deripaska bribed a government official, ordered the murder of a businessman, and had links to a Russian organized crime group.'

Deripaska denies any wrongdoing in general and these allegations in particular, calling them 'filthy lies'.

By the turn of the millennium everybody knew that many, many Russian businessmen were murdered in the 1990s and that some of the few who rose to the top may have done so by stepping over a whole lot of bodies. That makes the judgement of a series of British and American politicians about Deripaska so chillingly grim.

In 2005 Deripaska flew Peter, Lord Mandelson, and his pal, banker Nat Rothschild, to Siberia, where the oligarch arranged for them to be refreshed by being whipped with birch twigs after a sauna, an authentically Russian pleasure. The oligarch's security team had ensured that the British milord could waltz through Russian passport control, no easy matter, I can tell you from personal experience, but then Deripaska has a pal in the Kremlin. Serious questions about

Lord Mandelson's friendship over some years with Deripaska were raised. As EU Trade Minister, he had dropped two tariffs on aluminium. Had those actions benefited Deripaska? Lord Mandelson denies any wrongdoing. To be fair, down the track, Deripaska hired a former Tory MP and energy minister, Greg Barker, now Lord Barker, to do his bidding as chairman of En+.

In 2008 the haves and the have-yachts flocked to Corfu, the star attraction being Oleg Deripaska, on his boat, *Queen K*. On the guest list were Lord Mandelson, Nat Rothschild and then Tory Shadow Chancellor, George Osborne. David Cameron was not far away, floating on his lilo, but he seems to have escaped the big scandal. Mandelson, Osborne and Rothschild end up falling out and the banker accuses Osborne of soliciting a £50,000 donation for the Tory Party from the Russian oligarch. Osborne denied that but was on the back foot. He conceded he'd made a boo-boo on BBC Radio Four's Today programme: 'I didn't break any rules but I think I did make a mistake. In politics, it's not just what you say or what you do but it's how things look. If I am absolutely honest, this didn't look very good.'

Osborne is right about that. It didn't look good at all for him or Mandelson. They both deny wrongdoing, but the critical matter is that anyone with half an eye could work out that Deripaska was a Kremlin proxy and a bad man a long time before Mandelson went to the banya or Osborne put on his yachting shoes and went cap in hand, asking for Moscow gold. The idea that Osborne or Mandelson are naïve is absurd. One is left with the alternative hypothesis, that they smelt Deripaska's money and they liked it. The issue is that every single kopek of the oligarch's wealth was, is and always will be dependent on the goodwill of the master of the Kremlin.

That same year, 2008, Russia invaded Georgia and Putin's killing machine took a bite out of the smaller country. Two years later Osborne became Chancellor, Cameron Prime Minister, and there was a subtle change of posture. The Tory Party machine still carried on accepting Russian gold but the proxies were further away from the Kremlin's embrace than people like Deripaska. The new proxies lived on the outer edge of Putin's circle and so were deemed acceptable.

In 2017, when allegations surfaced that Oleg Deripaska had been funding Donald Trump's former campaign manager Paul Manafort, off the books, CNN reporter Matthew Chance chased the Russian oligarch around a conference centre in Vietnam. It was a great doorstep.

Chance: 'Mr Deripaska, it's Matt Chance from CNN. Is it true that Mr Manafort owed you millions of dollars when he was head of the Trump campaign? . . . Were you a secret back channel from the Kremlin to the Trump campaign? Mr Deripaska?'

After a lot of running around, Chance finally caught up with the oligarch. The Russian scowled at him and said in his voice, as deep as a grave: 'It's news for idiots. Get lost please. Thank you.'

Deripaska's seduction of figures like Mandelson and Osborne worked – but only for a time. The thing about Moscow's proxies is that they are like orcs from *Lord of the Rings*. One dies; another ten pop up to carry on the war. In 2010 the Conservative Friends of Russia threw a party at the Russian Embassy in London: raffle prizes included a bottle of vodka and the official biography of Vladimir Putin. Among the great and the good at the bash were Tory MP and future culture secretary John Whittingdale and his spad or special adviser, Carrie Symonds, the woman who later became the wife of the current prime minister, Boris Johnson; Matthew Elliott, the man who later was to run the pro-Brexit movement Vote Leave; and Sergey Nalobin, the Russian diplomat liaising with the Conservative Friends of Russia.

Nalobin is, of course, very likely to be a Russian spy. He denies it.

Luke Harding for *The Guardian* was the first reporter to set out the evidence that Nalobin, son of a KGB general, had all the hallmarks of an officer of the Russian secret state. After Harding's story ran, Paul Staines, the right-wing mosquito and founder of the Guido Fawkes blog, wrote a fascinating piece for *The Spectator* setting out what he knew about Nalobin: 'I first met Sergey Nalobin in 2012 at Soho House. He introduced himself, in accented English, as from the Russian Embassy. "On the Ministry of Foreign Affairs orientation course before coming to London, I was told to read Guido Fawkes blog and *Private Eye*. I enjoy yours more," he said flatteringly (I publish Guido Fawkes). A PR company had offered me an irresistibly large fee to give "a masterclass" to corporate marketing types in how to use social media. So it was that I found myself presenting PowerPoint slides in front of a boardroom of suits – with one short, heavy-set, cropped-haired Russian from central casting sitting right next to me. Later, over burgers, we exchanged banter. I immediately suggested he was a spy.'

If Paul Staines could arrive at that conclusion, so could Whittingdale, Symonds and Elliott. Staines continued that Nalobin 'was particularly interested in any gossip I might have about David Cameron and George Osborne'.

Of course, he was. It's what they do.

Staines saw Nalobin around Westminster, taking selfies with then foreign secretary William Hague and rising star Boris Johnson. Nalobin's Facebook page showed him at a fancy-dress party in Russian military uniform with 'KGB' written on the hat, a gun in one hand, a 'racy girl in stockings and suspenders' in the other. When Staines was asked to give a talk at the Russian Embassy, he told the ambassador that the Kremlin should release Russian opposition leader Alexei Navalny. That went down like a cup of cold sick. Nalobin popped up at the Tory summer party at the Hurlingham Club in 2014, but a few months later he was kicked out of Britain. Only four years too late.

Chapter Eleven

'So, sir, do you regret the killings in Ukraine, sir?'

Dusk is falling. I am standing in an endless cornfield in the middle of nowhere in eastern Ukraine, the land rising and falling slowly like a calm sea, looking at the nose of a passenger jet and plane seats and Air Malaysia logos and bodies in black bags being dumped in the back of a bin lorry. Paperbacks and bits of plane seats and luggage and Trunkis, those little wheelie suitcases that you pull a toddler along on, litter the ground. And every time I see a kid on one of those at Heathrow or Gatwick, I get a flashback and I start to cry.

I am being filmed by Darius Bazargan, a shooter-producer and a good friend. We've been in some tough places together but this is the worst by a long chalk. Generally, I can talk the front and back legs off a donkey but right now I am struggling to find some words that make any sense. We got here late and most of the corpses have been located and placed in body bags. As we stand, I count six body bags being loaded into the back of a lorry. The light is dying and I need to come up with words. Darius shoots some B-roll: a woman's red hat with a black band, a kid's black-and-white monkey, a part of the airframe bearing the words 'Impact Resistant Door.'

And then the words pour out: 'MH17 came from the west, where the sun is setting over there, from Amsterdam, heading east to Malaysia, and then the lives of nearly 300 people were extinguished.'

Down the hill it gets worse. Here, the mighty aero-engines and the landing gear fell to earth, the ground burnt black, the air thick. I tell the camera: 'You can't see it but the whole place stinks. It stinks of aviation fuel. It stinks of the dead. This is a monstrous crime.'

The Boeing was shot down on 17 July 2014 by a Russian BUK surface-to-air missile. What happens is the missile flies up at 3,500 miles per hour and rides alongside the target, then explodes, firing hundreds of metal golfball-sized bomblets into the enemy fuselage. The kinetic power of a plane flying at 500 miles per hour does the rest. The rocket-launcher is carried on a primary flatbed truck which tows a massive radar behind it. This particular BUK had been shipped across from Russia to eastern Ukraine into the hands of Putin's proxy pro-Moscow fighters via a pontoon bridge. The whole BUK unit, flatbed, rocket and radar was too heavy for the pontoon bridge so the Russian Army left the radar on the east bank. That degraded their ability to tell the difference between a Ukrainian fighter jet and a passenger jet full of holidaymakers. The soldiers thought they were killing the enemy. Instead, they killed 298 people, Dutch, Malaysians, Australians, British.

Down the track, I got to interview the Dutch far-right politician, Geert Wilders. I asked him what he thought was the single biggest terrorist attack against his country and he replied, thankfully, there hasn't been one. Then I mentioned MH17, where 193 Dutch citizens died. It wasn't Islamist extremists who killed those people. He didn't like that but then he is, as I told him to his face, a bit of a fascist.

There is no doubt MH17 was blown out of the sky by the Russian Army. Anti-Kremlin Ukrainians tweeted pictures of the BUK missile launcher on a red low-loader pulled by a distinctive white lorry cab with a blue-grey stripe driving inside pro-Kremlin-held territory. In a chain of photos, you can chart the missile launcher's progress: at one place it's pinned against a block of flats with a blue shed in the foreground; at another past a petrol station in the foreground with a yellow-fronted shop in the background. For our BBC Panorama investigation, Darius and I went to as many of these sites as possible to geo-locate the route of the lorry.

Pro-Kremlin occupied Donetsk was a dark place, the rebel fighters the dross of the earth, sporting skull and crossbones bandanas like some sick version of *Pirates of the Caribbean*, cradling their grenades, flying the Confederate Flag from their checkpoints. After the shooting down of MH17, the Kremlin denied any involvement, but told their proxies to allow the international press to report from the crash site. As the days wore on, the rebels' courtesy as hosts became more and more strained. One morning the *Daily Telegraph* splashed a photo of the launch-site, in a field not far from the town of Snizhne, east of Donetsk. Darius and I headed out with a fixer we had been working with for two or three days. We got stopped at the main rebel checkpoint outside Snizhne, the nastiest of the lot. At which our fixer got out his iPad and asked a heavy with a machine gun where, exactly, the Russians had fired the missile at the plane. The heavy laughed and told us to go back. We did a U-turn and, one hundred yards on, Darius and I both separately sacked our fixer on the spot. A good fixer is gold. This one could have had all three of us killed. I liked him as a human being but I wanted him and us to stay alive.

I took a break from the killing, went on holiday with my kids, then returned to Donetsk with shooter-producer Nick Sturdee, a fluent Russian speaker whose great-grandfather, Vice Admiral Sir Frederick Doveton Sturdee, sank Admiral Graf Spee's flagship, the *Scharnhorst*, off the Falklands in 1914.

Nick and I tracked down three eyewitnesses who saw the lorry towing the BUK missile launcher before it brought down MH17. Two witnesses were challenged by a Russian officer in an army jeep who spoke with not a local but a Moscow accent. Later, I told Dutch detectives investigating the massacre about the Russian officer. They flew me over to Schipol airport to get every detail. I checked with my Ukrainian sources and they were happy to tell the Dutch cops what they knew too. Journalism is not always about the heartbreak beauty queen.

The forensic people from the Netherlands and elsewhere found BUK missile warhead fragments piercing the wreckage. Bits of the missile that didn't explode fell to earth, complete with metal plates showing serial numbers or parts thereof. Bellingcat, the investigative website, made the definitive report on Russian responsibility for MH17. Anyone who doubts it is a fool or a Kremlin troll.

In the spring of 2014 Putin had launched a proxy war against Ukraine, first sending in Russian troops without their normal uniforms or ID, 'little green men', to Crimea, the diamond-shaped peninsula that pokes out of Ukraine into the Black Sea. Crimea is the historical home of the Tartars, a Muslim people, but also a place of quasi-magical power for Russian imperialism. It was during the Crimean War with

Russia where British military incompetence in the Victorian era was highlighted by Tennyson's poem, 'The Charge of The Light Brigade', but it is also true to say that the tsar's soldiers were defeated in the end by an alliance of the British, the French and the Ottoman Empire. In 2014 the successor of the tsar had better luck, taking over Crimea with barely a fight. Putin also stoked up tensions against Kyiv among the majority Russian-speaking population in the two eastern counties or oblasts of Donetsk and Luhansk. There were many people who had no truck with the Russian invasion by proxy but they were outgunned and outmanoeuvred by the Russian secret state. To ram home the message, the Kremlin created two proxy statelets, the Donetsk People's Republic and the Luhansk People's Republic. In the dark, pro-Kyiv citizens were murdered, tortured or hurried to the safety of free Ukraine.

If you're a war reporter, your other life follows you around the killing fields. I can't remember seeing evidence of some truly evil thing without some nagging problem from home. This time, it was down to BBC management. The morning of the day MH17 was shot down, the BBC's then Head of News, James Harding, announced 415 redundancies, identifying the London-based staff Panorama reporters among them. Of the four of us, I was the best known and so within hours my face and news of my certain redundancy was plastered over the internet. As a reporter, I took pride in knowing what the office gossip was and sensed something like this was going to happen so at the staff meeting I put on a brave face, said I had loved my time on the show, and offered to buy everyone a pint in the office boozer. When the MH17 story broke that afternoon, it gave me a proper perspective on the true nature of misfortune and I volunteered to report the story. So when

I turned up in Donetsk, all my mates from other news organizations said: 'But you've been made redundant.' Not yet, I replied.

One time when Nick and I were commuting between the Ukrainian and rebel-held lines Harding phoned. We stopped the car in no man's land while Harding explained that everyone whose post had been closed was allowed to apply for other jobs elsewhere in the BBC . . . 'James, I've got to go,' I said. 'Why?' 'There's two men with guns who want to talk to me.' We put our hands up, said sorry to the rebel gunmen, and hurried back to the safety of Free Ukraine.

Later, it came out that the only two BBC programmes with the budget and remit to take on us Panorama reporters, Newsnight and Today, had just filled up all their vacancies. Fancy that. Irritated by this clever 'apply for no vacant posts' sequencing, I stood my ground and the National Union of Journalists had my back. For the next two years I got seven redundancy letters which I ignored and BBC management could never quite bring themselves to sack me, lest the union go on strike. But the truth was that Director-General Tony Hall and his underlings wanted rid of me and for the next five years I struggled, desperately hard, to prove them wrong. It was like being in an abusive relationship and, inside, I was broken. For the time being, I was still on the BBC's books. Unless, of course, I was foolish enough to make a mistake.

Old-school Donetsk, the one before the Russians stole it in 2014, rocked. My ex and I didn't care for New Year's Eves. The random jollity and the enforced fun felt wrong, so we would pick random places to drop into. One year we hit the Lebanon, in 2012 Donetsk, two years before war destroyed much of it. The city sits atop Ukraine's coal and iron fields and was founded under the tsars by Welsh mining engineer John Hughes in 1860. Hughes, a force of nature from the valleys, worked his way up from the Welsh iron mills to Millwall in London where he made a fortune iron-cladding the wooden vessels of the Royal Navy. The tsar's men asked him to come out and forge a factory town in eastern Ukraine. They named it Hughesovka or Yuzovka in his honour. There is a glorious photograph taken in 1860-something of sixty oxen dragging a cylindrical iron boiler across the snow on sledges to the iron and coal city he would establish. He recruited hundreds of Welsh workers and their families to Hughesovka. The city as a Western-leaning economic engine started to die with the Bolshevik revolution in 1917. It became Stalino in 1923 and, the old monster disgraced, Donetsk in 1961.

Russians and/or Soviets killing Ukrainians in great numbers is nothing new. In 1933 Stalin's famine, caused by the forced collectivization of Russian and Ukrainian farms, led to the deaths by starvation of maybe seven million people, of whom perhaps four million were Ukrainian. Nobody knows for sure because nobody counted. Walter Duranty of *The New York Times* rubbished reporting about the famine and, thanks to his deference to the Kremlin, got an exclusive interview with Stalin for which 'scoop' he won a Pulitzer Prize. To this day, to the shame of *The New York Times*, the paper has not returned the gong.

Three Western reporters told the truth about Stalin's famine: Fred Beal, an American Trotskyist who had the guts to blow the whistle on evil; Malcolm Muggeridge, who was, for a time, the *Manchester Guardian*'s reporter in Moscow; and Gareth Jones, whose mother had been a Welsh governess to the children of John Hughes. Beal was ignored by the big papers in the States; Muggeridge was fired by *The Guardian*; Jones was, wrongly, vilified as a Nazi-sympathizer, and, in 1935, shot dead in China by, I believe, the Russian secret state. In 2011 I made a BBC Radio World Service documentary about Jones which led me to write a thriller about his war against fake news in Russia and Ukraine in 1933, *The Useful Idiot*. Here's just one scene, a fictional reworking of observed history:

'One hundred feet away stood Lenin, one arm outstretched, his coat-tails flapping in an iron wind, all of his upper surfaces coated in snow. A woman in black, pitifully thin, carrying an infant, walked up to the statue and knelt before him . . . She laid the baby down at Lenin's iron feet and crossed herself, over and over again. A GPU officer on the far side of the square started shouting at the woman, roaring with all the power of his voice, but the woman in black ignored him, then unwrapped the baby from its clothes. Only now did Jones realize that the baby was dead.'

This passage from my novel is based on fact. During the height of the famine, mothers would deliberately leave their dead children underneath statues of Lenin, making dark mockery of the Soviet regime's inhumanity. The West did precious little to stop the famine or stand up to Stalin's tyranny. To be fair, they had Hitler to worry about.

Not quite a century on, the West's reaction to the invasions of Crimea, Donetsk and Luhansk was similarly muted. The West set up sanctions but Putin calculated, correctly, that they would be of the light-tap-on-the-wrist variety. The shooting down of MH17 changed the mood music, somewhat, but the West's essential calculation, that it still had to do business with Putin's Russia, stayed unchanged.

*

Time to call the man ultimately responsible for the deaths of 298 people to account.

But first there was a wedding to go to. My niece, Laura, married her bloke Tim somewhere in the Home Counties. Drink was taken. I remember having slept for an hour and a half, and then a taxi to Gatwick, a flight at seven o'clock in the morning to Moscow, change of airports, and then a second flight to Yakutsk, nine time zones east of London. Producer Nick Sturdee had worked out that Putin was inspecting a museum of mammothology in Yakutsk. Nick said that we would never be able to doorstep Putin in Moscow – security is too tight – but in the sticks they sometimes get sloppy.

There is precious little food on the flight to Siberia so when we land I ask if we could get something to eat en route. I wolf a kebab. Hungover, jet-lagged, I do my best to fight the shakes. There is a line of professors of mammothology who seem to be shaking even more than me. I stand next to them in my wedding best, dressed up in my posh suit and green tie and long beard. The President of Russia pimp-rolls into the museum. I guess that Putin thinks I am a professor of mammothology when I jump out of the line of paleolithic boffins and hit him with my question: 'What about the killings in Ukraine, sir?'

The Kremlin media pool live inside a prefabricated bubble so they all assume (or appear to assume) that the question is baked into the schedule. They switch on their TV lights for the answer. Putin's spokesman, Dmitry Peskov, knows better and is furious. The down-table football manager lookalike scowls at me and tries to block Nick Sturdee from capturing what is going on.

I then hit Putin again: 'Thousands are dead, Ukrainians,

Russians, Malaysians, British, Dutch. Sir, do you regret the killings in Ukraine, sir?'

Too many cameras are on Putin for him to duck my questions and he's a pro, so Peskov's man-blocking doesn't work and Nick keeps filming. Putin gives a long and very boring answer in Russian which Peskov translates while looking daggers at me. Putin affects not to speak English but he can and he did. Peskov is so het up by my cheek that he forgets his English momentarily and Putin steps in to translate for the translator. 'Small cities, small cities,' he said. I'd book him.

In the flesh Vladimir Putin is nattily dressed, very short and a dead ringer for an Auton, the ultra-creepy monsters in Doctor Who that morph into wheelie-bins and gobble you up and spit you out as plastic. His cosmetic surgery is not a great advert for Botox but if you get to be the master of the Kremlin no one's going to tell you your skin-job sucks.

Close up, Putin can be quite the minx. At one point he gives a little pout, turning his plastic face into a moue. It is really strikingly effeminate. There is something a little submissive about his reaction to me. It is odd.

Putin's face fascinates because it is covered with this plastic sheen, apart from a little bit of skin just under his eyes, the last non-Botox bit. I want to touch his face and say, 'Are you really plastic all the way through?' But that would be the end of me. So I'm fighting this mad compulsion to touch his face and he's staring at me and I'm staring at him. I'm way taller than him. He's a small man, five foot six, something like that. I'm five foot eleven and a half. But there's another problem. The kebab was squiffy and I'm feeling, 'Oh my god, I'm going to throw up over Vladimir Putin.' Now the Ukrainians would love this. I'll never have to pay for a drink in Kyiv again. But the Kremlin muscle is standing directly behind him. They're all looking very angry at me. And I say to myself, please, John, don't throw up over Vladimir Putin. He gets to the end of his long monologue, setting out that the argument that the war in Ukraine is all the fault of the government in Kyiv because of their failure to talk to the (Kremlin-backed proxies) people in the East.

It's clever because he's using a long speech, giving the appearance of answering my question, while in reality killing proper scrutiny.

I have a follow-up question, 'Why are there so many fresh graves of Russian soldiers killed in Ukraine?' But he just turns and, like a piece of ballet, all of the bodyguards stand in front of me, forming a wall of muscle. Peskov glowers at me and Nick and then a big man says, 'Come with me.' And we follow the guide downstairs into a basement, down a long corridor, and when we get to the end, we're put in a room, and there's frosted glass, and in the room there's coffee and croissants, so things have improved since Stalin's day. But there's a click as a key is turned in the lock and we can't get out. Through frosted glass, you can see the shadow of a big man. So things haven't changed as much as you think.

Back in London, BBC management are fizzing with anxiety. Why did Sweeney do this? What's happened? Where is he? Our mobile phones don't work because we're in a basement. And after an hour or two, they let us out again.

A little later that day Putin opens some gas pipeline with a Chinese deputy prime minister. I start walking closer to the stage and I get within 200 feet of him when one of the Russian goons comes up to me in the crowd and hand-chops me in the guts, discreetly of course, so no one can see it.

So that is what it's like to doorstep Vladimir Putin. But I

didn't throw up over him. I regret it now. To be honest, I wish I had.

The evidence is compelling that when I confronted Vladimir Putin about MH17, the President of Russia, by blaming the tragedy on Ukraine, told me a big fat lie. James – Jim – Fallon is a neuroscientist who studies murderers, psychopaths and dictators. He's professor of psychiatry at the University of California and has made a study of Putin's mind, body and soul. I recorded an interview with him for the 'Taking On Putin' podcast. The prof and I hit it off so I shall call him Jim.

First of all, Jim sets out that he has never had the opportunity to do a direct diagnosis, face to face. But he has gone out of his way to talk to people who have dealt with Vladimir Putin and this includes a former President of Ukraine, a former Prime Minister of Chechnya, big players in Belarus and other countries who have spent time with Putin over the years. Jim listened to his sources and logged Putin's 'personality traits, the ones that everybody agrees on. So I put them together and tried to determine from afar, by trait analysis, if he fits any of these pernicious personality disorders, especially psychopathy and also narcissistic personality disorder.'

I ask Jim to explain some of these traits that he's looking for.

'Psychopaths are very good at lying. Most people, when they're lying, they have tells, tics. They have all sorts of tells that people can read. The thing is, if you don't care about morality, if you don't really deeply believe what you're doing is immoral, you don't have those tells. They don't think what they're doing is immoral or wrong. They don't have the tells. So they are very glib liars. And they have no problem with it. You can't get them on lie detectors. And even the police or people around them will say, well, he is innocent and he's telling the truth because they have no tells.'

I tell Jim about my doorstep of Putin about MH17, how he lied so smoothly.

'Yeah, I've seen that clip, it's very typical of all psychopaths and also people with narcissistic personality disorder. They have a similar type of presentation. So when I say they're glib, they're not thinking about the impact, the negative impact of the lie that's going on. So they're very smooth and fast about it because there is no conflict in them. Plus, if you believe what you're doing is ultimately the moral way to go, you think you have moral superiority. So not only are you glib, you have no tells that you're lying. You don't care. People can't tell you're doing this and this becomes a practice trait from childhood. So they become professional liars. You can't tell by looking at it. They believe it. Another part of these personality disorders is blame externalization. They're always ready to blame what they do on somebody else. They always have a case ready for the blame. It's like: "Well, you did it." Psychopathic murderers will say, "Well, there was a gun there, and I was holding it, but that person deserved to die and the bullet came out." It's very strange, because they don't connect themselves with the crime. And they've done this all their lives. So, listening to you talking to Putin and him glibly saying it was basically their fault, that's a trait of a psychopath right there.'

So as far as the smooth liar goes, Putin ticks the box. What are the other traits that you're looking for in a psychopath?

'Well, a grandiose sense of self. This tremendous confidence in the self, in your own self-identity: they all have that. So they are very convincing, very confident, they have grandiose ideas about themselves. They have what is called fearless dominance. This is somebody who's got such balls, such guts, they are willing to take great chances. And psychopaths are very good at taking chances.'

There is one other factor that Jim Fallon suspects may be in play in Putin's psyche.

'First of all, every psychopath, and almost all the dictators I've ever studied, have all had very troubled early lives. They were abused, abandoned, especially between two and three years old. All of them except for Pol Pot. He's the only one out of the hundreds of them. That's true for Putin. In his early life, he was abandoned, abused, bullied. He was a petty street criminal. And so he fits that pattern of abandonment and abuse, of having early epigenetic environmental abuse, that permanently fixes somebody with these personality disorders.'

I tell Jim that I have one source who told me that Vladimir Putin was sexually abused as a child. Jim's sources echo mine: 'They all said that he was abused and abandoned early on, in his first two to three years.' I return to the disputed story that Putin was a bastard, abandoned by his natural mother in Georgia. Jim has a fascinating but different take.

'The most consistent story was the abandonment and the abuse primarily happened in Leningrad. I heard the Georgian story.'

This raises the possibility that Putin was abandoned by his natural mother, not in Georgia, but somehow in Leningrad. Jim continued: 'This is similar to other psychopaths. There's something unexplained, some unanswered question because the person themselves will deny it or somebody in the family will deny the real story, to protect the family. You get this problem in court cases and in biographies of psychopathic killers. They will always protect the secret. So you always get this denial thing, "No, I was brought up fine." But in reality someone brought up after their mother abandoned them, raised in an environment that's abusive, this is a very common thing with psychopaths. So there's always this question of exactly what happened. So which one is the most true story? The one I heard most consistently is that the abandonment and abuse occurred very early on.'

We don't know the whole story, and probably never will. But we do know that Vladimir Putin exhibits multiple signs of being a psychopath: smooth lying with no tics; fearless dominance; blame externalization; unexplained early life.

The shooting down of MH17 by a Russian surface-to-air missile in July 2014 was the moment when I thought that Vladimir Putin had shot his bolt, that this time he had gone too far, that this time the West would finally stand up to him.

And about that, I was wrong. The West's appeasement of the Kremlin continued, as before.

CHAPTER TWELVE

The Leader of the Opposition Has Been Shot

The man who almost became the master of the Kremlin instead of Putin, Boris Nemtsov, bright, bubbly-haired, funny, the former theoretical physicist turned democratic politician, was on cracking form. The oligarchs had built a road from the coastal town of Sochi to the ski resort in the mountains at an extraordinary cost of five billion dollars for Putin's Winter Olympics. I caught up with Nemtsov in Moscow in December 2013, some weeks before the opening ceremony. He joked: 'It would have been cheaper to have paved this road with Louis Vuitton handbags.'

I explained to Nemtsov that I'd met Anatoly Pakhomov, the Putinist mayor of Sochi, and challenged him on the issue of how gay Olympians would be treated. He'd told me with a straight face: 'There are no gays in Sochi.'

Pakhomov's claim – an echo of the Radio Stars' 1977 hit 'No Russians in Russia' – was preposterously untrue to anyone who knows anything about the beach resort in Russia's deep south. This nonsense delighted Nemtsov: 'No gays in Sochi? Unbelievable, unbelievable.'

He started giggling and couldn't stop, and in our Panorama film on 'Putin's Games' we had to trim the laughter because it went on so long. Of all the figures in the public eye I've met as a journalist, the only one to touch Nemtsov's delight in the absurd is the Dalai Lama and he's a god-king.

It's when Panorama freelance producer Nick Sturdee and I tried to hear stories at first hand that the gloss came off Putin's 2014 Winter Olympic varnish. We rolled up to a checkpoint in the middle of the village of Akhshtyr, east of Sochi, not far from the border with Georgia. It's a nowhere kind of place, not special, but it didn't use to be quite as ugly as it is now. High up was a massive quarry, where rock for the Olympics had been hewed, and now the big hole in the ground was to be a landfill dump. Lorries thundered through the checkpoint all day, engines roaring as they inched past our car, but we couldn't move.

The soldiers were FSB and the lead grunt barked at me in Russian that we could not pass. But to do our job, we had to. The villagers say the fancy $5 billion road from Sochi to the ski resort has isolated the village from Sochi. The children used to have a twenty-minute commute to school. Now they have to drive for an hour down a muddy road because a promised access road was not built.

I looked the FSB grunt in the eye and said: 'President Putin promised the International Olympic Committee that journalists would be welcome in Sochi.' Nick translated and a look of unease clouded the FSB grunt's face: he was young, blonde, and had a big gun. But nor did he want to fall out with some stranger who quoted the president. He took our passports and questioned our status: 'How do we know you are journalists?' We didn't have Russian press passes because, although we had sent in applications three weeks before, the Foreign Ministry in Moscow was unable to print our passes or communicate that difficulty to us.

A villager walked past and palmed something to me: the business card of Robert Roxburgh, press officer of the International Olympics Committee. I called the number on the card on my mobile and told Roxburgh that the FSB had taken our passports, and asked him what the IOC was going to do about it. He scolded us for going to Akhshtyr without Russian press passes. I explained that problem lay with the Russians, not us. The FSB subsequently kept our passports but allowed us to walk on foot through their checkpoint to film the villagers. They complained about the quarry, owned by Russian Railways, which was in turn owned by oligarch Vladimir Yakunin, an old St Petersburg mucker of Vladimir Putin.

When we got back to the FSB checkpoint, the grunt said that to get our passports back we had to sign a document admitting that we had illegally entered 'the border zone'. No deal. I called Roxburgh again. He huffed and puffed. A solution emerged when one of the FSB agents suggested we sign 'I refuse to sign' on their document. That we did and then we were free.

Workers claimed that they had been cheated of their wages. Few were willing to say so on camera, but electrician Mardiros Demerchan was an exception. He told us that when he complained, the police arrested him on a trumped-up charge: 'They started to beat me, one from one side and one from the other. I fell to the floor and I started losing consciousness, and they hauled me back up and sat me on the chair. One of them said, "Have you had enough or do we have to beat you some more?"'

Demerchan claimed he had been tortured and sexually assaulted with an iron bar. He was trying to bring charges against the police. They were suing him for libel.

I didn't mention Moonglade to the FSB. That's my translation from the Russian of Lunnaya Polyana, a secret base high up in the mountains, accessible only by helicopter, which sounds like a Bond villain's lair. Built in a former national park, Moonglade is officially a meteorological research station, but it appears to be a hush-hush skiing lodge for the president. Green activist Yevgeny Vitishko hiked up to Moonglade. He told us: 'Vladimir Putin liked it and decided to build himself a country house there.' Vitishko campaigned against more lodges being built nearby: 'This holiday home fever is something that must really be fought – which is what we're doing, and why the court found us guilty.' Vitishko was referring to his trial for hooliganism for allegedly painting a graffito on a fence, a charge he denied. After Vitishko appeared on our Panorama programme 'Putin's Games' – he took the decision himself, fully knowing that it was apiece with his activism – he got sentenced to three years in prison.

The way I liked to work on Panorama was to push everything to the limit, so that when the bosses pushed back, adding cold milk as they always did, the viewing public would still get something with a bit of flavour. For the Moonglade section of 'Putin's Games' I suggested that we should use the John Barry soundtrack from his song 'Capsule in Space', the bit in the Bond movie *You Only Live Twice* when the SMERSH satellites gobble up the Soviet and American satellites. It's a brilliant and creepy riff. The BBC underlings were so terrified about the rest of the show they somehow forgot to water this down and it stayed in.

Just sayin'.

Our detention by the FSB, the anger of the cut-off villagers, the torture of the electrician, the arrest and sentencing of the brave Green activist all summed up 'Putin's Games' for me: the authorities pretending to be all smiley, but every now and then the guard dropped, and you had a glimpse of a police state, robbing the powerless, serving the powerful.

Boris Nemtsov hated Vladimir Putin's war against Ukraine, the seizing of Crimea and the masked invasions of Donetsk and Luhansk in the east. He fired this shot directly at the Kremlin in the spring of 2014 on his Facebook page:

'Putin has declared a war of brother against brother in Ukraine. This bloody folly by a crazed KGB man will cost Russia and Ukraine dear: once again the deaths of young boys on both sides, bereft mothers and wives, children turned into orphans. An empty Crimea, which tourists will never visit. Billions, tens of billions of roubles, taken from old people and children and thrown into the furnace of the war, and then after that even more money to prop up the thieving regime in Crimea . . . The ghoul needs a war. He needs the blood of the people. Russia can look forward to international isolation, the impoverishment of its people, and repressions. God, why should we be cursed like this??? How much longer can we take it?!'

A little more than a year after I interviewed him giggling his head off, Boris Nemtsov was shot dead, gunned down on 27 February 2015 on the bridge over the Moskva river, a hundred yards from the Kremlin. I remember I called my Panorama executive producer, Andrew Head, and sobbed down the phone. Seven years on, no one who commissioned the killing has been charged. Nemtsov was an extraordinary man, the sweetest, funniest and most human Russian I've ever met. His brutal snuffing out caused me to sink into a profound depression. I knocked out a thriller, *Cold*, about modern Russia and I dedicated it to three Russians who I'd met and who had been shot: Politkovskaya, Estemirova, Nemtsov.

In the *London Review of Books* Keith Gessen reflected on Nemtsov's Facebook post against the war in Ukraine and wrote this after he was assassinated: 'He was killed for his opposition to the war. Since the start, critics have been warning that the war in Ukraine would eventually come home to Moscow. No matter who pulled the trigger on the bridge, it has.'

Nemtsov was no fool. He sensed what was about to happen to him. One month before his murder he blogged that his mother, then eighty-seven years old, feared Putin would have him killed. Was he himself afraid, someone asked? 'Yes, not as strongly as my mother, but still . . .' Nemtsov being Nemtsov, he went on: 'I am only joking. If I were afraid of Putin, I wouldn't be in this line of work.'

He wasn't joking. Two weeks before his murder, Nemtsov told his old pal, journalist Yevgenia Albats, that he was afraid of being killed, but he set out the reasons why it would not happen: he had been a high-up in the Kremlin, a deputy prime minister, and killing him would set a precedent in bloodletting.

Nemtsov was wrong about that. He was shot in the back several times one hundred metres or so from the walls of the Kremlin, one of the most closely CCTV-filmed areas on earth. The official narrative was that a bin lorry obscured the Kremlin's cameras from capturing the killer or killers. Attentive readers will have already got it, but for the avoidance of any doubt the official narrative is a load of old hogwash. In my four decades-plus of reporting, I have never been detained by police officers more often than outside the Kremlin. You cannot move five yards without a cop demanding to see your passport. The idea that Nemtsov was assassinated but that none of the Kremlin's cameras captured critical evidence is absurd. Putin's press officer, Dmitry Peskov, twisted the knife: 'Putin noted that this cruel murder has all the hallmarks of a contract hit and is extremely provocative . . . In political terms he did not pose any threat to the current Russian leadership or Vladimir Putin. If we compare popularity levels, Putin's and the government's ratings and so on, in general Boris Nemtsov was just a little bit more than an average citizen.'

Once again, for the avoidance of any doubt, Nemtsov was trouble for Vladimir Putin. The one person who benefited from his murder was the master of the Kremlin.

The police investigation into the assassination of the unofficial leader of the Russian opposition went exactly as attentive readers would expect: Moscow's finest galloped off in the wrong direction. The night after the killing, police raided Nemtsov's flat and confiscated his computer hard drives. Of course they did. The victim was the enemy. The Russian-born American reporter Julia Ioffe predicted what would happen: 'We can be sure that the investigation will lead precisely nowhere. At most, some sad sap, the supposed trigger-puller, will be hauled in front of a judge, the scapegoat for someone far more powerful. More likely, the case will founder for years amid promises that everyone is working hard, and no one will be brought to justice at all.' The Kremlin, she wrote, was already 'muddying the waters'.

Smart people in Moscow were divided about who, exactly, ordered the hit. Nemtsov was a long-time thorn in Vladimir Putin's prickly side. But, like Anna Politkovskaya before him, he was also a forthright critic of the psychotic Chechen quisling, Ramzan Kadyrov. Russian opposition activist Ilya Yashin suspected that Kadyrov had Nemtsov killed. The word was that there were FSB officers who found hard evidence that the Chechen satrap commissioned the hit and were frustrated that Putin, after days of indecision, ordered them to close down their investigation.

I say it to my Ukrainian friends again and again: there is another Russia. The problem is that the alternatives to Vladimir Putin are either dead or not very alive.

In December 2016 I was back in Moscow, hanging out with one of the intellectual colossi of Vladimir Putin's Russia. With his long hair and beard and iconic Slavic looks, Alexander Dugin, then aged fifty-four, is variously described as 'Putin's Brain' or 'Putin's Rasputin'. At the time he had his own pro-Kremlin TV show which pumped out Russian Orthodox supremacy. Imagine Goebbels-style rhetoric inside a Songs of Praise format and you get a flavour of the holy-moly mind-fuck. Dugin is the apostle of Eurasianism, the ideology that Russia is a stand-alone country, spanning both Europe and Asia, and so it must hold itself aloft and away from the seductive, weakening diseases of human rights, democracy and the rule of law. It's Orthodox fascism wrapped up in fancy gibberish but, that said, Dugin is widely believed to have the ear of the Kremlin. When I met him he was under Western sanctions for the ferocity of his statements in favour of the Russian invasion of Ukraine and his denial of Ukraine's nationhood. At that point in 2016, Putin's war in the Donbas had only cost 10,000 lives.

Dugin's big shtick was that the greatest dangers to Western civilization were enfeebling liberalism and Islamist extremism.

Others were sympathetic to his view, including President Donald Trump's chief strategist, Steve Bannon. In 2016, Trump and Bannon seemed to be masters of the universe. Bannon had aired his views in a right-wing mind-fest on the fringes of the Vatican in 2014, claiming that so-called Islamic State has a Twitter account 'about turning the United States into a "river of blood"'.

'Trust me, that is going to come to Europe,' he added. 'On top of that we're now, I believe, at the beginning stages of a global war against Islamic fascism.'

The danger is that in allying yourself with the Kremlin in the way it fights 'Islamist fascism' in say, Aleppo, you could end up siding with Russian fascism. It is a risk about which Alexander Dugin did not seem willing to reflect. My interview with him in Moscow did not end well.

First, he dismissed the chances that the Russians hacked American democracy in the 2016 US presidential election as 'strictly zero'.

Sweeney: 'People ask questions about Vladimir Putin's commitment to democracy?'

Dugin: 'Please be careful. You could not teach us democracy because you try to impose to every people, every state, every society, their Western, American or so-called American system of values without asking . . . and it is absolutely racist; you are racist.'

Sweeney: 'What happens is, if you are critical of Vladimir Putin you may end up dead.'

Dugin: 'If you are engaged in Wikileaks, you can be murdered?'

Sweeney: 'Julian Assange is dead, is he?'

Dugin: 'No.'

Sweeney: 'So hold on a second, please, tell me about Boris Nemtsov. He was murdered one hundred yards from the Kremlin.'

Dugin: 'By Putin? You think he was murdered by Putin?'

Sweeney: 'He was critical of Putin. Can you list the number of American journalists who had died under Barack Obama. You can't, can you?'

Dugin: 'It is a completely stupid kind of conversation. Very nice to meet you but I don't like to continue.'

Then Dugin ripped off his sound-mike and walked out of the interview.

And we had been getting on so well.

Later, he posted a blog to his 20,000 followers, illustrated with my photograph and accusing me of manufacturing 'fake news: I've kicked a BBC correspondent out. A notorious bastard! An utter cretin ... John Sweeney was in charge. His name tells it all: he's a "globalist swine". They are making a fake news documentary on how Russians helped Trump become President. Their only evidence that Putin had worked in the KGB. Complete imbeciles. Zero journalistic skills! Nazi-style propagandist. Stay away from them!'

Such is the language of the new world order.

From then on, everywhere I went in Russia I was followed.

Chapter Thirteen

Taking On Putin

Shot.

Stabbed.

Tasered.

Beaten by silent thugs.

Hit over the head with an iron bar.

Half-blinded.

These verbs tell the story of what it is like to take on Vladimir Putin, to stand up for Russian democracy. What is so admirable is that the opposition to the Kremlin work with style and panache and a dark sense of humour. And unbelievable courage.

Shot? Nemtsov.

Stabbed? Tasered?

In the spring of 2018 the master of the Kremlin was running to be elected President of Russia, again. Team Navalny were doing their bit to show that the election was a dark farce, at great cost to themselves and, ultimately, their leader.

Even mockery was dangerous. Take the road cleaner who dared to wear a Vladimir Putin mask at opposition demonstrations. Vladimir Ivanyutenko, from St Petersburg, became famous for sporting the mask and a T-shirt with a rude caption which you could translate, politely, as 'Putin is a plonker'. In December 2017 he was walking to work at six o'clock in the morning when two men attacked him. One man zapped him with a Taser, the second stabbed him twice. They ran off and left him to die in the snow. Yet he survived. Ivanyutenko believed the Russian state was behind the attack. He told me: 'I can only connect it with my opposition activities. I back the critics of the Putin regime and I think he is a kleptocrat. He is not a legitimate president.'

No one has been charged for the attack on Ivanyutenko. Of course not.

Beaten by silent thugs? In January 2018 Dinar Idrisov was live-streaming Russian police disrupting a Navalny rally. But his live-feed video meant it was child's play to geo-locate him, whereupon he was attacked by three men. They knocked him to the ground and kicked him in the face, head and torso, keeping silent all the while. He suffered a broken rib, arm and cheekbone, and his face was beaten to a pulp. Idrisov believed the attackers were from Russia's state security services. Normal thugs yell at you as they hit you, but his silent assailants did not: 'These people were emotionless.'

No one has been charged for the attack on Idrisov. Of course not.

Hit over the head with an iron bar? Nikolai Lyaskin was a senior aide to Alexei Navalny. In September 2017 he fell to the ground: 'At first, I actually thought that something had fallen off a roof, maybe the building is collapsing. I turned around and saw a man hit me on the head again with an iron bar.' After the attack, Lyaskin got a funny peculiar text message: 'Done.' The Russian police accused him of setting up the iron-bar attack himself, of paying his assailant to hurt him. Some days after the attack, the police raided the offices where he worked, which so happened to be the HQ of Team Navalny. 'It was completely absurd. I got hit on my head with an iron bar and they just confiscated all the flyers, all the stickers, all the stuff with Navalny's name on it from our office.'

No one has been charged for the attack on Lyaskin. Of course not.

Half-blinded? The man who feared for a time that he would lose the sight of an eye, his right one, is Alexei Navalny himself. I first encountered Navalny by Zoom in 2016 when my Russian pal, Roman Borisovich, living in exile in London, put me in touch with Team Navalny's Anti-Corruption Foundation, known by its initials in Russian, FBK. They had made a funny and yet also dark forty-minute video about the then Russian prosecutor-general, Yury Chaika, and his sons. The gist of the film was that Russia's top law-enforcement official and his sons were in bed with organized crime. If ordinary Russians tried to fight back, they could end up dead. Nick Sturdee and I made a short BBC Newsnight film, using the fact that Chaika means seagull in Russian. Our film opened with a shot of frozen wastes and bleak water, with me holding a chip aloft, to be gobbled up by a diving gull, all to the tune of Stalin's version of the Soviet national anthem. I intoned to camera: 'Welcome to Lake Baikal.' The sound glitched and I came clean: 'Oh, all right, welcome to Southend-on-Sea.' Chaika and his sons denied the FBK's charges, with the then prosecutor-general himself saying on film that the video was 'a hatchet job' and that 'the information presented [had been] deliberately falsified'.

Over Zoom, Navalny told me that Vladimir Putin presided over a Russia rotting from the top: 'He is the tsar of corruption.' I came away from the interview impressed by his courage. It was one thing for us to set out these charges from the safety of London, but for Navalny and his team to do it from inside Russia was brave beyond belief.

In the run-up to the 2018 presidential elections everyone knew who was going to win. Any candidate with a chance of beating Vladimir Putin wasn't in the game. Nemtsov had been shot and killed, Kasyanov sex-shamed, Navalny barred because of a nonsense of a trial featuring absurd evidence from the state, the captive judge mumbling out his lines dictated by the Kremlin.

But Team Navalny caused the Kremlin grief, no question. Navalny's schtick was a bizarrely clever one, to pretend that Russia was a functioning democracy and act accordingly. In April 2017 he was just outside his office in Moscow when an attacker threw green medical dye, *zelyonka* in Russian, in his face. The dye is regularly used as a disinfectant, if you've grazed your skin for example, and is not toxic. But there was some other substance mixed in the dye, a caustic chemical agent of some kind, and that caused corrosive burning to his right eye. He had to go to Spain for medical treatment and close-up, it's clear that his damaged eye still looks affected, less mobile than the good one.

The Russian police have not been able to identify and trace the attacker, which is odd because Team Navalny did. There's CCTV footage of the attacker running from the scene. The police had the footage, yet someone had blobbed out the face – but not the clothes or body of the attacker. They had blobbed out, too, a second man, walking slowly away from the scene so as not to attract attention. He's holding his mobile phone in his hand. One of Navalny's supporters found a version of the CCTV footage on the internet where the blobbing of the second man didn't work for a frame or two. They identified him as Aleksei Kulakov, a former major in the Moscow police and an activist in a sinister pro-Kremlin group called SERB, an acronym which stands, bizarrely in English, for South-East Regional Bloc. They are from the occupied south-eastern part of Ukraine, plying the Putin line on the war there, that they are freedom fighters and the government in Kyiv consists of Nazi usurpers. By identifying Kulakov, Team Navalny managed to trace the man they believe was the corrosive attacker, Aleksandr Petrunko. All concerned deny any wrongdoing. They have not been charged.

SERB's stated goal is to 'support a cult of traditional Russian family values and put an end to the moral decay of society being forced upon us by the West and America'. To counter that moral decay, they have thrown green dye, piss and shit at the opposition, but the police never seem interested in stopping their harassment. SERB enjoys a licence from the Russian state to monster anyone with impunity who questions the Kremlin, as I was about to find out.

Producer Nick Sturdee, our fixer and I arranged to meet the SERB activists by the statue to the great WW2 Soviet general, Marshal Zhukov, just to the north of the Kremlin. SERB's leader is a failed actor called Igor Beketov, a strikingly tall man with some stage presence, sporting a red woolly hat with SERB written on it in white letters. He talked rubbish, fast and loud. On the day we met it was snowing and we were all wearing thick coats and jumpers, but even so it was clear that Beketov had a stab vest on too. There were only four of them: Beketov, a crotchety geezer in a trilby, a man in a woolly hat like a tea cosy, and the fourth was former police major Kulakov, the second man seen on the green-dye attack CCTV walking calmly away from the scene. Kulakov was lean, fit, silent and wall-eyed. He spent the whole time filming us on his mobile phone fitted to a telescopic stick thingy. What we didn't know at the time was that we were also being secretly filmed from afar because long-distance video of our meeting with SERB later popped up on state TV. It made great B-roll.

Beketov led us first to the spot where Nemtsov had been gunned down on the bridge over the river, a stone's throw from the Kremlin's great red wall. It was bitterly cold but even so there was an old chap guarding the shrine to the slain politician. If you love Russia, there's always a moment when the issue is raised that there isn't just a problem with the man in the Kremlin. There is something rotten, some people say, with Russians as a whole. It's the swamp, not the monster. To counter that stereotype, I always think of the guardians of the Nemtsov shrine: an impromptu affair of candles, a framed photograph of Nemtsov's film-star face, some flowers, a wreath. The Kremlin started sending in the local street-cleaners to demolish the shrine. Every time that happened, the shrine would magically grow back. To really stick it to the Kremlin, Nemtsov's supporters organized a 24/7 watch. Throughout the year – come sun, rain and a helluva lot of snow – the guardians made sure the shrine was respected. The SERB activists came along and picked a fight with this old chap guarding the shrine that day. He may have been old but he was having none of it: 'All the leaders I wanted to vote for were killed.' He listed them, starting with Galina Starovoytova – the liberal MP who called Yeltsin 'Boris the Bloody' after starting the first Chechen War, shot dead in 1998 – and ending with Nemtsov, shot dead in 2015.

Nonplussed, Beketov went into a rant that the old chap dared to call this the Nemtsov Bridge rather than by its correct formal name. It was out of all proportion, that he was picking an argument with a man protecting a shrine to a murdered democrat. I put to Beketov a charge made that SERB is effectively financed and run by Centre E, the anti-terrorist or anti-extremist section of the Russian police force. He denied it. We walked on south and arrived after a time in the neighbourhood where Nemtsov used to live. The owner of the building where Nemtsov once lived has refused permission to put up a photograph of him on his wall, but the owner of the next-door building said it was okay. So, five feet from Nemtsov's old building is a little shrine to the murder victim, a framed photograph on a wall and a wreath hanging from it. Beketov objected to the shrine being put up on the wrong building, walked over to the Nemtsov photograph and wreath and ripped them from the wall. He kept the photograph on him but dumped the wreath in a nearby plastic toilet. As he took it all down, I said loudly and clearly in English: 'Aren't you desecrating a shrine?' This was translated so Beketov and the former police major who was filming everything would be in no doubt as to what I thought of their vandalism.

On this trip, every single time our Panorama team moved in Moscow and St Petersburg, we were followed by strangers in unmarked cars. In the extreme cold, they were comically easy to spot: sitting in the gloom, with interior lights always off but engines running.

The day after SERB desecrated the Nemtsov shrine we interviewed Andrei Soldatov, an expert on the FSB, in our van with dark windows. As usual, we were being followed by an unmarked car. This one had a registration number starting X369. I have never been so blatantly followed in my entire life. As we drove by the Lubyanka, the FSB headquarters, which sits in the dead centre of the Russian capital like a yellow-grey toad, I asked Soldatov how many people had been executed in the basement: 'Thousands. We are doomed in a way. You have fear installed in your memory. You cannot get people interested in freedom because you have this disaster in the past and nobody wants to talk about it. We are still in fear of Stalin's secret police.'

Jon Coffey, our Panorama producer, stuck in the hotel wiring back our rushes – the video we had already filmed – to the edit in London via the internet using an encrypted system, called me to say that four Russian police officers were waiting to talk to camera op Seamus McCracken and I. We had no idea why. Seamus and I dropped Soldatov off but I didn't fancy taking that day's rushes to our meeting with the police, lest they search us, confiscate the SD cards, and then find Soldatov's uncut interview with us. We went to the BBC Moscow office, our plan being to drop off the SD cards, then meet the police.

The BBC Moscow office had other ideas. I explained that we had been filming Soldatov and we wanted to put our rushes in a safe place to protect him. We were told: 'Leave the Moscow bureau and take your rushes with you.'

I appreciate the Corporation has a duty to protect its own, but we were also part of the BBC family. In my view, this action not only endangered us but also our source, Andrei Soldatov.

Flabbergasted, I found a friendly Russian – not someone employed by the BBC Moscow office – who hid our rushes, and Seamus and I kept our appointment with the cops. They interviewed our fixer and Seamus first, leaving me to dwell on my sins in a room on my own. It was a nice room, as rooms in Russian police stations go. It had a window overlooking a courtyard through which I could see three cops having a fag break in the snow. But I wasn't free to leave.

A newsflash popped up on my mobile, that a Russian TV channel close to the FSB-KGB was reporting that I was going to be charged with vandalizing the Nemtsov shrine. I didn't know what was going to happen next and, although I did my absolute best to suppress it, I felt afraid, that this time I had pushed the secret policemen who rule Russia that bit too far. The problem for me in that knife-slash of time, and more generally for the Russian opposition and the democracies, is that those secret policemen have no limits. Or if they do, no one knows what those limits are.

And that is scary.

While in the cop shop, the police took our passports to make copies, then returned them. Before we were free to go, someone anonymous on Telegram, a Russian online channel, put up the passport photo pages showing Seamus's and my details: photo, date of birth, passport numbers. We had to cancel them as soon as possible.

Out in the snow, walking away from the police station, we were immediately doorstepped by a team from Russian TV, camera lights and all. Seamus, who is no milquetoast, whipped out his camera-phone and started shooting the other side. I turned on the hapless reporter and gave him a lick with the rough edge of my tongue: 'Are you part of the police state?' The reporter gulped at me, like a goldfish in his bowl. I turned to Seamus's camera phone and said: 'These colleagues from Russian state TV have tried to doorstep us but they have done it so incompetently they are now walking away.' It made it into our Panorama programme, 'Taking On Putin', which got three million viewers.

Our Panorama team had been chased around the streets of Moscow and St Petersburg by the secret police; I had been framed for vandalism; we had been held for an afternoon in a Moscow nick; our passports had been compromised; our fixer was declared an extremist and had to leave Russia for good. While Putin is in power, I can't go back. Back in London, I protested about our team being thrown out into the cold by the BBC Moscow bureau, but to no avail. I should have read the tea leaves. Management wanted rid of me, their troublesome reporter.

I still believe the BBC to be a noble thing; I defend it. But placing bureaucracy above journalism is not good.

The one thing that we had not got in the bag was an interview in Russia with Navalny. Intent on making as much trouble as possible for the Kremlin, Navalny isn't that bothered about his image in the West. Seamus and I had met him once already, very briefly, in Strasbourg, where he attended a court case at the European Court of Human Rights in late 2017. The court found for him and against the Russian state – not that it was bothered. Navalny had ten minutes to spare before flying back to Moscow where – who knew? – he might get arrested yet again.

In the flesh, Navalny is tall, lean, oozes charisma, and has grey staring eyes. What saves him from messiah status – and the darkness that can flow from that – is his sense of humour and love of the absurd. As Seamus fixed the sound mike on Alexei's lapel, I explained that Seamus was from Northern Ireland. Seamus stopped what he was doing. Navalny started to grin, smelling my fear but also enjoying the comedy of the moment as the BBC reporter was desperate to get a sound bite in the can. Navalny and I were suddenly not politician and reporter but two big dogs, sniffing each other's bottoms. I gave out a high-pitched giggle and explained that Seamus 'is from the island of Ireland and that we British are still learning to deal with the legacy of imperialism', at which Seamus started working again and Alexei laughed his head off.

Navalny started out as a lawyer, then made his own anti-corruption blog which became fabulously successful, with hundreds of thousands of followers. Along the track he had made some mistakes. In the late 2000s he flirted with Russia's xenophobic far right but since then has veered back to the centre ground. He took part at a course for leaders at Yale University in Connecticut for a few months in 2010 with Marvin Rees, the black mayor of Bristol. Rees told me the two men became friends and that Navalny had a car but he hadn't, to begin with, and Navalny would drive him to the supermarket so that he could do his shopping. When their wives and kids came out to the States, the two families would go apple-picking together. 'At no time did I feel anything other than respect from Alexei.'

Courage and a way with words has got Navalny far. In 2011 civil Russia was outraged to discover that Vladimir Putin and Dmitry Medvedev were swapping jobs, again. Putin had been elected to two four-year terms, from 2000 to 2008, but under the then constitution he was barred from standing for a third term. Hey presto! His then prime minister, Medvedev – one of very few Russian politicians who is actually shorter than Putin, hence his elevation – announced he would run for president. And, for prime minister, he would go for Putin. President Obama and others fell for the trick, treating Medvedev seriously, whereas in fact he was merely a stooge. Professor Donald Rayfield put it best when I asked him what he made of Medvedev? 'Al Capone's lawyer.'

Come 2011, Putin announced that he and the smaller man would swap job titles again, and angry Russians hit the streets.

Navalny, not tainted by power or the chaos of the Yeltsin years, rose to prominence. He called United Russia, the vehicle for Putin and Medvedev, the 'party of crooks and thieves' – an insult which stuck because it rang true. Once Nemtsov had been shot in 2015 and Kasyanov sex-shamed a year later, Navalny became the effective leader of the opposition. Naturally, the Kremlin used, or, in fact, abused the rule of law to knock him out of the running for the presidential elections. When I finally caught up with him at his office in Moscow, Navalny gave it to the Kremlin with both barrels: 'This is not an election. You cannot participate in it because it's disgrace, it's immoral, it's awful, it's ugly. We cannot call this procedure an election.'

'Is Russia a police state?' I asked him.

'Absolutely, 100 per cent.'

Chapter Fourteen

The View from the Spire

In March 2018 a rare fall of snow settled in southern England but, as ever, it soon turned to slush. No better time, one might think, for two Russian sports nutritionists to fly from Moscow to check out the spire of Salisbury Cathedral, twice, on two days running. Putin's favourite lapdog, sorry, journalist, Margarita Simonyan, caught up with the two holidaymakers on RT, formerly Russia Today, the Russian TV channel controlled, like all the others, by the Kremlin.

> Margarita Simonyan: 'Salisbury?'
> Ruslan Boshirov: 'Yes.'
> Simonyan: 'What makes it so wonderful?'
> Boshirov: 'Our friends had been suggesting for a long time that we visit this wonderful town. There's the famous Salisbury Cathedral, famous not only in Europe but in the whole world for its 123-metre spire' – that's 404 feet in old money.

What's funny peculiar about this interview is that the two sports nutritionists don't look like medieval architecture buffs at all. They're thickset, grim, cold-eyed. To be frank with you, they look like common murderers. And did they actually go up the spire? Good question. You can climb it. It's 322 steps. I know because I climbed all of them. The view from the top – well as close to the top as non-human flies can get – is extraordinary, the patchwork majesty of England's green and pleasant land set out under a blue sky.

The two Russians never got close to the spire. A chain of CCTV images shows they went in the opposite direction, towards the home of Sergei Skripal.

That name might ring a bell for some of you. Sergei Skripal was in the GRU, Russian military intelligence, the heaviest of the heavy mobs. It's common ground that the GRU is the most murderous element of the Russian secret state. Skripal was a Russian spy working for the GRU first in Malta, then in Spain – but at some point in the 1990s the British secret service, MI6, make him an offer. He accepts but then is called back to Russia in the early 2000s. But he's eventually betrayed and locked up for thirteen years in 2006 for spying for the British.

In 2010 the FBI swoops in on nine American citizens who are no such thing. They call themselves Donald Heathfield and his wife Tracey Lee Ann Foley, Richard and Cynthia Murphy, Juan Lazaro and Vicky Peláez, Michael Zottoli and Patricia Mills, and Anna Chapman. They fly the Stars & Stripes from their suburban lawns or sip cocktails in Upper East Side bars, but they are living a deep lie. They are Russian sleepers, the most memorable of whom is Chapman, born Anna Kushchenko in Kharkhiv in what is now free Ukraine. The daughter of a Soviet KGB officer who served in Kenya at the Soviet Embassy, Anna has the looks of a catwalk model. She had moved to London, where she met a British chap called Alex Chapman at a rave in the Docklands, married him and took his surname. After the marriage fell apart she moved to New York and set up a whole new life until the FBI came a-knocking.

The spy swap took place at Vienna airport. The CIA plane landed next to the Russian plane and a covered jetty was used so that no outsider could photograph who got the fat and who got the lean. Four Russians who had spied for the Americans and the British, Skripal included, were swapped for the Russian sleepers.

The swap meant that, according to the rules of the spy game, Sergei Skripal was no longer on the board. If it was a chess game, Skripal was a discarded knight, no longer in play. MI6 bought him a small, nondescript modern two-up-and-two down in Salisbury, gave him a bit of a pension, and asked him the odd fruity question about his past life now and then. He lived quietly but not in hiding. Skripal, like MI6, assumed he was safe. But the Russian secret state, and in particular the GRU, don't play by the rules of the game.

Skripal was not safe. Nor was his family. His wife died of cancer in 2012, his son of a mysterious illness on a trip to St Petersburg in 2017 when he was just forty-three. Attentive readers will worry about anyone who dies of a mysterious illness in those circumstances. Skripal's house was about half an hour's walk from the spire. I know because I walked the route the Russians took. On 4 March the CCTV shows the two men with slush on their boots coming out of Salisbury railway station at 11:46, stopping to take pictures as they cross the River Avon. At 11:58 they're caught by the CCTV at the Shell petrol station on Wilton Road, five minutes' walk from Skripal's home.

The CCTV images don't show the petrol station because the camera is looking outwards, but they do show a distinctive metal drain grid and then a double yellow line. The two Russians move past the grid and double yellow, not towards the cathedral, but towards the home of Sergei Skripal.

The Russians smear the poison on the door handle of Skripal's home. It's not in liquid form but a kind of gel. You can't see it or smell it. The poison is Novichok, a chemical nerve agent and a weapon of mass destruction, invented and manufactured only in Russia by the Russian secret state. The two Russian sports nutritionists are, in fact, poisoners, working for the GRU, Russian military intelligence.

The hit didn't work.

That day Sergei and his daughter, Yulia, visiting him from Russia, had pizza and a pint for lunch in Zizzi's, a chain restaurant, and then they came to a little park overlooking the River Avon. They had some bread left over from lunch and they gave it to three little boys who fed the ducks with it. Then they sat down on a park bench and passed out. A NHS nurse, off-duty, saw Yulia first. She could see the whites of her eyes, froth coming out of her mouth. She dialled 999 and the Skripals, father and daughter, got the very best first aid imaginable, a jab of atropine, which originally comes from the poisonous plant deadly nightshade (belladonna). It slows down the nervous system and stops it from crashing. It is routinely given to junkies. The Skripals were also lucky because of great old British weather. It had been damp, very, plus heavy fog, and that's not good for nerve agents.

When the news broke that the Skripals had been poisoned with a nerve agent, the family with the three boys who had fed the ducks got in touch. They were rushed to hospital where they were checked but found to be okay. The point is, of course, when it comes to the lives of others,

Vladimir Putin and the Russian secret state don't give a damn.

The Skripals weren't the only victims. Wiltshire Police sent in a good copper, Detective Sergeant Nick Bailey, to carry out a forensic search of Sergei Skripal's home. He got contaminated with the Novichok too, his recovery was long and hard-fought, and eventually he had to leave the police service.

After the Skripals were poisoned, Salisbury's town centre was sealed off and experts in HazMat chemical warfare suits did a fingertip search. Anything contaminated by the Novichok was destroyed. But the killers had one more surprise for the shire. More may come out at the inquest into the killing of Dawn Sturgess due to be held in late 2022, but the evidence points to the poisoners carrying the Novichok in a fake Nina Ricci perfume bottle, and then dumping it in a Salisbury park. Four months later Charlie Rowley found what he believed was a perfume bottle in a charity-shop bin and thought it would make a nice gift for his girlfriend, Dawn Sturgess. He didn't know the true origin of the present.

It was from Russia but not with love.

Dawn Sturgess rubbed the perfume into her wrists and passed out very quickly. The emergency services had no idea what they were dealing with and so she wasn't jabbed with atropine. The dose was fatal and she died in hospital. Dawn, too, is a victim of the Russian poison factory.

For the avoidance of any doubt, the Organization for the Prohibition of Chemical Weapons, the international body set up to monitor poisons like Novichok, reported the nerve agent was of 'high purity'. Later that year Switzerland's Intelligence Service announced that two Russian spies had been identified trying to hack into a laboratory in the Swiss town of Spiez, a lab tasked by the OPCW to confirm that the Salisbury poison was indeed Novichok. The spies were based in the Netherlands and expelled.

Did the President of Russia show any remorse? Putin was asked about Skripal at a conference in Moscow six months after the first wave of poisonings. 'I see,' he said, 'that some of your colleagues are pushing the theory that Mr Skripal was almost some kind of human rights activist. He was simply a spy. A traitor to the motherland. There is such a concept – a traitor to the motherland. He was one of those.'

The follow-up question, 'Was Dawn Sturgess a traitor to the motherland, too, Mr President?', was never asked because, in Vladimir Putin's Russia, there are no follow-up questions.

On Russia's Channel One, TV anchor Kirill Kleimyonov warned traitors, 'Don't move to England . . . Something is not right there. Maybe it's the climate, but in recent years there have been too many strange incidents with a grave outcome. People get hanged, poisoned, they die in helicopter crashes and fall out of windows in industrial quantities.'

The TV anchor is referring to the list of mystery deaths first reported by BuzzFeed. The hanging (2013) refers to Boris Berezovsky; the poisoning (2006) to Alexander Litvinenko; the helicopter crash (2004) to multi-millionaire Stephen Curtis, the British money man for YUKOS, owned by Khodorkovsky, once Russia's richest man, who dared to challenge Putin and ended up in the slammer for ten years; the fall from the window (2014) refers to Scott Young, a British associate of Berezovsky. Mr Young may have killed himself. Or he may have been pushed. In plain English, the Kremlin's patsy media was taking the piss.

As always with a fancy operation by the Russian secret

state, there are a ton of conspiracy theories galloping off in the wrong direction. Two academics at King's College London, Dr Gordon Ramsay and Dr Sam Robertshaw, investigated twenty yarns spun by the Russian disinformation factory:

1. The Novichok used is or could be from Porton Down [UK military chemical weapons research establishment, eight miles from Salisbury].
2. The Novichok used was not made in Russia.
3. The Novichok used may be Russian, but was not made by the state.
4. All Russian Novichok stockpiles had been destroyed prior to the attack.
5. The Novichok could be from another post-Soviet state.
6. No proof that the nerve agent used was actually Novichok.
7. The Novichok could have been stolen.
8. The Novichok could be from a Western country.
9. The nerve agent used was definitely not Novichok.
10. The Novichok may have belonged to Sergei Skripal.
11. The Novichok programme never existed.
12. Any laboratory could be used to produce Novichok.
13. Porton Down can't identify the nerve agent as Novichok or Russian.
14. Novichok specifically created by the UK and US, not Russia.
15. The UK does not have any Novichok to identify it.

16. Porton Down has confirmed to the UK government that there's no evidence the Novichok was made in Russia.
17. The Novichok could be from Iran.
18. The UK is deliberately withholding samples of Novichok.
19. Porton Down is trying to destroy its own stocks of Novichok.
20. The Novichok was definitely developed in the US.

None of these assertions was ever backed up by evidence. All of the above are nonsense. To address one or two of these, I had a natter with Dan Kaszeta, an American who worked for the US Secret Service, protecting President George W. Bush from being poisoned. Kaszeta now lives in Britain, helps vaccinate people against COVID, and is a sidesman at St Martin-in-the-Fields, the great church overlooking London's Trafalgar Square. Kaszeta started by setting out his background in the US Secret Service: 'We were paid money mostly to worry about chemical terrorism as opposed to somebody secreting something into the president's food and drink. I'm not going to get into the technical details of how the President of the United States is protected. But I was mostly worried about a chemical bomb going off, somebody throwing a mysterious liquid at the limousine or on the President, a waft of gaseous vapour through a room and everybody starting to pass out. I was worried about those scenarios. I was working inside this Venn diagram where chemical warfare, terrorism and assassination run together.'

Dan's book, *Toxic: A History of Nerve Agents from Nazi Germany to Putin's Russia*, is a dark yet fascinating read. The idea that the Novichok came from Porton Down is nonsense.

Some people floated the possibility that it came over the ether, that it somehow moved five miles as the crow flies, then just so happened to settle on the doorknob of a former GRU colonel, rather than the doorknobs of the other 120,000 people who lived in the Salisbury area, not one of whom was considered a direct traitor to the Russian secret state.

Dan's view is that a Russian state assassination and/or intimidation effort against somebody like Skripal or Navalny works on several different possible levels. To understand that, you have to get inside the heads of people inside the Kremlin bubble: 'It could very well be OK if the target dies. That's not a bad thing. But if he lives and he's afraid of us and other people are afraid, that's possibly even more value than him having died. Let's have a look at the Skripal poisoning. His survival and that of his daughter was more down to luck than anything else. If they had just stayed at home, watched television, had a bottle of wine instead of going out, they probably would have both died on the sofa.' By which time the traces of the Novichok may have gone: 'It might have been days before anybody knew. It would then been very suspicious, two people dead on the sofa versus one, but they could have got away with it.'

The Kremlin did its best to wriggle out of the overwhelming evidence against it, but that attempt, like the poison itself, told you more than you might think about the source. When the CCTV appeared of the two Russian spire-fanciers, Margarita Simonyan interviewed them on Russia Today. The show from the Kremlin's dark theatre of the absurd was an obsidian spectacular. What you see tells you a little bit about the cruelty at the top of the Kremlin power game. If you're a lowly player, and you make a mistake, things will not go well for you. The two GRU officers are very publicly humiliated.

Simonyan gets it out of them that they shared a single bed, the implication left hanging in the air that they might be gay. In London no one would give a damn, but the two men are not Londoners. They are – although it is never articulated by the Russian media – officers of the special services. And the Russian secret state has a problem with gay people. Frankly, its attitude towards gay life and gay culture is Neanderthal. So the moment it's implied that these two guys are gay, then everybody who knows the Russian secret state may well conclude that they can't possibly be spies.

Radio Free Europe/Radio Liberty (RFERL) ran a piece online titled: 'Novichok Suspects: Gay or Not Gay? That Is Russian State Media's Question.' The article explained how Simonyan broke into a suggestive smile: 'What, so to speak, unites you then?'

After the men asked that details of their private lives be left out, she added: 'No need to justify yourselves. Whether you had a single or double bed is the least of the world's concerns right now.' RFERL reported that lit the fuse and then 'Russian state-controlled media wasted no time peddling rumors about the men's sexuality – an apparent effort to counter the idea they could be GRU officers.' Life News, very close to Alexander Dugin and the Russian secret state, reported: 'The LGBT community has come out in defense of Petrov and Boshirov.' A columnist in *Zavtra*, a nationalist online newspaper, wrote: 'Instead of dangerous killers – timid gays.' That evening, Russia 24, a flagship TV show, broadcast a sarcastic report about Salisbury's spirit of 'modern European tolerance', portraying it as a place overrun with gay clubs and parades. Simonyan took to Twitter, saying that the two men 'didn't hit on me ... I don't know if they're gay or not gay. They're stylish, as far as I can tell – with little beards and cute haircuts, taut trousers and jumpers that tighten around impressive biceps.'

That is funny peculiar because there is evidence that suggests they may not be gay at all. 'Hitmen's Hookers: How Russian Hitmen Smoked Drugs and Had Sex with Prostitute' was the headline in *The Sun*. The two Russians had checked into the two-star CityStay Hotel in London's East End. A fellow guest recognized one of the duo and told the red-top: 'I could smell weed from their room. Later there was a woman in there. I think it was a prostitute. They were having sex. Definitely. I heard them having really loud sex for a long time. It was definitely a woman. I don't think the men were having sex with each other. I could still smell the pot.'

Bellingcat, the glorious British-based investigative open-source website, went to work with independent Russian journalists based in Latvia working for the website, The Insider. They discovered the true identities of the duo. The one who banged on about Salisbury's 123-metre-high spire was Colonel Anatoliy Chepiga of the GRU. His mate was Dr Alexander Mishkin, also of the GRU, a medic along for the ride to make sure Chepiga, presumably the primary poisoner, didn't kill himself. Bellingcat then identified a third Russian GRU officer, 'Sergey Fedotov', cover name for Major General Denis Sergeev, who was also in Britain at the same time as the two poisoners. Bellingcat tracked back Sergeev's movements and connected him to a suspected failed attempt to poison an enemy of the Kremlin in 2015. This time the target was Emilian Gebrev, a Bulgarian arms dealer whose company exports to Ukraine.

What remains extraordinary about the Salisbury poisonings is the seeming stupidity of it. How so? Novichok is, like polonium-210, a very expensive poison. The two murderers were sent to Salisbury with their poison bottle but with no regard to the simple fact of modern British life, that the country is littered with six million CCTV cameras, more units per person than any other country apart from China. Whoever sent the GRU officers is a fool. Reflecting on this anomaly – multi-million-dollar secret poison delivered on candid camera – makes me draw a harsh and, perhaps, novel conclusion about the Russian secret state in the twenty-first century. Kim Philby burrowed his way through the British Establishment to rise to near the top of the British Secret Service, starting in 1933, the year of Stalin's great famine. Soviet spies like Philby secured the West's nuclear secrets and betrayed hundreds, maybe thousands, of Western agents. I once interviewed John le Carré for *The Observer* and learned from him, and his extraordinary novels, especially *The Spy Who Came In From The Cold* and *Tinker Sailor Soldier Spy*, that he had great professional respect for 'Karla', the figment of a novelist's imagination, but also for the real thing, the KGB.

The West has locked that truth in a room, turned the key and walked away. I remember arguing with the late, great Phillip Knightley, the author of the definitive book on Britain's greatest traitor, *Philby, KGB Master Spy*, about this very thing. But the truth is the world has indeed changed. The ideological power of Communism's appeal to people like Philby is long dead; so, too, is its darkest enemy, Hitler; so, too, is the state that created the KGB. In its place you have the Russian Federation, an ethno-nationalist kleptocracy run by a pleonexiac with too long a table. The West should not be surprised that the quality of the servants of the Russian secret state in the twenty-first century is, frankly, a bit rubbish.

Vladimir Putin has been micro-managing the big war

against Ukraine, ordering his defence minister to 'seal' the steelworks at Mariupol in mid-April, only for all of us to see the Russian Army try and take it in May. He can't bear not to stick his nosy beak in it – wherever or whatever it might be. That leads me to my working hypothesis, that Putin has not been a casual backseat observer of the Russian secret state's most daring, or rather, most disgusting crimes against humanity. I suspect that the Moscow apartment bombs in 1999, the Moscow Theatre siege of 2002, the Beslan siege of 2004, and certainly the poisonings of Shchekochikhin, Tsepov and Litvinenko, all bear his fingerprints. Remember what Jim Fallon, the professor of psychiatry at the University of California, said about the psychopath's habit of deploying blame externalization: 'They're always ready to blame what they do on somebody else.' So Chechen terrorists blew up Moscow, besieged the theatre, besieged the school; MI6 poisoned Litvinenko. One Kremlin line was that MI6 poisoned the Skripals.

Then, against the evidence and common sense, Russia Today runs an interview with the two Salisbury poisoners implying that they are gay. I have been wrestling whether to share this story for it breaks rule one of investigative journalism, that you must have at least two sources for a story. I have only one source and that source is at one remove. But you will understand from the context why that might be. The story goes, says source X, that source Y told him that he met a couple in Moscow who told him that in the early 1990s they met Putin when he was Mayor Sobchak's bagman. Putin came on to the woman but, the couple realized, it was a feint. Putin was interested in the man. It's Sweeney policy not to give a damn what other adults do for sex. I'm no Puritan. But if the story is true, then Putin is bisexual but in denial of his sexuality. This makes me broaden out my working hypothesis, that the master of the Kremlin not only planned the black op spectaculars against the Russian people but also wrote the script for the Simonyan interview, implying that the Salisbury poisoners were gay when they were not.

To be clear, this is not established fact. But look once again at the footprints in the snow: an extraordinarily expensive poison is delivered on CCTV. Only Vladimir Putin could have ordered the poison; only Putin could have forced through the delivery of the package against the common sense of the officers of the Russian foreign intelligence service, the SVR, who have eyes in their heads and read the papers and know that Britain is awash with CCTV. Only Putin is so all-powerful that people lower down in the decision tree of the Russian secret state would not dare to speak out about the stupidity of the plan.

Inside the Russian secret state, you do not argue with the boss.

But that isn't the end of the story. In the wake of the Skripal poisonings, the British government expelled twenty-three Russian diplomats, and our allies around the world threw out another hundred more. So that taught Vlad the Poisoner a lesson. Or did it?

Bill Browder made a ton of money back in the days of the Wild East, once working out he could buy the old Soviet Arctic fishing fleet for a mere $100 million though it was worth $1 billion. But in 2009 his Moscow-based lawyer, Sergei Magnitsky, was bludgeoned to death by the Russian state. Magnitsky had been investigating a massive fraud by corrupt Russian officials. Since then, Bill has gone out of his way to speak truth to the Kremlin's power. And he got thirty-five countries to pass legislation, known in the US as the

Magnitsky Act, making it less easy for some – but by no means all – of Putin's thugs, before the big war in Ukraine, to park their yachts in St Tropez or their money in the City of London. Browder's been on the Kremlin's wanted list for years. Before the big war, I asked him if the West was really serious about sending a clear 'Stop mucking around' message to Putin?

Browder told me: 'I don't think so at all. The most dramatic and stark example is the case of the Salisbury poisonings. Actors from the Russian state, dispatched by Vladimir Putin, came to the UK with a military-grade nerve agent and they created a massive public health emergency in a British city. We ended up with the death of a totally innocent bystander and a police officer whose life was ruined. And what was the consequence of that? They expelled a bunch of diplomats. The unspoken secret about expelling diplomats is that they then replace them with other diplomats. So there was no consequence. Why? Because deep down the British government and many other governments are scared of Putin. They don't want to pick a fight with him. So they want to seem to be doing the right thing but they don't actually want to do the right thing. And so we end up in a world where Putin gets away with murder, literally, on a regular basis around the world.'

Expelling diplomats would have caused the Russian spy personnel department a bit of extra work for two weeks. This is like playing poker when you're staking pounds sterling but your opponent is playing with Monopoly money. Or, in this case, Britain is staking the lives of its citizens and Vladimir Putin is staking diplomatic passports.

Chapter Fifteen

A War We Don't Know We Are Fighting

One of Britain's great diplomats, a former ambassador to Moscow and a fine historian in his own right, Sir Roddy Braithwaite, tells this story about Chris Donnelly, the Kremlin watcher-in-chief to four NATO Secretaries General and a former senior Ministry of Defence civil servant: 'Last time I saw Chris he was sitting around a hole in the ice on some river in Siberia, fishing, surrounded by Russian generals, all of them drinking vodka. There's a man who knows his stuff.'

Chris is a gruff Lancastrian who studied Russian at Manchester University, can sing the Soviet national anthem, Stalin version, and has a small private museum of Russian alcohol second to none. More than any other person I know, Chris has devoted his mind, body and soul to understanding what is going on inside the Kremlin and the Russian secret state that controls it. Some people wake up in the middle of the night worrying about the threat from Russian nuclear weapons. Chris lives and breathes inside that nightmare; he listens to the heartbeat of the Russian imperial psychosis; he walks the echoing halls of the Kremlin's paranoia. Now formally retired, in 2009 he set up a think tank, the Institute for

Statecraft, to monitor and explain what is going on inside the Moscow beltway. It was hacked by the Russian secret state, causing him and his fellow analysts some annoyance, but his work, shining a light on, as de Custine put it, 'government that lives by mystery', continues.

Before the big war, the February 2022 invasion of Ukraine, I asked him how he would characterize what is happening between the West and Russia?

His answer is grim: 'We are at war with Russia and the Russians understand that. So from a Russian point of view, we are at war with them. From a British or a Western point of view, we most certainly are not. And that is the disparity between the attitudes and in the relationship.'

'How well are we doing at this war we don't know we're fighting?' I ask.

'We're losing.'

'Why?'

'Firstly, because we are not aware that the war is on. And if you don't know you're fighting, you are at a disadvantage from the start. Secondly, if you're going to fight any war, you need a wartime mentality. You need attitude, different procedures, different priorities. So if we're fighting a war but with a peacetime mentality, we aren't going to be doing very well. We are fighting an opponent who has very much a wartime mentality and can therefore more effectively use the weapons in this war. It's not just about things that go bang – tanks, ships, plane bombs and bullets – but virtually everything else in the arsenal of a state, information, economics, cyber, bribery, corruption, politics, just about everything.'

'You missed out assassination.'

'Yes, the Russian term is "active measures", and within that, wet jobs, *mokryye dela*.'

Puzzled as to why Putin and his gang are so aggressive, so reckless when it comes to poisoning their targets, I ask Chris why they take these risks?

'Firstly, if the enemy . . . if the opponent, let us say, doesn't realize that it is under attack, the risks are not that high because generally, human beings tend to see what they're looking for. And if you're not looking for an attack, if you believe that this isn't an attack, or if politically it's highly inconvenient to acknowledge that there's an attack on you, then the risks are not high at all. To understand the murder of Litvinenko and the attempted murder of Skripal, it's wrong to see these as crimes. These aren't crimes, they're acts of war. They only make sense in an actual war because in war, you have to take risk. And the Russians don't have any understanding of risk management, in the sense that it's become a disease that now afflicts Britain across the board. They balance risk and advantage. And you have to do it in wartime. You will always have casualties in war. All you can hope to do is reduce them. Things will always go wrong. People will always make mistakes. Things won't be perfect. You will have collateral damage, like Dawn Sturgess.'

The idea of a war we didn't know we were fighting – before February 2022 – is such a big, counter-intuitive mind-jump that I have trouble getting my head round it. I ask Chris, surely it was insane for the GRU, Russian military intelligence, to use Novichok against Skripal because they were going to be discovered. True?

'It's not necessarily true. If you look at the Russian intelligence service tradition, a lot of what they do is effective because it's intimidatory. If it's designed not only to punish in this case the individual, but to be a lesson to others, it has to be visible. It has to be seen. People have to know you've done it. In a strange, bizarre way, the Russians have always gone in for obscure, dramatic, high-profile ways of killing people. Novichok is one example, polonium as a poison is another. It fits the pattern. They want to be known to have done it. They don't want to be caught in the act and embarrassed that way. They don't like being caught but they only want a degree of secrecy to protect the operation itself, until it's been successful. It's not even necessary in this instance that Skripal should die. The very fact is, that they have demonstrated to the principal audience, which is their own people, to the secondary audience, which is their own intelligence officers, and to the third, tertiary audience, the Russian diaspora abroad, that, whoever you are, we will come and get you if we want to.'

'They want you to feel afraid?'

'Yes. What was that Latin expression? *Oderint dum metuant*. Let them hate so long as they fear. That would fit the Russians pretty well.'

For Chris, off the top of my head, I run through my list of people critical of or dangerous to Vladimir Putin, his regime or people, who just got in the way and who ended up dead or not very alive. For this book I have refined and re-categorized that list. First, there is the list of those people who may have been poisoned or indeed were poisoned in Russia, Britain or elsewhere. Some survived, most died: Anatoly Sobchak, Yuri Shchekochikhin, Lecha Islamov, Roman Tsepov, Anna Politkovskaya, Alexander Litvinenko, Badri Patarkatsishvili, Vladimir Kara-Murza, Emilian Gebrev, Sergei Skripal, Yulia Skripal, Detective Sergeant Nick Bailey, Dawn Sturgess, Charlie Rowley, Alexei Navalny, Roman Abramovich.

The second list of Putin critics who have been shot: Sergei Yushenkov, Anna Politkovskaya, Natasha Estemirova, Stanislav

Markelov, Anastasia Baburova, Boris Nemtsov. Keen readers will have noted that Anna Politkovskaya was both poisoned and later shot.

Cars, helicopters and planes are dangerous ways of getting around. A third list is of Putin critics who suffered mystery car or air accidents: Artyom Borovik was a Russian reporter on the trail of the story that Putin may have been born a bastard who spent his early years in Georgia, or that Putin was a paedophile. Shortly before the March 2000 presidential election, the private jet flying Borovik out of Moscow airport fell to the ground, killing all nine people on board. General Alexander Lebed was a hero from the Afghan war and a potential rival to Putin until his helicopter fell out of the sky in Siberia in 2002. Khanpasha Terkibayev, the lucky Chechen terrorist who managed to slip out of the Moscow Theatre siege in 2002, was unluckily killed in 'a car crash' in Chechnya after he was identified as an agent provocateur by Politkovskaya. Stephen Curtis was the YUKOS lawyer whose brand-new, extremely safe helicopter fell out of the sky as it approached Bournemouth airport in 2004.

The fourth list are those people who were critics of Vladimir Putin and his cronies and who died in fishy circumstances: in 2000 Antonio Russo was an Italian journalist, also on the track of the Putin the bastard story, and, separately documenting Russian Army war crimes in Chechnya, who was found dead on a road not far from a Russian military base. He had been tortured and a number of his videotapes had gone missing. Boris Berezovsky was presumed to have hanged himself in his home near Ascot in Berkshire in 2013, but no one who knew him well believes that. In 2017 reporter Nikolay Andruschenko died of injuries after being beaten up by mystery assailants in St Petersburg. He was a long-time critic of the master of the Kremlin from the time when he, Andruschenko, was a local politician in Russia's second city and Putin was deputy mayor. He had said that Putin's politics were about money and nothing else. In 2018 three Russian journalists investigating the mercenary Wagner Group in the Central African Republic – Kirill Radchenko, Alexander Rastorguyev and Orkhan Dzhemal – were murdered, allegedly for their possessions. But nothing of value was taken from their vehicle. In the same year, the head of Russia's GRU military intelligence agency, General Igor Korobov, the boss of the two Salisbury poisoners, died, aged sixty-two, after a long, extended illness. The word in Moscow is that Korobov might have suffered from Putin's wrath after the Salisbury operation went so badly wrong.

A fifth list is composed of people who fell out of windows: Russian journalist Ivan Safronov, fifty-one, fell from his fifth-floor apartment in Moscow in 2007. He had been investigating covert Russian arms sales to Iran and Syria via Belarus. His editor at the Russian business paper, *Kommersant*, said: 'I don't want to fuel speculation but I can say for sure that I knew him well and he showed absolutely no sign of being suicidal.' Russian journalist Olga Kotovskaya fell from the window of her fourteenth-floor apartment in Kalingrad in 2009. Berezovsky's British fixer, Scot Young, fell from a fourth-floor flat in Marylebone in London in 2014. Russian journalist Max Borodin fell from his fifth-floor apartment in Yekaterinburg in 2018. I shall set out the story behind the story of the defenestration of Borodin in the next chapter.

Of course, all these deaths could just be coincidences. Or maybe not.

Let's just take, say, the poison victims who had British

passports: Alexander Litvinenko, Sergei Skripal, Detective Sergeant Nick Bailey, Dawn Sturgess and Charlie Rowley. How come, I ask Chris Donnelly, the British authorities haven't been joining the dots on this stuff?

'In truth, I don't know. A surmise might be that to do so would force them to acknowledge the problem. And to acknowledge the problem would be embarrassing and awkward and maybe financially disadvantageous to the City of London which has a lot of influence on the government, and which is a very large recipient of Russian money.'

Now that Russia has invaded Ukraine and sought to take Kyiv, it's bleeding obvious that the West is at war with the Kremlin. But I believe that Chris Donnelly was right, that for the best part of two decades we were at war with Russia and we didn't know it. Or, worse, perhaps our leaders did know it but they looked the other way because Vladimir Putin offered them something cold and shiny and dark.

Moscow gold.

A few days after then Prime Minister Theresa May blasted the Russian secret state for the Salisbury poisonings, Russia's gas giant Gazprom held a highly successful bond sale in the City of London. The Russian Embassy in London mocked the United Kingdom, tweeting that demand for the bond sale was 'three times higher than the placing [€750 million]. Business as usual?'

It was a vanishingly rare moment of honesty from the Kremlin's envoys in London.

And absolutely on the rouble.

Chapter Sixteen

The Kremlin Candidate?

Take it away, Fats.

I found my thrill
On Blueberry Hill
On Blueberry Hill
When I found you.

That's not Fats Domino. The crooner murdering 'Blueberry Hill' – in the musical sense that is – happens to be Vladimir Vladimirovich Putin.

It's just before Christmas 2010 at a charity bash in St Petersburg. You can find this clip from US National Public Radio if you look in your search engine for 'Putin sings Blueberry Hill'. You'd have thought from Putin's hideous torture of a lovely song he would have been booed to the echo – but you would be wrong. Clapping like sea lions at feeding time at the zoo are some of Hollywood's clapped-out, sorry, greatest stars: Sharon Stone, Kevin Costner, Mickey Rourke, Goldie Hawn, Kurt Russell, Gérard Depardieu, Vincent Cassel and Monica Bellucci.

Sad to say Sharon Stone & Co aren't the only useful idiots in this story.

In the United States, first George W. Bush then Barack Obama went out of their way to give Vladimir Putin a home run. Bush the Second's nickname for his opposite number in Russia was 'Pooty-Poots', but he read Putin wrong. Obama over-invested in Putin's proxy-in-chief, Dmitry Medvedev, not seeing the truth about a man best described by Professor Donald Rayfield (in chapter 13) as 'Al Capone's lawyer'. Chris Donnelly looked on in despair as Western politicians played kissy-kissy with the killer in the Kremlin: 'They do tend very often to be naive. They think the best of people. They often think that people like me exaggerate when I tell them that they're actually under attack. And the people they deal with are really working them. They're being fooled.'

I challenged Chris, putting to him that his belief that the West was at war with Russia was crazy. He replied: 'A lot of people would think that because they don't understand what war is. They're confusing war and battle. It's amazing how many Western politicians, but especially US presidents, have a reset with Russia. They're going to sit and look Putin in the eye. And they won't make the same mistakes? They have no idea what they're dealing with. They simply haven't understood the situation.'

Donald Trump is by far the biggest fish in the Kremlin's net, if Trump is a trout, if the Kremlin has a net. I've met him three times and each time we met we hated each other a little bit more. The first time was in 2012 when I was making a film about Mitt Romney's run for president. To get a bit of showbiz pizazz, shooter-producer James Jones and I decided to interview Trump in Trump Tower on Romney. Trump

Tower was tacky, very, a poor man's idea of a rich man's home. The 1980s gilt had lost its gloss. Trump himself was oily, eager to please, boring on Romney, and we dumped him, leaving his offerings on the cutting-room floor.

One year later I was back, following up a wonderful documentary, 'You've Been Trumped', by the British film-maker, Anthony Baxter. He followed Trump's purchase of a natural beauty spot to build a ghastly golf course in Scotland, his seduction of then SNP leader Alex Salmond, and the New Yorker's contempt for his neighbours. In the course of documenting Team Trump's bullying of the locals, Baxter got nicked by the police. The star of the show was a mordantly funny crofter who wrote a very rude message to Trump on the roof of his haybarn. Our Panorama team followed Baxter's film and we interviewed him for it. I'm never wholly comfortable copying someone else's journalism and started looking into Trump's brushes with the New York mob. I became fascinated by *Village Voice*'s legendary reporter Wayne Barrett, who documented the connections between Team Trump and Team Genovese Crime Family. Its main man, Anthony 'Fat Tony' Salerno, Wayne Barrett reported, sold mobbed-up concrete to construct Trump Tower. Not only that but there was evidence that Trump and Salerno shared the same lawyer, Roy Cohn, a smooth-tongued villain who had been chief counsel to Senator Joseph McCarthy, the witch-finder general against Reds in the 1950s – a dark passage in American history that led Arthur Miller to write his great dramatic allegory, *The Crucible.*

When I finally got to interview Wayne Barrett for BBC Newsnight in 2016, I asked the legend about 'Fat Tony'. On cue, the great New York storyteller punched out the perfect reply: 'Fat Tony was faaaaat.' It's my favourite sound bite from an interviewee, ever, and if you dial in 'Donald Trump's business links to the mob' you can find it on YouTube.

I loved Wayne Barrett. In the spring of 2016 he was dying of cancer. A great reporter to the end – he died in January 2017 – he could smell the stink of the disaster to come, that Hillary Clinton antagonized the blue-collar voters, that Trump seemed to many of them like a champion of ordinary Americans. Wayne knew the first law of politics, that to win you must steal the other guy's clothes, and sensed what was going to happen.

'Are you afraid that Trump might win,' I asked him.

'I am full of fear,' he replied.

In spring 2013 it was time to meet Trump again. Ever attentive to the media, with whom he has had a love-hate relationship his whole life, he invited us to his golfing estate at Bedminster in New Jersey. We got footage of Trump driving a golf cart, me riding shotgun, over a small cliff of a bunker and, just as the sound pack reached the end of its limit, you can hear me squeak: 'I'm a bit worried about the driver.'

Trump also arranged for us to go for a ride in the Trump helicopter. Transactional as ever, the rides in the golf buggy and the chopper seemed to give him a sense that he somehow owned part of me, that he expected the fealty that was his due. I am not for sale, or, if I am, I'm not that cheap. I don't like golf and I've been in lots of helicopters.

Trump and I traded blows about him being nasty to his Scottish neighbours, but our hearts were not in it. He struck me as a narcissus with psychopathic lining, cunning, streetwise, malevolent. The nastier he gets, the softer he speaks. I had agreed with my producer Judith Ahern that I would ask him about the Scottish story first and then I could ask him my questions about his links with the mob.

So I hit Trump about his business relationship with Felix Sater, the managing director of Bayrock Group LLC and a senior adviser to Donald Trump and the Trump Organization when Bayrock and Team Trump built the $450 million forty-six-storey Trump SoHo apartment complex in 2006. Investors who had been lured into the project by Trump's name were disconcerted to read in *The New York Times* in 2008 that his business partner was a Russian-born son of a gangster. And that Sater was a bit of a gangster himself. Sater was the son of Mikhail Sheferovsky, who, according to the FBI, was an underboss for the Russian mafiya 'boss of bosses' Semion Mogilevich. When Sater was eight the family left Russia, ending up in the United States. In 1991 Sater, by now a Wall Street broker, stabbed another broker in the face with the broken-off stem of a margarita glass, causing the victim to need 110 stitches. Sater was convicted of first-degree assault and spent fifteen months in prison. In the late 1990s he was arrested for his part in a $40 million Wall Street pump-and-dump scam involving four Mafia families, including the Gambinos. Sater turned stool pigeon, gave evidence against the mob, pleaded guilty, and the FBI kept his role secret until *The New York Times* broke the story. But even afterwards, Trump and Sater were a thing. In 2010 Sater was handing out business cards touting himself as 'Senior Advisor to Donald Trump' with an email address at TrumpOrg.com. The former gangster and Donald Trump were as thick as thieves – that's a very old English language metaphor and there is, of course, no suggestion of any wrongdoing, blah blah blah.

Trump's big shtick, before he became president in January 2017, was playing the reality TV star host of the US TV version of *The Apprentice*, hiring but more often firing wannabe business partners with the catchphrase: 'You're fired!' It gave me no pleasure to use Trump's catchphrase against him.

Sweeney: 'Shouldn't you have said: "Felix Sater, you're connected with the Mafia and you're fired!"'
Trump: 'Well, first of all we were not the developer there, that [Trump SoHo] was a licensing deal.'
Sweeney: 'You stayed in bed, if I may say so, with Felix Sater and he was connected with the Mafia.'
Trump snarled: 'Again John, maybe you're thick but when you have a signed contract, you can't in this country just break it.'

Among my mates at Panorama, this phrase – 'John, maybe you're thick' – had a certain cachet for some months in the office boozer.

Trump went on to belittle his relationship with Sater: 'I know who he is', but he wasn't a big player. Then, suddenly, he had another meeting to go to: 'I hate to do this John, but there's a lot of people waiting for me upstairs', and then he stood up and offered me his hand to shake. I gave him a flat palm and said, 'One more question, Mr Trump. Why did you buy your concrete from Fat Tony Salerno?'

My producer Judith Ahern put her head in her hands and said: 'Oh, no, John.'

Team Trump – who had been videotaping the whole interview, waiting for such a moment – put out an attack video, showing Judith's clip and dripping poison on me. But a few years later Trump's attack video on me, after I had challenged him about his relationship with Sater, caused him trouble. Sater was seriously well connected with both Trump and the Russian secret state. Sater was an old friend of Trump's attack-dog lawyer, Michael Cohen. *The New York Times* reported in 2018 that Sater emailed Michael Cohen saying he guided Donald junior and Ivanka around

Moscow, fixing for Trump's daughter to sit in Putin's chair in the Kremlin.

In the autumn of 2015 the Sater and Cohen duo swapped emails about a new project, dubbed Trump Tower Moscow, to be funded by one of the Kremlin's piggybanks, VTB Bank, the whole deal backed by none other than the master of the Kremlin. In November 2015 Sater emailed Cohen boasting that he had access to Vladimir Putin: 'Buddy our boy [Trump] can become president of the USA and we can engineer it. I will get all of Putins [sic] team to buy in on this. I will manage this process.'

Sater contacted around a hundred figures in Russia, pushing Trump Tower Moscow, one of whom just happened to be retired General Evgeny Shmykov, formerly of the GRU. Shmykov had enrolled in the Federal Security Service Academy – Russia's spy school – going on to work with anti-Taliban fighters in Afghanistan in the late 1990s and early 2000s while serving in the GRU. In autumn 2015 Trump signed a non-binding 'letter of intent' to proceed with Trump Tower Moscow. In December of that year Sater emailed Cohen, saying he had General Shmykov on the phone and that he needed passport details for both Cohen and Trump so they could get visas. Sater explained that not the Kremlin but VTB Bank would sponsor the Americans because it was for 'a business meeting not political'. VTB Bank has denied it was ever involved in the project and Trump Tower Moscow never went ahead. The investigation by ex-FBI director Robert Mueller never found the smoking gun proving that Donald Trump was definitively in bed with the Russian secret state. Trump is a technological dinosaur and does not use emails. Perhaps he was lucky. But it is true to say that the Russians had several lines in to Team Trump. Sater was only one.

A second line from the Kremlin was via George Papadopoulos, a lowly minion on the edge of the Trump solar system. In April 2016, as the US presidential election campaign was hotting up, Papadopoulos met Professor 'Ambassador' Joseph Mifsud in London. Mifsud was no diplomat but a dodgy Maltese academic-cum-conman who was milking the University of Stirling in Scotland at the time. Mifsud told Papadopoulos that the Russians had 'dirt' on the Democratic contender, Hillary Clinton. The Maltese told the Trumper that 'the Russians had emails of Clinton, they have thousands of emails'.

Lo and behold, some months later those very emails popped up magically on the internet. It was almost as if the offer of delivery was considered by Team Trump, then politely declined, perhaps with a suggestion that if they were to appear elsewhere that better suited plausible deniability. This is, of course, just me wondering aloud.

Mifsud is a fascinatingly seedy character straight out of a Graham Greene thriller and, for BBC Newsnight, my colleague Innes Bowen and I looked into him in depth. Mifsud left a job at the University of Malta under something of a cloud in 2007, then led a new university in Slovenia. He left that too, disputing claims that he had fiddled expenses worth €39,332 ($48,550 or £34,320). Next stop was the London Academy of Diplomacy in 2013. It was a rum outfit, now bust, linked to the University of East Anglia and then the University of Stirling.

At one conference he was described as 'Ambassador Mifsud' but, although he worked for six months in the private office of the Maltese foreign minister, he was never a diplomat. Mifsud became a selfie king of the diplomatic circuit. Boris Johnson, then British foreign secretary, and former Foreign Office minister Tobias Ellwood were photographed with Mifsud, as was the then Russian ambassador to London.

Along the way, according to BuzzFeed, Mifsud fathered a daughter with a Ukrainian lover.

Papadopoulos, a fool, could not stop telling people about Mifsud's offer of 'the dirt' on Hillary. He told two Australian diplomats in London and soon the FBI was investigating potential Russian interference in the 2016 US election. One intelligence community source told us: 'It's clear that Mifsud knew something before the world did. And that raises questions.'

In April 2016 Mifsud had introduced Papadopoulos via email to Ivan Timofeev, who works for a think tank close to the Russian Ministry of Foreign Affairs. That same month, Mifsud was in Moscow on a panel run by the Kremlin-backed Valdai Club with Timofeev and the third man, Dr Stephan Roh, a German multi-millionaire. Mifsud and Roh interlock: in 2014 Roh became a visiting lecturer at the London Academy of Diplomacy. Roh bought Link Campus University, a private institution in Rome where Mifsud was part of the management, and Mifsud became a consultant at Roh's legal firm. Roh and his Russian-born wife, Olga, had homes in Switzerland, Monaco, London and Hong Kong. And then there is a derelict castle in Scotland. Buying it made Stephan and Olga the Baron and Baroness of Inchdrewer. Olga Roh was a star in Fox's reality TV show *Meet the Russians*, in which, surrounded by the trappings of extreme wealth, she purrs: 'My family was always achievements orientated.'

The baroness was extraordinarily well-connected, running an upmarket fashion company in London's Mayfair. Among her customers was Britain's then prime minister, Theresa May. There is a photograph of Theresa May meeting the Queen in an Olga Roh coat.

But this Baron Inchdrewer – Stephan Roh – has a funny

peculiar business history. In 2005 Dr Roh bought Severnvale Nuclear Services Ltd from its one-man-band owner, British nuclear scientist Dr John Harbottle. He kept Dr Harbottle on, then invited him on an all-expenses paid trip to a conference in Moscow. But the nuclear scientist was alert to the danger that visitors to Moscow can be targeted or even honey-trapped in compromising situations: kompromat. Dr Harbottle said: 'We smelt a rat. It didn't sound as if it would ring true and I decided that I wasn't going to go to this meeting.'

Shortly afterwards, he was fired. Under Dr Harbottle the company's turnover had been £42,000 a year. Within three years under Dr Roh, Severnvale Nuclear, with just two employees, was turning over more than $43 million (£24 million) a year. Dr Roh declined to respond to repeated attempts by the BBC to ask him to explain how he had transformed the business. Professor Mifsud too didn't respond to Newsnight's attempts to contact him. When approached by the Italian newspaper *La Repubblica* the mystery professor said: 'Secret agent! I never got a penny from the Russians: my conscience is clean.'

Then Mifsud vanished from the face of the earth, abandoning his pseudo-diplomatic career, abandoning his daughter by his Ukrainian lover, abandoning his old circuits where he hobnobbed with Boris Johnson and all. My working hypothesis is that Mifsud may have gone to ground in Russia. To mark the launch of this book I am announcing a £1,000 award for a contemporary, 2022, photograph of dodgy Professor Mifsud. Anyone with such a photograph should contact me via my website and I will hand the dosh over in used fivers in the back of a boozer in Soho. I'm serious about getting that photo, mind.

A third line from the Russian secret state to Team Trump

was through its one-time election tsar, Paul Manafort. The US Senate Intelligence Committee said in August 2020 that Manafort's connections to proxies for the Russian secret state while he was Trump's campaign manager 'represented a grave counterintelligence threat' by creating opportunities for 'Russian intelligence services to exert influence over, and acquire confidential information on, the Trump campaign'. Manafort was jailed for lying to the FBI investigation. Shortly before Trump left office, he pardoned Manafort. There is, of course, no blah blah blah.

Was Trump the Kremlin candidate? In January 2017 I reported a Panorama programme on that very subject with that very title. Our documentary looked at the secret report by former MI6 officer Chris Steele, alleging that the Kremlin had a kompromat tape of Trump in 2013 watching a porn show with prostitutes being urinated on, defiling the very Moscow hotel bedroom in which Barack and Michelle Obama had once slept. Trump had been in the Russian capital for the Miss Universe pageant.

Trump denied the report, but Chris Steele, the former head of MI6's Russia house, knows his Moscow. Later, the FBI prosecuted one of his sources for lying to the agency, but that, for me, does not knock flat Steele's report. The Russian secret state has ways of terrifying people that go far beyond what the FBI can do. The FBI has its faults but it is a law-enforcement agency which must properly work inside the rule of law. Britain's one-time ambassador to Moscow, Sir Andrew Wood, was so concerned about the Steele dossier that he gave it to Senator John McCain, by hand. Wood told the BBC: 'Trump is a sexaholic.'

Others – good people who know their stuff – fear the Steele report was based on disinformation. Trump's later conduct with Putin makes me believe that the Russian secret state may well have had something on him. Steele may have got the wrong end of the stick but there was a stick.

For our Panorama programme, 'Trump: The Kremlin Candidate?', Michael D'Antonio, author of the unauthorized 2015 biography *Never Enough: Donald Trump and the Pursuit of Success*, told me, 'Trump has said: "I am the star of my own comic book." He believes he's Superman or Batman. Or maybe he's a villain. He believes in "truth, justice and the American way" but it's a 1950s framework. In that time it was never anyone but a white older male who was in charge and the bad guys didn't have the chiselled jaw and the beautiful hair. The bad guys were disfigured, recognizably evil. I think he likes to identify people as recognizable enemies and then go after them simply for opposing him. So the American way is Donald Trump, and the enemy is the person he defines as the enemy.'

Scarily, D'Antonio thought the same of Putin: 'He is also a comic book character. He's head of a country whose economy is half that of the State of California and yet on the world stage he looms large because he's puffed himself up. He's also a strong man and Trump really admires strong men. He admires the exertion of power and the fact that Putin doesn't seem inhibited about using it.'

The unauthorized biographer tracked down a fellow New York property developer who said this of the 45th President of the United States: 'Trump won't do a deal unless there's something extra – a kind of moral larceny – in it.' That chimed with both what I knew about Trump's murky business affairs and Putin's modus operandi. Trump and Putin are weirdly similar. One Trump-watcher suggested that his family, especially son Donald junior and daughter Ivanka, will restrain their father from doing something rash. I put that to

D'Antonio. 'I interviewed his children and they all occupy offices one floor below his and when they spoke of him, they automatically said "Our Father" and looked up as if to heaven. Ivanka is most worshipful. The children are lesser gods but Donald is the seat of all knowledge, all power and all that is good. There is a cult-like quality to the Trump organization.'

There's no doubt in my mind whatsoever that Vladimir Putin wanted Trump to win in 2016. The Russian secret state took a good number of Democratic Party pawns off the board to secure victory for their champion. When our Panorama programme went out I wrote a piece for *Radio Times* which concluded: 'Faced with two comic-strip baddies being the most powerful men on Earth, I'd hide under the bed if I were you. But line the bed with lead and put it in a hole in the ground 100 feet deep. Let's hope I'm dead wrong.'

The Russian Embassy in London posted an entire blog condemning our Panorama programme and my journalism. The rant began: 'The BBC's another low in outright post-truth propaganda in the defence of the unsustainable status quo in Britain, US and worldwide. Not a single shred of evidence on any issue raised. John Sweeney's praise for Christopher Steele's "kompromat" report, "even if it is a pack of lies", explains it all.'

Of course, I never reported that I thought Steele's report was a 'pack of lies'. On the contrary, I suspect his report was most likely true. But the Russian Embassy post made something very clear.

I was now a target of the Russian state.

Once in power, Trump did pretty much everything the Kremlin would have wanted him to do: sow division in NATO, weaken the European Union, kowtow to Putin.

The evidence is stark. In 2018 Trump and Putin met in Helsinki and had a two-hour conversation behind closed doors. By this time the whole world knew that the Russian secret state had hacked Team Hillary's emails, that Paul Manafort had been in hock to a Kremlin proxy, that the Russian-born Sater had worked in Trump Tower, that Russia had interfered with the presidential election in 2016. The latter point was the stated finding of the US's intelligence community.

At the joint news conference after their private chat, Putin denied that he had any kompromat on Trump. Of course he did. Putin argued 'that he did not even know Trump was in Russia for the Miss Universe pageant in 2013' – the time when, according to the Steele report, video of Trump was secretly recorded to blackmail him. A reporter asked Trump point blank to denounce Russian interference in American democracy. Trump replied evasively, concluding: 'My people came to me ... they said they think it's Russia. I have President Putin. He just said it's not Russia. I will say this: I don't see any reason why it would be ... I have great confidence in my intelligence people but I will tell you that President Putin was extremely strong and powerful in his denial today.'

Democratic Party Senator Chuck Schumer socked Trump: 'Millions of Americans will continue to wonder if the only possible explanation for this dangerous and inexplicable behaviour is the possibility – the very real possibility – that President Putin holds damaging information over President Trump.' People in the US intelligence community suggested that Trump was a 'Russian asset', a 'useful idiot' and 'Putin's puppet'.

James Clapper, an ex-director of National Intelligence, asked 'if Russians have something on Trump', and former

CIA director John Brennan accused Trump of 'treason', tweeting: 'He is wholly in the pocket of Putin.' Senator John McCain said it was a 'disgraceful performance ... No prior president has ever abased himself more abjectly before a tyrant.'

One year later President Trump met President Zelenskiy at the UN headquarters in New York City and told him: 'I really hope that you and President Putin can get together and solve your problem.' Ukraine's problem was that Russia had invaded in 2014 and seized Crimea, Donetsk and Luhansk. Zelenskiy looked grim.

On the evidence of his conduct at the Helsinki summit and his advice to Zelenskiy at the UN in New York, Donald Trump was Moscow's man.

Chapter Seventeen

Useful Idiots

Maxim Borodin was a brilliant investigative journalist, thirty-two years old, a bit of a dandy in bow tie and worsted jackets, based in Yekaterinburg in the Urals, but he had just got the job of his dreams in Moscow. He had made his name working for the city's New Day website, angering far-right monarchists who violently objected to his reporting of a controversial drama, *Matilda*, which touched on the murder of Tsar Nicholas II and his family by the Bolsheviks in July 1918. Max explained that in 2017 he had been hit on the head with an iron bar by the far-right activists.

One April day in 2018 at five o'clock in the morning he called his friend, Vyacheslav Bashkov, saying that 'there was someone with a gun on my balcony and people in camouflage and masks on the staircase landing'. Max lived on the fifth, top floor of his apartment block. For a fit gunman to drop down from the roof would be child's play. A few hours later Max called Bashkov back. The story changed, it was just some security men doing an exercise. A day later his body was found on the ground outside his building. The police investigated and concluded that while drunk he had fallen out of the window. They declared his death a suicide.

Or, at least, that's the official fairy story.

The alternative version of Max's death goes like this. In February 2018 Russian mercenaries in the Wagner Group were ordered to capture oil-rich land in Syria under the control of the anti-Assad, anti-Russian Free Syrian Army. The Wagner mercenaries have a deservedly grim reputation for carrying out brutal killings, rapes, robberies and torture at one remove from the Kremlin. But this is a convenient fiction. In reality they are a proxy army, run by one of Vladimir Putin's favourites, Yevgeny Prigozhin, jailed for twelve years in 1981 for robbery, fraud, using teenagers to commit crime. He is now a billionaire. His nickname is 'Putin's chef', so-called because he ran one of Putin's favourite restaurants in St Petersburg. His official gig is that his company supplies the food to the Russian Army, some of which is years past its eat-by date. Prigozhin's unofficial gigs include allegedly financing the troll farms and hacking labs that burrowed their way into the US Democratic Party emails which helped secure the 2016 presidential election for Donald Trump. Prigozhin is also suspected to be the backer of the Wagner Group, former Russian soldiers paid to kill first in the Donbas, in eastern Ukraine, then Syria, Libya, the Central African Republic and Mali. The group is named after Hitler's favourite composer; its titular leader, Dmitry Utkin, is tattooed with Nazi SS flashes and in 2016 he was photographed in Putin's company. If the Kremlin was serious about 'de-Nazifying Ukraine' it should lock up its own private army first.

But the Wagner operation in Syria went horribly wrong because the United States military was helping the Free Syrian Army. As the Americans saw the Wagner mercenaries advance towards the FSA oilfields, they contacted the Russian Army liaison officers to warn their fellow countrymen to stop. The warning was never passed on, the Americans opened fire and reportedly something like 200 Russian mercenaries were killed. A group of the Wagner men killed came from Asbest, forty miles from Yekaterinburg. Max Borodin interviewed relatives of the dead, angry at the loss of their loved ones. One of them, Elena Matveyeva, the widow of Stanislav Matveyev, called the Wagner unit commander on the phone. The commander opened up with her, not knowing that Max was listening and videotaping the call. The unit boss told Elena: 'In one battalion there were 200 people killed right away. We only had AK47s, nothing in the way of anti-aircraft weapons. They beat us, they gave us hell. The Yanks said, "Russians, we're coming."'

I reported a short film on Max's mysterious death for BBC Newsnight. Vyacheslav Bashkov told us: 'Max was kind, funny, I would never think of him as suicidal.'

It is impossible to say, definitively, what happened to Max, but my working hypothesis is as follows: that the massacre of the 'Wagnerites' by the Americans was a humiliation for Prigozhin and his SS-tattooed commander, Utkin, but they had worked hard to keep the story out of the headlines in Russia; that Max's story, backed up by the tape of the unit commander telling all, doubled down on that humiliation; that Max, because he was just starting out as a reporter, did not have a proper register of the extreme red-zone risk he was running; that when Max told his friend Bashkov that at five in the morning there was a man with a gun on his balcony, there was a man with a gun on his balcony; and the same goes for the other men in camouflage; that the story about security men conducting an exercise was a lie, told by Max under duress; that it's highly likely the Wagnerites tortured Max so that he played along with the exercise story;

that the Wagnerites then killed Max by throwing him out of the window; that the local police did not want to open a can of worms.

Not long afterwards, three Russian investigative journalists in the Central African Republic, looking into claims that the Wagner Group were committing human rights abuses, were killed in mysterious circumstances. The message was pretty clear: if you are an investigative journalist and you want to die before your time, you ask the wrong kind of questions of the Wagner Group.

I was greatly troubled by Max's killing. I had wanted to write an online piece about it for the BBC website to go with my Newsnight film, but I was told it would not work. Once again, I felt that BBC colleagues were giving too much benefit of the doubt to the Kremlin's proxy killing machine. This was a fear shared by colleagues in the BBC's Ukrainian Service who deliberately sought me out, worried that the BBC Russia Service and the BBC in Moscow was not reporting the cold hard facts about Vladimir Putin's rule. One colleague told me: 'John, you're the only reporter who really sticks it to the Kremlin, you're the only one.' Professor Donald Rayfield told me that back in the days of the Soviet Union the BBC Russia Service had been excellent, but that lately: 'I believe that it has been compromised and infiltrated.'

I felt that too. I felt that I was under pressure, too. My luck held, for a time.

When I wrote my thriller about the Holodomor, *The Useful Idiot*, I dedicated it to Max Borodin and made him one of the key characters in the story. In my novel, Stalin's secret police put it about that the fictional Max Borodin had jumped out of his fifth-floor window. That was a lie, of course. They had murdered him in cold blood.

But if you sing the Kremlin's tune, then all sorts of possibilities can open up for you. It is fair to say that the Russian secret state succeeded in getting worryingly close to serious political leaders in the United States, Britain, Germany, France and Italy. Time and again the Kremlin turned Western democracy into a game of matryoshka dolls. Lift out the Donald Trump or Nigel Farage or Jeremy Corbyn or Matteo Salvini or Marine Le Pen dolls, and you come face to face with Vladimir Putin – smirking up at you.

The Kremlin's most naked useful idiot is Gerhard Schröder. The former Social Democratic Chancellor had not even left office in 2005 when he supported a deal backing the Nord Stream pipeline project which would pump Russian gas direct to Germany. The black magic for the Kremlin is that Nord Stream, by running along the bottom of the Baltic Sea, would bypass transit countries, enfeebling their ability to stand up to the Russian bear. The moment he was out of office, Schröder took a fancy job with Gazprom, the Russian natural gas giant. Schröder has denied any wrongdoing. The US Democrat Tom Lantos, then chairman of the House Foreign Affairs Committee, called him a 'political prostitute' for accepting the gig. Schröder had been married four times when he got the nickname Audi Man, a reference to the German car manufacturer's symbol of four interlinked rings. Fifth time he got married, he became 'Olympic Man' or 'Lord of the Rings'.

The German media has oftentimes taken photos of Schröder out on the lash at the expense of the Kremlin or its cronies. The danger is that such revelries can lead to a trap where a Western politician could be the target of kompromat. I put that to Chris Donnelly, who said: 'Let me give you the two sides of the argument. One side is that at the high level of politics a lot of agreements and understandings can be reached in informal settings. You can take the view, and it's not a silly view, that senior people can reach a degree of understanding in an informal setting and achieve a relationship that would be very beneficial. When I was working at NATO, the meetings in the headquarters were often very formal, very stilted, rather awkward. But when I brought the same Russian group back to my house at night, and Jill [Chris's wife] made them supper and we had a few drinks, you could get agreements on things which you could never do in formal circumstances. That's the one side of it. But at the same time, if you're doing this with a country like Russia, it's important to understand that the people you're dealing with have been trained and are working to a strategy. So if you are going to have that kind of diplomacy, you've got to be very alert and very good at your job. Otherwise you may find yourself at a disadvantage.'

'The other side, the KGB people,' I ask Chris, 'they've been trained in understanding human weakness?'

'Indeed. They are savvy. They will happily exploit sex, drink, drugs, power. And pride and flattery and all of these things. It is not just sex. Kompromat can be very much more sophisticated. Think of Chancellor Schröder and the relationship that he developed with Putin. He had four wives with no children. Then Putin organized him to adopt two orphans from the Petersburg orphanage.'

'Putin worked out exactly what Schröder wanted?' I suggest.

'It doesn't have to be sex and drugs and money. It can be

something that's clever, really clever. You have to admire the professionalism.'

Tom Tugendhat, the British Conservative MP and chair of the Foreign Affairs Committee, believes that Putin's Russia is best understood as a country that has been captured by its intelligence service. Everything is run through the prism of a spy factory. No wonder, then, that the Kremlin spies, trained in the study of human weakness, awash with cash, have managed to ensnare and entangle so many Western politicians, most, but by no means all, on the right or the far right of the political spectrum.

The French radical right politician Marine Le Pen was fairly skewered by President Macron in their debate before the 2022 elections in France when he described Vladimir Putin as her 'banker'. Her political party, called the National Front on its foundation in 1972 by her father but since 2018 euphemistically renamed National Rally, is paying back a $12 million loan from a Russian entity now under US sanctions. The precise history of how much Moscow gold has ended up in the pockets of the French far right is, at the time of writing, not fully known. But it is a lot.

The same goes for Matteo Salvini, the Italian far-right wunderkind and leader of the League Party. In 2018 three Russians and three Italians, one a close aide to Salvini, were caught on tape in Moscow's Metropol Hotel – a gold bullion bar's throw from the Kremlin – discussing how Russian generosity could benefit the party of Salvini, who was at the time both deputy prime minister and minister of the interior. Had this happened, it would have been a breach of Italian electoral law which forbids parties from accepting any large donation from a foreign source. Long-time Salvini aide Gianluca Savoini had been photographed the day before with my old friend Alexander Dugin, Putin's Rasputin. The following day Savoini was taped saying: 'We want to change Europe. A new Europe has to be close to Russia as before because we want to have our sovereignty.' Salvini himself did not show up for that meeting but he was in Moscow at the time. The potential deal the six men discussed was for a Russian petrochemical major to sell $1.5 billion of fuel to Eni, the Italian oil company. The hidden part of the deal, which would happen via secretive go-betweens, would be a $65 million bung for the League.

Challenged about the tape by Alberto Nardelli from BuzzFeed News, Savoini replied: 'Sorry but I don't have time to waste on these things.' Blown out of the water by great Italian journalism, this particular deal never saw the light of day. The suspicion remains that the Kremlin has been funding its far-right pals so that they can enjoy 'La Dolce Russian Vita'.

In 2000, after I had come back from Chechnya and called Vladimir Putin a war criminal, there were two public figures in London who spoke out against his brutal war, and I admired both of them: the first was the actor Vanessa Redgrave and the second Labour MP Jeremy Corbyn.

Vanessa was a thing of beauty, using the raw power of her voice to condemn what Putin was doing. She strode into the wooden cockpit of the Globe theatre, a floppy hat on her strawberry hair, long flowing coat, wielding a long heavy wooden stick. She immediately thrust the stick at us, swinging it high and sweeping it down low, then a prod and a probe. It was a challenge, a dare, a 'come on, let's see what you're made of'. The *Observer* photographer John Reardon stood his ground, but I ran away and hid behind the Globe's PR person. There's making an entrance.

And then there's Vanessa Redgrave waving her stick at you.

Back then she was sixty-two, entitled to a Zimmer frame and knitting needles, but there was no sign of her getting soft or slowing down. She ascended to the gods to catch a last pool of April sunlight and the years dropped away. She looked astonishingly young and alive, a life force to be reckoned with.

The stick and the floppy hat were there because she was rehearsing her role as Prospero in *The Tempest.* Photographs taken, she gave me a lift across London to her flat in Chiswick. It was a thrilling, roller-coaster ride, as the tiny VW Polo lurched forward and suddenly stopped. She started, suddenly, and raved at the London Eye, hovering over the Shell Building like 'an alien spaceship', and then returned to Chechnya. There's driving in London.

And there's being driven by Vanessa Redgrave.

At her flat she showed me a letter, on it the names of the founding supporters of the International Campaign for Peace and Human Rights for Chechnya, including Yelena Bonner, the widow of the Soviet dissident Andrei Sakharov, and her own name. And then she started speaking, her voice low, her face staring ahead, wreathed in smoke from her Silk Cuts: 'Thomas Mann wrote a powerful attack after the Munich Agreement. He was absolutely forthright that Chamberlain had destroyed the German opposition that could have halted Hitler. I fear the same thing in the case of Russia. In destroying the Chechen people in a genocide, Putin has sent out a message: "Look at what we did to Chechnya. And, if you are Russian, look at what we did to Babitsky."' Andrei Babitsky was the Radio Free Europe reporter who led the world in telling people what was really going on inside Chechnya. He was arrested, tortured and, worst, forced to listen to others being tortured, including a woman screaming in agony. He was then handed over to quisling Chechens loyal to Adam Deniyev, the man the Chechen government-in-exile holds responsible for the murder of six Red Cross nurses in 1996. Babitsky was only released thanks to huge international pressure.

'Babitsky,' Vanessa continued, 'is a glowing flame to what is still good about Russia.' The flattening of Chechnya, Babitsky's arrest, 'These are actions of a fascist character. My view of Putin's regime is that it is Hitlerian.'

She was distressed that Robin Cook, the then British Foreign Secretary, and Tony Blair had both kissed Putin's hand. 'I've met Mr Blair. He's extremely attractive as a human being, a very nice man. I thought the arrest of Pinochet wonderful and I supported the war against oppression in Kosovo. Cook and Blair think they can control him. And they are making the same mistake as Franz von Papen, who thought he could control Hitler.'

Back in 2000 Vanessa, who has been famously associated with the Workers' Revolutionary Party for much of her life, reflected on the evidence that Putin would cause trouble in the future: 'In order to get ordinary Russians to hate the Chechen "sub-humans" state TV showed "Chechen bandits" cutting the throat of a Russian soldier. I've seen the footage, and it is so shocking it can probably never be shown on British TV. That it was repeated on Russian TV is firm evidence of a hate machine working at full blast.'

The Chechens have long been blamed for murdering the Red Cross nurses and the beheading of four British telephone engineers: 'You've got to ask, who gains?' she asked. 'The Chechens? No. The Kremlin? Yes.'

She paused to light another fag. 'I read about the Holocaust again and again to find how to stop it . . .'

Some people got exactly who Vladimir Putin was, very

early on. Jeremy Corbyn was a second seer. In December 1999 he sponsored a parliamentary motion condemning Putin's war in Chechnya: 'That this House condemns the Russian military action in Chechnya and calls for troop withdrawal and a political solution that recognizes rights of self-determination; is also concerned that the Russian action is partly motivated by demand for control of oil and gas pipelines running through Chechnya; and is concerned that the criticisms of Russia have not focused sufficiently on supporting peace and anti-war groups in Russia.'

And that makes Jeremy Corbyn's subsequent betrayal of the anti-Putin coalition all the darker. In 2014 *The Guardian* journalist Seumas Milne chaired a meeting of Kremlin patsies at the Valdai Club in Sochi where the main speaker was Vladimir Putin.

Not everyone at *The Guardian* thought that attending the Valdai Club was a good thing. Luke Harding, the paper's former Moscow correspondent, wrote that to go to Valdai was to play 'a puppet in the Kremlin's theatre, there to make Putin look good'. Milne and Harding clashed at the paper's editorial conference. In the middle of the row, Milne's phone rang, at which Harding said: 'That must be the Kremlin.'

One year later Corbyn became Labour leader and hired Milne as his PR man. In 2018, after the Skripal poisoning in March, Corbyn asked then Prime Minister Theresa May in the House of Commons: 'How has she responded to the Russian government's request for a sample of the agent used in the Salisbury attack, to run its own tests?'

It was like asking for the axe-murderer to be given his axe back. A host of Labour backbenchers stood up to condemn their leader's wishy-washy appeasement of the Kremlin. Yvette Cooper said that the Russian state involvement, as the

UK government concluded, 'should be met with unequivocal condemnation'. Several Labour MPs signed a motion saying: 'This house unequivocally accepts the Russian state's culpability for the poisoning of Yulia and Sergei Skripal.'

Behind the curtains, Milne dug his master's grave deeper, telling the Westminster lobby under his mask as the spokesman for the Leader of the Opposition: 'I think obviously the government has access to information and intelligence on this matter which others don't; however, also there's a history in relation to WMD and intelligence which is problematic to put it mildly. So I think the right approach is to seek the evidence; to follow international treaties, particularly in relation to prohibited chemical weapons, because this was a chemical weapons attack, carried out on British soil. There are procedures that need to be followed in relation to that.'

What Milne was doing was very clever and very stupid, both at the same time. His reference to WMD was a dig at the Blair government's great mistake on Saddam still having the chemical weapons he had used against the Iraqi Kurds. But Blair was long gone. Theresa May may have been ditchwater-dull but she was no liar. And, once again, the chances of a nerve agent being glued to the doorknob of a former GRU officer by any agency other than the Russian secret state – proprietor: Vladimir Putin – were vanishingly small. The great British public saw Milne's appeasement for what it was and voters, especially traditional Labour working-class ones, started to dump Corbyn, big time. I give credit to Corbyn for taking the stand that he did in 2000, but he lost it all, and more, by appointing a Kremlin patsy like Milne to be his PR man and then lost it all over again by giving the Kremlin the benefit of the doubt over the Salisbury poisonings. Corbyn's tragedy is that his politics got locked in the early 1970s when he saw left-wing causes, especially that of a free Palestine, broken by US power. When the American and British establishments were at one with Putin in the early years, he was against Putin. As American and British politicians slowly began to see Putin for who he really was, Corbyn decided to echo, albeit in a faltering and weak voice, some of the Kremlin's messaging. This was because he was navigating simply by holding himself in constant opposition to American power. By doing so, he made himself yet another of the Kremlin's useful idiots. George Osborne and Peter Mandelson cosied up to Kremlin proxies for their own self-interest; Corbyn lost his bearings because his political ideology was so strong it twisted reality.

Boris Johnson's friendship with Evgeny Lebedev – now Baron Siberia – and his father, Alexander, has nothing to do with political ideology. The bunga-bunga parties the Lebedevs threw at the Palazzo Terranova near Perugia in central Italy were out of this world: among the guests were Peter Mandelson, Sarah Sands (the then editor of the BBC's Today programme), Amol Rajan (at one time an editor of *The Independent*, owned by the Lebedevs, and now a rising star at the BBC), Elton John, Shirley Bassey, Stephen Fry, Michael Gambon, Elizabeth Hurley, Rupert Everett, Ralph Fiennes (who plays M in the Bond movies), Boris Johnson and even topless model Katie Price – according to James Cusick in a brilliant piece of reporting for OpenDemocracy in 2016.

Sarah Sands and Amol Rajan are two important cheerleaders for Evgeny Lebedev. Sands was Evgeny's editor at the *Evening Standard*, then got control of BBC Radio Four's flagship Today programme but has now left. Rajan remains the corporation's media editor and regularly presents Today.

While at the *Standard*, Sands said Evgeny Lebedev's 'taste is exquisite'. Rajan, when at *The Independent*, said 'he has a terrifyingly good memory and, as someone who works for him, he can be terrifyingly sharp'.

Evgeny Lebedev wrote in the *Mail on Sunday*: 'Various papers produced Stalinist lists of "enemies of the people"; influential Russians in the UK who, it is implied, advance the Kremlin's agenda . . . I am proud to be a friend of Boris Johnson, who like most of my friends has visited me in Umbria. And I hate to disappoint, but nothing happens there that produces "kompromat".'

We have the word of the son of a KGB colonel for that.

However, the word on the streets of Perugia is that anything goes at these parties. Evgeny Lebedev is a libertine with a capital L, he likes to play Lord Misrule and he makes no bones about it. In 2012 Evgeny, when he had recently bought *The Independent*, wangled an interview with the Kremlin patsy president, sorry, dictator of Belarus, Alexander Lukashenko, for the BBC. The Corporation sent along my old colleague Natalia Antelava to keep an eye on Lebedev, but his subject matter threw both her and the tyrant of Minsk.

'So, what's your opinion on group sex?' Lebedev junior asked the strongman. Lukashenko sidestepped the question, but Natalia came away thinking that Lebedev junior was not 'terrifyingly sharp', just a narcissus and a fool. At his palazzo, there's a fancy-dress box and guests have to pick what they are going to wear blind, which is why one very famous partygoer ended up as a gimp in a gimp suit. A butt-plug with a Vladimir Putin face on it has been spotted. Beautiful men and women are at hand, at beck and call. Katie Price, Jim Cusick reported, hit the champagne a little too heavily and got her breasts out for then Foreign Secretary Boris Johnson.

There is, of course, no suggestion that Johnson wore the gimp suit or, indeed, the Vladimir Putin butt-plug, and no suggestion whatsoever that he wore both at the same time.

But behind the scenes the possibility remains that the Lebedev parties might be a target for intelligence gathering by the Russian secret state. Remember, Alexander Lebedev was a KGB spy in London, helped Vladimir Putin secure the keys to the Kremlin by putting Yuri Skuratov under surveillance, fell out with Putin over his Moscow newspaper story about his mistress, Alina Kubaeva, and has now somehow climbed his way back into the Kremlin's affections. Remember the Italian parliamentary intelligence oversight committee report airing concerns that Alexander Lebedev may not have ended his association with the Russian secret state, that the KGB was like Hotel California, an agency you can never leave. Alexander Lebedev still has active business interests – that is, money – in Russia and, reportedly, Russian-occupied Crimea. In 2017 he threw a media bash at his hotel complex in Alushta, Crimea, 'to correct an impression of Crimea put out by a biased Western media'.

The impression of Russian invasion does not need correction.

At the time of writing, mid-May 2022, Alexander Lebedev has not tweeted any comment whatsoever on Russia's February 2022 invasion of Ukraine.

Would the Russian secret state dare to violate the privacy of, say, a British foreign secretary while on the lash at a bunga-bunga party in the home of a former KGB colonel?

One former MI6 officer reflected on the strange friendship between the Lebedevs, father and son: 'If Boris goes to the Lebedevs' palazzo in Italy and shags someone, there's got to be a sporting chance that someone's filming it . . . Imagine if Putin was knocking off a woman in a place in Moscow owned by a British businessman, then, in my old job, I would be onto that immediately, I would be all over it like a bad rash.'

Two years on from the Katie Price incident, Boris Johnson was back at Palazzo Terranova, intriguingly just after a NATO summit in response to the Skripal poisoning. Both in 2016 and 2018, Johnson, then foreign secretary, dumped his Metropolitan Police minders. The detectives that follow him around are there to protect him from a terrorist attack, but they also have another, more discreet function: to protect the British state from being betrayed by one of its servants. If left in London while the foreign secretary is under a Russian roof, the Met detectives can no longer do their job properly. Journalists in the know, like Adam Boulton of Sky News and Gordon Corera at the BBC, both reported stories that Boris Johnson had lost control over MI6 because of his dodgy conduct. The Foreign Office put out a murky denial.

The true extent of the relationship between the Lebedevs and Boris Johnson remains opaque. But in 2020 Johnson, now prime minister, put Evgeny forward to be a member of the House of Lords. The committee that vets potential members of the House of Lords turned him down on advice from Special Branch. That advice was later reversed and Evgeny 'Group Sex?' Lebedev became Baron Siberia. As I reported for *Byline Times*, the House of Lords Appointments Commission was troubled by this dramatic change and awaited the long-delayed publication of the Intelligence and Security Committee's Russia Report. It caused the Commission yet more unease. The report stated: 'The extent to which Russian expatriates are using their access to UK businesses and politicians to exert influence in the UK is ***: it is widely recognised that Russian intelligence and business are completely intertwined. The Government must ***, take the necessary measures to counter the threat and challenge the impunity of Putin-linked elites.'

The asterisks mask security-sensitive details. So we, but perhaps not the Kremlin, are left in the dark.

Once ennobled, Baron Siberia socked it to his critics in the *Mail on Sunday*: 'To all those who sneer at my Russian background, I say this: Is it not remarkable that the son of a KGB agent and a first-generation immigrant to this country has become such an assimilated and contributing member of British society? What a success for our system. Don't you think?'

Others say nyet, Baron, nyet.

Professor Donald Rayfield told me: 'Is Evgeny Lebedev a potential security risk? Yes. Especially because of the role of his father, who goes back and forth to Russia. Remember it's very difficult to retire from the KGB. They don't have a procedure for that.'

Evgeny Lebedev makes a big point out of not having met Putin, but Rayfield doesn't believe this invalidates the question. 'You don't have to meet the man to be in his clutches. Twenty years ago the British authorities would not have given Evgeny Lebedev residency let alone a place in the House of Lords. Evgeny makes much of his ownership of *The Independent*, but it occasionally veers into the territory of Russia Today, suggesting that Putin is not our enemy.'

Is it possible that Johnson might have been a victim of sex kompromat? It is. The former MI6 officer said: 'Boris Johnson may well be compromised. No one believes he went to the palazzo just to sip orange juice.'

For OpenDemocracy, Jim Cusick reported that, in

November 2018, Evgeny Lebedev's dog – a white Borzoi called Vladimir – died in mysterious circumstances. 'Lebedev,' Cusick wrote, 'has told associates that he believes the dog was poisoned and that it was a message from Moscow.'

Who killed Evgeny Lebedev's dog and why is another good question. Is it possible that the secret Russian state wanted to send Evgeny a message? It is.

For *Byline Times* I contacted the Lebedevs and 10 Downing Street but received no reply on the record.

The break-up of the European Union is a Kremlin goal and Brexit was a great Kremlin success. Russia's former ambassador to London, Alexander Yakovenko, boasted that Russia had 'crushed' the British after the public voted to leave the EU in 2016. In his book, *Shadow State*, Luke Harding reported that while nattering to a fellow diplomat, Yakovenko said: 'We have crushed the British to the ground. They are on their knees, and they will not rise for a very long time.'

That remark raises questions about whether the Russian secret state helped pay for Brexit. This is a question that I kept on asking in my last years at the BBC and, I'm sad to say, that my doggedness won me few friends, in particular with Nigel Farage and Arron Banks. Farage – the last syllable rhymes with Raj, not the back bit of garage – got so angry with my reporting that he hand-delivered a letter to Broadcasting House calling for me to be investigated. He wrote for the *Daily Telegraph* that my reporting caused him 'more misery than any other in my 25 years in politics'.

The story starts with the death of Arek Jozwik, a forty-year-old Polish worker in Harlow, Essex, in August 2016, not long after the Brexit vote. I reported the immediate aftermath of the killing for BBC Newsnight – the film is on

YouTube titled 'Harlow: A town in shock over killing'. It told how Jozwik was having a drink with some mates in the new town's square when his phone rang and he started speaking Polish. This grabbed the attention of a gang of English youths, someone shouted 'fucking Polish', and Arek was punched by a fifteen-year-old and fell back, cracking his head on a low stone and dying. It was manslaughter but the atmosphere was toxic for immigrants after the Brexit vote and Essex Police treated Arek's death as a hate crime. I interviewed one Polish man, a friend of the deceased, who said Farage has 'blood on his hands'. I then went on to say that Nigel Farage has always denied this allegation. My report also reflected the reality of anti-social behaviour in the town square, how English people were frightened by the young gangsters.

There was CCTV in the square, but the audio pick-up was poor so that the detectives dropped the charge of hate crime and prosecuted the youth with manslaughter. The jury found him guilty. At the sentencing hearing a statement from Arek's mother, Ava, was read out: 'Every day I miss him. There are moments I do not want to live anymore . . . In moments like this I cannot hold back my tears.'

The defence brief, seeking to get a reduced sentence for his fifteen-year-old client, said that Arek had used a racist word in the fight before the fatal punch. This was not a finding of the court but a claim amplified post-trial. Nigel Farage seized on this point and went on the attack, calling my reporting a slur. Speaking on his LBC radio show, Farage said: 'I want an apology and if I don't get one then I think I'll be compelled next year to feel why should I pay the licence fee.' The *Daily Mail* followed up with a story headlined 'The Great Hate Crime Lie'.

A BBC spokesperson said: 'The BBC's reporting reflected,

like other media, that racial motivation was a line of inquiry the police were looking at and our coverage also featured vox-pops giving differing views including anti-social behaviour as a possibility.'

Farage didn't get an apology from the BBC, nor did he get one from me.

Ekaterina 'Katya' Paderina, born in Russia, was so poor that when she arrived in Portsmouth and went sun-bathing on Southsea Beach – which is not exactly San Tropez – she used butter, not suntan lotion. She asked a passing merchant seaman, Eric Butler, twice her age, to help with the butter and soon they were married. Butler told me that when the happy couple were on the steps of the Registry Office in Portsmouth he stepped on her dress by mistake and said, 'Sorry dear', to which she replied: 'I don't love you, I'm not married to you in Russia. If you come at me, you will feel the full power of Russia.'

Butler then said that Special Branch popped around to their flat, not far from the Portsmouth Royal Naval base, lifted up the carpet, and found a large stash of dollars. Katya then had a love affair with local Portsmouth MP, Mike Hancock; then she hit Butler so hard with a lightshade the police charged her; then they got divorced; then she married Arron Banks who, later, gave £8 million, Britain's single biggest political donation ever, to the Brexit campaign Leave.EU.

Nothing to see here, folks. Or maybe there just might be.

In 2014 Arron Banks stood next to Nigel Farage in the grounds of his mansion he nicknamed Downton Abbey and declared that he would give the Brexit Party £1 million. The money kept on flowing, leading to the Brexit vote when Britain did exactly what the Kremlin wanted it to do and voted out of the European Union. Did the Kremlin rig the vote? No one knows for sure. But there are anomalies aplenty.

The clock struck thirteen for me when I rocked up at Banks' James Bond-style lair on Catbrain Lane, Bristol. 'Catbrain' comes from Anglo-Saxon for the local clay but somehow it summed up the whole Arron Banks shtick. In 2017 he ran a series of insurance businesses with low premiums but high add-ons, perhaps the best-known being 'Go Skippy', housed in an unbelievably naff headquarters, just off a dual carriageway roundabout. Banks cheerfully admits to it being very David Brent, the naff boss from the BBC mockumentary, 'The Office'.

Everything about Arron Banks oozes catbrain clay. Companies House records show that Banks has set up thirty-seven different companies using slight variations of his name: Aron Fraser Andrew Banks; Arron Andrew Fraser Banks; Arron Fraser Andrew Banks; and Arron Banks. In 2013 the auditors of one of his companies, Baker Tilly, resigned, stating 'a breakdown in the relationship has occurred because, by failing to supply accurate information, management is imposing a limitation of scope on our work'. Banks says the auditors resigned because of a conflict of interest.

Some of his other businesses hit choppy waters. Banks was managing director of African Compass Trading, which sold the Star 150 sexual enhancement pill, a kind of herbal Viagra. Its slogan was 'Naturally, every man wants to be a superman in the bedroom'. The MHRA, the medicines regulator, said that in 2014, as part of a criminal investigation, it seized Star 150 pills worth around £50,000 from an address in Bristol. After the pills were seized, the investigation was halted and no criminal charges were pressed. Banks told our BBC investigation team, led by Innes Bowen, with Phil Kemp doing the leg work and me the pretty face, that he did invest £100,000 in the business but that operations were discontinued due to 'stiff competition'.

The joke is classic Banks. Katya Banks for a time drove a car with the number plate XMI5 SPY. You laugh, then you worry, then you laugh. He is a funny old toad and lots of people who don't agree with his politics one little bit have a sneaking liking for the human being. That goes for the brilliant journalist Carole Cadwalladr whom he is currently suing for libel, for Martin Fletcher who spent four hours with him for a piece for the *New Statesman*: 'As an ardent Remainer,' Fletcher wrote, 'I am expecting to dislike the man intensely, but I find him disarmingly humorous and frank. We chat for nearly four hours. Whether he is merely generous with his time, or loves the attention, I cannot tell.'

And for me? Banks' anti-establishment sensibility was groomed at a run of dodgy third-rate private schools from which he was expelled for a pub crawl and stealing lead off a roof. Or some such.

The grand anomaly with Arron Banks, eight-million-pound Brexit donor, is that if you look closely at his empire it does not smell of big money. Far from it. He held his first big press conference in what he likes to call Downton Abbey, Old Down Manor overlooking the Bristol Channel, which he bought from musician Mike 'Tubular Bells' Oldfield. But when we at BBC Newsnight inspected the books in 2017, we found that he had a hefty mortgage on it. At the time he actually lived in a much smaller house down the road, again with a hefty mortgage. His insurance businesses were not high end and are not awash with cash or premium income. He had a couple of diamond mines in southern Africa but they, too, had their problems. They were not producing big or many diamonds. So how could Banks afford to be so extraordinarily generous to Leave.EU?

And then there were the men with snow on their boots. In September 2015 Banks was approached by 'a shady character called Oleg' from the Russian Embassy at the UKIP annual conference, according to his ghosted book, *Bad Boys of Brexit*. Oleg 'was introduced to us as the First Secretary of the embassy – in other words, the KGB's man in London,' wrote Banks. That led to a boozy lunch with the Russian ambassador, Alexander Yakovenko.

'Our host wanted the inside track on the Brexit campaign and grilled us on the potential implications of an Out vote for Europe. Diplomatic relations only improved when our new friend produced a special surprise. It was a bottle of vodka which he claimed was "one of only three in a batch made for Stalin personally".'

Banks told Newsnight: 'No money came from the men with snow on their boots.'

But he actually downplayed the number of meetings between his group, Leave.EU, and the Russian Embassy: there were eleven in all.

With our Newsnight team, Banks repeatedly came up with funny replies to our questions. Asked about his political donations and the African Viagra story, he sidestepped the substance and fired back: 'Since the referendum result and my support for Donald Trump, I have been the subject of politically motivated attacks by the "mainstream media" and Remain-supporting institutions. It comes as no surprise that Newsnight would join the party at this late stage with their own particular type of trashy "News of the World" journalism.' He concluded that after allegations by some that he was a 'Russian spy ... part of a worldwide conspiracy to subvert democracy ... the only surprise is how long it's taken Newsnight to have a pop at me! BBC Fake news is alive and well!'

People started to wonder what was the true source of the £8 million. To comply with British law, the origin of political donations must lie onshore, not offshore. The Electoral Commission fined Leave.EU and asked the National Crime Agency to investigate. Later, the NCA ended up clearing Banks and the Electoral Commission reached a settlement with Banks, who said that he had been 'completely vindicated'.

In 2018, before he had been cleared by the NCA, Banks gave an interview to Andrew Marr, then still at the BBC, and to prove his innocence that the £8 million came from his own British companies, not offshore, not Russia, he sent the team at the Andrew Marr Show a huge batch of emails. Not having the time to pore over them at length, the Marr team sent them on to me. One email from Banks to a minion read: 'Redact the reference for Ural Properties and any references which include sensitive info e.g. the account numbers that the money was sent from.'

Fascinated, we started digging. What was Ural Properties? Who owned it? What did it own? Did it have anything that the men with snow on their boots would be interested in? The Urals are a mountain range that roughly mark the end of European Russia and the start of Siberia. We worked with an online website, Source Material, which got hold of the accounts of Ural Properties in Gibraltar and passed them on to Newsnight. The company was effectively owned by Arron and Katya Banks and it, in turn, owned two flats in Gunwharf, Portsmouth, overlooking the sea lane into the Royal Navy base, something the men with snow on their boots would be interested in, very much so. But the flats were also an attractive business proposition.

Asked about Ural Properties, Banks, true to brand, made no substantive reply but he did fire back: 'This is the seventh [Newsnight] programme designed to smear me and discredit Brexit. I have repeatedly stated that I am a UK taxpayer and the funds were from UK. The NCA have had "full disclosure" of the relevant bank accounts and an explanation of where the money came from. We will be doing a victory lap of the TV studios once this matter is resolved and look forward to being interviewed by John "the Trot" Sweeney or the ever "professional" Kirsty or Emily.'

For the avoidance of any doubt, I am not, nor have I ever been, a Trotskyist or a Communist.

Chapter Eighteen

The Underpants Poisoner

On 20 August 2020 Alexei Navalny is flying from the Siberian city of Tomsk to Moscow when he gets up to go to the toilet. Before he can make it his legs collapse from under him, he falls onto the floor and lets out a piercing scream. It's not just the sound of Navalny in agony. For me it's the sound, too, of democracy in Russia – dying.

Then three miracles happen in the right order that save his life. The first miracle is that the pilot of the plane understands that the effective leader of the Russian opposition is mortally ill, so he carries out an emergency landing in the city of Omsk. The second is that an ambulance picks Navalny up after he's brought down from the plane and the medics on board jab him with atropine, the very same drug that helped save the Skripals in Salisbury. And the third miracle is that German Chancellor Angela Merkel gets on the phone to the Kremlin and asks permission to fly Navalny to Germany to be treated. After a long delay, as the hospital in Omsk starts filling up with funny peculiar strangers in cheap suits, Putin agrees to the medical evacuation to Germany. Once Navalny has arrived there, the doctors go to work and do tests and they discover that he's been poisoned with Novichok, the same nerve agent used to poison the Skripals and, accidentally, kill Dawn Sturgess.

The prime suspect is the master of the Kremlin.

A few months later, in December, Bellingcat's Christo Grozev and The Insider identify the poisoners, officers of the FSB. The investigation is an extraordinary piece of open-source journalism, establishing who poisoned Navalny, then backtracking the suspects' movements to show that the FSB Poison Unit had been following him – and, presumably, considering how to kill him – for three years. Navalny, recovering in Germany, told *El País* newspaper: 'It is difficult for me to understand exactly what is going on in [Putin's] mind ... twenty years of power would spoil anyone and make them crazy.'

That December, Navalny did his own bit to make mad Vlad that little bit madder. It's the early hours and you're a grunt in the FSB, a military chemist by the name of Konstantin Kudryavtsev. Some high-up calls you and starts barking at you, whereupon you tell everything you know.

High-Up: 'Konstantin Borisovich?'
Kudryavtsev: 'Yes, yes.'
High-Up: 'This is Ustinov, Maxim Sergeevich, aide to Nikolay Platonovich Patrushev. I received your number from Vladimir Mikhailovich Bogdanov. I apologize for the early hour, but I urgently require ten minutes of your time.'

Oh no it's not. It's Navalny himself pretending to be a high-up. The call is taking place at daybreak and the gormless FSB goon gives the game away. Navalny is a cocky one. 'Maxim' the high-up wants to know how the team poisoned Navalny. After some preliminaries, the call continues.

Navalny (pretending to be Maxim, the high-up): 'And on what bit of fabric did you focus on? Which item of clothing had the highest risk factor?'

K: 'The underpants.'
N: 'The underpants.'
K: 'A risk factor? What do you mean?'
N: 'Where it [the Novichok] would be the most concentrated?'
K: 'Well, the underpants.'
N: 'Do you mean inside or outside?'
K: 'Well, we were working on the inside. That is what we were doing.'
N: 'Well, imagine a pair of underpants in front of you. Which part did you treat?'
K: 'The inside, where the groin is.'
N: 'The groin?'
K: 'Well, the crotch, as they call it. There are some sort of seams there, by the seams.'
N: 'Wait, this is important. Who gave you the order to treat the codpiece of the underpants?'
K: 'We figured this out on our own. They told us to work on the inside of the underpants.'
N: 'I am writing it down. The inside. Okay . . . Do you remember the colour of the underwear?'
K: 'Blue. But I am not sure.'
N: 'And they are whole, I mean theoretically we [the FSB] could give them back? We are not going to do this, but they are undamaged and everything is okay with them?'
K: 'Yes, they are all clear.'

*

Navalny's sting made another thing clear, too: Vladimir Putin is the underpants poisoner. He didn't treat Navalny's underpants with Novichok but only he had the clout to authorize the poisoning of the second most powerful political actor in Russia.

There is a film called *Navalny* made by HBO and CNN that records his war against the Kremlin. Watch it.

I had a natter with Dr Ben Noble, Associate Professor of Russian Politics at University College London and co-author of *Navalny: Putin's Nemesis, Russia's Future?* First of all Ben explained how Bellingcat and The Insider cracked who the poisoners were. 'Through accessing various bits of information, including flight manifests, which they have acquired from various different sources, they can work out that there's a group of people who have been tracking Navalny for years, and importantly, since he stood as a candidate for the 2018 presidential elections. In the end, he was blocked but he campaigned for quite a while.'

In Russia, every government department and business company is so corrupt that you can buy, for the right price, anything: flight manifests, car registration databases, passport databases. The resistance to Putin is using the master's corrupt practices to expose his killing machine. It's kind of beautiful.

Ben continued: 'So there is the specific group of people who Bellingcat claim are an FSB assassination unit who follow Navalny. Bellingcat then sees that this unit is linked to other poisonings of opposition politicians in Russia. They've also looked into the group's expertise when it comes to handling poisons. And so they release this extraordinary bombshell investigation, which again for many people is just confirming what they already suspected. The details that

Bellingcat include are really quite something, but the cherry on the cake is Navalny himself calling up somebody who is part of this FSB assassination unit. Again it's a sign of Navalny's balls that he would call up and in the moment, say "I'm this incredibly important person." He gets the tone, the language exactly right. Navalny gets the member of Team Poison to say, "Well, look, we put the poison in his underpants." And that is just an extraordinary admission.'

Bellingcat and The Insider carried on investigating, linking the poison unit that tracked Navalny to other deaths, including activists Timur Kuashev in August 2014 and Ruslan Magomedragimov in March 2015, and politician Nikita Isayev in November 2019. Another joint investigation found that Russian opposition politician Vladimir Kara-Murza was followed by the same unit before his suspected poisonings in May 2015 and February 2017.

In January 2021 Navalny flew back to Russia, to certain arrest and certain conviction and uncertain life, by which I mean probable death. But for this brave man, there was no other option. He knew that if he stayed in exile, he would never evict Putin from the Kremlin. The moment he lands in Moscow, he's arrested and ends up in court. He's locked inside a glass cage and as he is about to be led away to the penal colony, he makes a heart sign with his fingers to his wife, Yulia. It is a beautiful, romantic moment, a signal of grace under pressure and a reminder, once again, that another Russia is possible.

Navalny had one more trick up his sleeve. Once he was safely behind bars, up he popped on YouTube, presenting an extraordinarily funny film called *Putin's Palace*, about a one-billion dollar-plus palace on the Black Sea, paid for by Putin's cronies, protected by Putin's Presidential Guard. Navalny's

Anti-Corruption Foundation had gone to town, flying drones over the secret palace, using photos shot inside and making use of architects' plans to show the obscene amount of money pissed away on the project. After the film was broadcast, Putin and his patsy media dismissed it but, to date, more than 123 million people, many of them Russian, have seen it. The bits that stick in the mind are a €780 gold toilet brush, an aqua-disco – whatever the hell that is – and Navalny's chunky Tonto, Georgy Alburov, avoiding all the checkpoints on land by driving a RIB with a powerful outboard motor down the coast of the Black Sea close enough so that he could launch a drone to fly over the palace. It's investigative journalism at its ballsiest.

Navalny remains in prison but he's still alive. Why on earth doesn't the Kremlin kill him, people ask me. The answer is simple. If Navalny, a fit forty-six-year-old man, dies then the best of Moscow and St Petersburg will hit the streets to protest and the master of the Kremlin is morbidly afraid of that very thing. He's also morbidly afraid of something else too: dying himself.

And that's a little ironic because there is evidence – this being Russia it is always opaque – that he might be doing just that.

Chapter Nineteen

The Kremlin Patient

The night before the big war started I was invited to a super-model party in a flat off Kreshchatyk, Kyiv's fanciest street. There were no super-models. On a table, a hunk of saveloy, plastic cups, bottles of wine and vodka. Standing around were a group of freelance journalists digging for hope in the alcohol. It felt like 2 September 1939. Joe Biden came on the telly and said out loud what we all knew in our hearts was going to happen, that Vladimir Putin had given the order to invade.

It was bloody grim. I went outside, found a bar, started drinking – previously I had just been taxiing down the runway – met two Ukrainian women, told them the war was going to start in a few hours. They did not believe me. I bought them a Big Mac each as a kind of consolation prize, went back on my own to my Airbnb and woke up with a hangover. I've had worse hangovers but not on day one of a war.

Nearly all my Ukrainian friends, whom I adore, believe there is something preternaturally wrong with Russia and the Russian soul, that Putin is just one monster among many from the swamp to the East. With love and with respect, I don't agree with them. This is Vladimir Putin's war. Like his wars in Chechnya, Georgia and Syria. Like his war without tanks and bombs against the West. Like his poisonings. It's down to him.

I had left the BBC in 2019 and in Kyiv I was freelance, my own editor, my own boss, but also my own security man. Still, I had my lucky orange hat. There were only three times when I felt fear in the nigh on three months I spent in Kyiv from mid-February to mid-May 2022. One time was when I made a little film for Twitter at night in the middle of an air-raid siren going off and there must have been a catch in my delivery, a sense of unease, of vulnerability, something I do my best to hide. Someone tweeted 'RIP John Sweeney'. My son rang me, anxiety in his voice. I assured him that I was very much alive, but I was worried that my family was worried and I couldn't sleep well that night.

A second moment of fear was when I was sent an email which looked very much like a successful phishing attack, the sender geo-located to the Kremlin, Moscow. It was when I was setting up my podcast, 'Taking On Putin', and I lost two whole days resetting my email passwords and doubling down on my digital security which, of course, protects not only me but my sources. To give you a sense of this, I have a 13-digit code to fully open my phone. Only after two days did I get a message from a friendly techie that I had not been phished, that the Kremlin geo-locator was a spoof, a fraud, but one sent to people with high profiles, with lots of followers on Twitter, who were strongly critical of the Russian secret state.

The third moment of fear came when Vladimir Putin held his National Security Council meeting at the Kremlin, a couple of days before the war, everything televised for the world to see. Putin was in complete psycho Bond villain mode, keeping his fearful minions thirty feet away from him, snarling at the head of the Foreign Intelligence Service, the SVR, Sergei Naryshkin. On the official menu was whether the creeping and crawling things would agree with the master of the Kremlin that the two eastern oblasts or counties, Donetsk and Luhansk, should be recognized as independent states. Unofficially, it was a show of strength by Putin that Russia would give its blessing to the dismemberment of Ukraine and, also, a very public pinning down of his henchmen that they, too, supported his strategy and, implicitly, his war to come. But Naryshkin – yet another old pal of Putin from St Petersburg and early KGB days, a lightweight nonentity with very little time at the intelligence coalface – was somehow off-message. When asked to rubber-stamp the taking apart of Ukraine, Naryshkin, punch-nosed, gaunt, red-eyed, started to stutter. It was as if some part of his mind was rebelling against the very idea of a stupid war.

Putin snapped: 'Speak clearly.' Fear scribbled on Naryshkin's face as he sensed his betrayal by stutter would not go well for him. He over-corrected, jumping ahead in the script by three or four pages, saying that the breakaway republics should be accepted as 'part of Russia'. Putin's snarl switched to a sadistic smirk as he said that annexation by Russia was 'not under discussion'. Switching film references now, it was like a scene from *The Godfather* when the *capo di tutti i capi*, played by Marlon Brando, noted the anomaly and required fealty.

The Putin I had challenged in 2014 was a different man, subtle, supple, willing to engage with a difficult BBC reporter, albeit only to lie so calmly. The Putin of 2022 was hyper-aggressive. But the reason I felt fear was something else. The Putin I had met in 2014 looked like a ferret or a reptile, thin-faced, lean. The 2022 Putin looks like a hamster, his cheeks stuffed, unhealthy. He looks like a man on steroids and that made me full of fear.

Steroids are part of modern medicine's toolkit. They are good for killing pain. Abuse them and they can make you extraordinarily aggressive. I first came across 'roid-rage' in the nineties when I investigated a Liverpool drugs baron, Curtis 'Cocky' Warren, and his henchman, Johnny Phillips. The latter was a bodybuilder who had overdosed on steroids and became so insanely aggressive he used to enforce drug debts by buggering lesser dealers on the streets of Toxteth. He was widely suspected of starting a gang war in Liverpool by shooting dead a rival gangster, David Ungi, in 1995. He died when his own heart blew apart, the coroner saying that he had never seen such an over-extended heart in all his career.

At some point in the early years of his rule Vladimir Putin fell off his horse while riding and injured his back so badly that he was out of commission for days. Steroids would be the obvious medical treatment. But steroid misuse can lead to kidney problems and liver damage, even tumours. Has he got a cancerous tumour? Is it possible that Vlad the Poisoner could have ended up poisoning himself?

It is. And such a fate would be both grimly ironic and funny ha-ha so long as the Kremlin Patient does not have control of the world's biggest arsenal of nuclear weapons, however rusty they may be. But he does.

When Vladimir Putin gets up close with anyone, the story goes, the other party must undergo isolation for two weeks beforehand, do regular PCR tests for COVID, and submit to a test of their own faeces so that the Kremlin's doctors know they are in good health. Proekt, the extraordinary Russian investigative website led by Roman Badanin – the reporter who told me about Putin's first mistress, Lady Crooked Legs, also known as Svetlana Krivonogikh – ran a story about Putin's morbid fear of ill-health and how a battery of doctors follow him around. Proekt reported: 'Cancer surgeon Dr Evgeny Selivanov is one of the most frequent medical attendants on Putin. Over four years, the doctor has flown with or to him 35 times and spent a total of 166 days with the head of state.'

When Putin falls ill, he never vanishes from the TV screens of main street, Russia. That's because of what Proekt calls 'canned footage': the broadcasting of pre-recorded meetings between Putin and his subordinates. The canned footage trick allows him to disappear from time to time when he is ill. Proekt had another scoop, too, that Putin, worried about his bad back after the fall from the horse, has dabbled in occult medicine. Word is that he has bathed in Siberian antler's blood which is famous for its restorative powers, although the method of extracting the magic liquid is extraordinary cruel, but that, of course, may be part of its charm.

In mid-March I moved Airbnbs to a flat overlooking Kreshchatyk with a jacuzzi which, tragically, didn't work. I was tempted to give the place a rubbish review on Tripadvisor but then thought that, in the middle of a war, that did not feel proper. But what I did do – partly to keep up my own morale, partly to cheer up my British, American and Ukrainian friends – was to throw a party. Thanks to martial law, the sale of alcohol was still banned, so I was rather proud of having several bottles of good Italian red wine, Irish whiskey, vodka, gin and advocaat for my pals. My 'translator' Eugene used food colouring to dye the gin blue and with the advocaat we made Zelenskiy cocktails which the gang forced me to drink. What did it taste like? Disgusting isn't strong enough a word. Suffice to say, the president is better than the cocktail we named after him. Vlad the Driver brought his kids along and it was weirdly and delightfully normal to be in a room with kids messing about, eating too much chocolate, being cheeky to their parents in front of the stranger in the silly orange beanie. For a moment we started to forget about the war. Fool, Sweeney, fool. My phone pinged, telling me that a friend, let's call her K, was about to arrive downstairs. I took my phone, got in the lift, went downstairs, whereupon two passing police officers stopped me and asked for my passport. Foolishly, I had left it up in the flat. My inability to prove who I was instantly, and perhaps my minor annoyance at the request, made one cop suspicious. He wanted me to go to the nearest police checkpoint, just inside Kreshchatyk metro station. I called Eugene to get my passport and while we were all waiting, K arrived. I said hi, and then the whole posse, the two officers, Eugene, K and I went into the police checkpoint where they checked my passport against the Ukrainian national database. Frankly I was a bit irritated and cranky – the Zelenskiy cocktail can't have helped – and Eugene reminded me of my own advice, that at checkpoints you should always crack a joke. K suppressed a smile. To my certain knowledge she worked for or inside Ukrainian military intelligence until recently, or still does. All she had to do was lift a finger and then this charade would stop. But it was smarter and more time-efficient to play along, so I started 'God Save The Queening' with a smile on my lips, and soon the system found me and we were free to leave.

Back in the party, K and I had a private conversation while the others systematically emptied whatever alcohol was left while rocking along to Boney M. She knew a Russian oligarch, very close to the Kremlin, she told me. The oligarch told her a few months ago that Putin has cancer of the liver.

'When I met him, he had just had Botox,' I said. 'He looked

a bit plasticky but his cheeks were normal. Now he looks like a hamster.'

'That's the steroids,' K said.

'Is he dying?'

'We don't know for sure.'

I turned back to the party, ash in my throat.

Michael Weiss is a friend of mine, a New Yorker, half Jewish, half Irish. 'I can smash up the bar at night and then amortize the damages in the morning,' is one of his better lines. During COVID lockdowns we put out a simple conversation podcast, 'Two Boozy Hacks', where we drank from different sides of the pond and put the world to rights about Trump, Brexit, Putin and all. As a reporter, Mike has long walked the shady corridors of the US intelligence community. He is working on a long-awaited book about Russian military intelligence, the GRU, and knows all the right people in Ukraine.

In April he told me that he had heard that Putin has cancer. 'Snap!' I said, or something like that. But the story he had heard was that Putin had cancer of the blood. Mike had more sources, so I put him in touch with some geezer I met in a pub a long time ago. The name of said geezer is Ashley Grossman and he is professor of neuro-endocrinology at Oxford University. He said: 'Some of my friends and I have been looking at his face. It's got much rounder in the past couple of years. That would best go with lymphatic cancer. A regular treatment for that is prednisone, a steroid. Side-effects would include mood swings, aggression, confusion. You gain weight in your abdomen, the back of your neck and your face. So if he is taking prednisone that would account for his more erratic behaviour in the past months.'

K told me cancer of the liver, Mike had been told cancer of the blood, and Ash and his gang at the Oxford posse were thinking cancer of the lymph system. All three are connected by blood. Ash mused some more: 'Thyroid cancer is easily treatable. Blood cancer is also treatable but lymphatic cancer is much more serious, especially if it has metastasized to the spine. I had read that the spinal problems were to do with him falling off a horse but, if this is the case, it's a very serious diagnosis. He has an additional problem in that the quality of medicines in Russia is poor, even for someone like him.'

I told Ash that when I had met Putin in 2014 his face looked like that of a reptile; now he looks like a hamster.

'That would be the steroids,' said Ash. 'Putin looks like another leader back in the day. In 1963 JFK had a hamster-face because he was being over-treated with steroids for Addison's Disease.' Ash, because he really is a professor of medicine, added that Putin was not his patient and his remarks were based on remote observation.

Mike wrote his story up for *New Lines Magazine* and it caused a sensation around the world. He cited a story from a Telegram channel called 'General SVR', seemingly from a retired officer of Russia's Foreign Intelligence Service, which says that Putin is set to undergo surgery for an unspecified form of cancer in the near future. While he's under the knife, Nikolai Patrushev, ex-KGB man, aged seventy-one, will run the shop. But Mike went one better and got hold of a tape from the oligarch K talked about. The story was slightly different but, in my lengthy experience, that makes it more, not less, credible. A Western venture capitalist had taped the oligarch – Mike gave him the false name of 'Yuri' – in mid-March without Yuri's consent. Yuri is not a happy bunny, saying Putin 'absolutely ruined Russia's economy, Ukraine's economy and many other economies – ruined [them] absolutely. The problem is with his head . . . One crazy guy can turn the world upside down.'

The oligarch spelt out what he knew about Putin's health, saying that he is 'very ill with blood cancer'. Mike, by the way, is not 100 per cent convinced that the story is true. It could be disinformation, bandied about by the Russian elites, 'because they want to undermine his reign'. Christo Grozev of Bellingcat has reported that the FSB are under instruction to treat all such stories about Putin's ill-health as disinformation which, of course, suffers from the law of unintended consequences, that they start believing it to be true. My take is that Putin is, indeed, seriously ill. In late May the Telegram channel 'General SVR' claimed that Putin underwent surgery in the middle of the night on 16 May. Putin was out of reach, the story goes, for everyone apart from his trusted stooge, the National Security Council boss, Patrushev. The rumour machine in Moscow has generated a fifth cancer, that of the abdomen.

So, of the five possibilities – cancer of the liver, the blood, the lymph system, the thyroid, the abdomen – which is it? We do not know. Remember, dear reader, that Russia under Putin is government by mystery. Hard facts are not just difficult to come by. The whole Kremlin system works to prevent the gathering of hard facts, not least by poisoning the fact-gatherers. So apologies, but you have to remember that opacity – not being able to see clearly – comes as standard when you are trying to understand the ill-health of a Russian autocrat.

Towards the end of April, Putin had a one to one with his sidekick, General Sergei Shoigu, the Russian minister of defence, in which he told him not to attack the steel mill in Mariupol, the last redoubt of the Ukrainian army in the besieged city. Within days, the steel mill was being pounded by Russian artillery and, eventually, after a truce brokered by the UN and the International Red Cross, most surviving Ukrainian soldiers were allowed to leave – but to Russian territory. Their fate at the time of writing is uncertain. So much for Putin's honesty. But the most striking thing about the chinwag with Shoigu was Putin's posture. He sat down with the general at a comically small table, the kind you might put a chessboard on, but the side of his body seemed to be frozen, his right hand gripping the table hard. His grip was so fierce it reminded me of the way my grandma, Granny Sweeney, used to hold on to things, lest she fall.

He is not a well man. And that raises a question. Would Vladimir Putin, knowing that he has not long to live, kill us all?

Chapter Twenty

This Ends in Blood

How does this end? What will some kind of peace look like? What will Ukraine accept? And what kind of endgame could Vladimir Putin live with? Or will there be the ultimate unhappy ending as a dying man hits the nuclear red button?

The Kremlin goon show takes place nightly on Russian state TV. What you see is a host of voices, arguing, sometimes passionately, with one another. No one ever says Putin is a crook and a poisoner; no one ever mentions Navalny by name. It's a rigidly controlled circus, the ringmaster watching from the shadows, waiting for one of the clowns to crash the clown car in the wrong kind of way, waiting for a trapeze artist to let out an off-message scream as she falls to earth. Some of the time, if the light slants the right way, the circus provides a frosted window into Vladimir Putin's soul. The chief goon is Vladimir Solovyov, Squealer in *Animal Farm* but without the charm. He loves to quote the ringmaster, Putin, from an interview he conducted back in 2018: 'What is the point of a world in which there is no Russia?' There's a second quote from Putin in the same year: 'If they start a nuclear war, we will respond. But we, being righteous people, will go straight to Heaven, while they will just croak.'

Croak. Clock the gangsterspeak. By the way, a hat-tip to Masha Gessen, who riffs on the Kremlin's media circus in the May 2022 edition of *The New Yorker.* Martin Amis has written beautifully about violence, how the person offering it knows that you don't want to go there, that every decent human instinct is to run away. That's what Putin's Squealer wants us all to do. The Ukrainians have no choice. They have nowhere else to run.

Borodyanka gives you a good clue to the chasm between Ukrainian democracy and the Kremlin goon show. A decent-sized town around forty miles north-west of Kyiv, to get there we sashayed past numberless car wrecks, shot up, each one with 'dyeti' – 'kids' – clearly written on the windscreen: war crime after war crime after war crime.

Four blocks of flats overlook the main square. One block has been demolished by a Russian air force missile. It was fired from a jet, early on in the war, as the invaders punched down from theoretically neutral Belarus through the Chernobyl radioactive zone towards Kyiv. Borodyanka was on – or, rather, in – the way. Liza Kozlenko, Mike Weiss, Alex Zakletsky and I mooch around the kids' playground, not quite taking in what we can see with our own eyes. A second block was also hit by a missile, knocking a great hole in it, but somehow the roof held so the building looks like a polo mint. It is both obscene and darkly fascinating: how on earth could that roof hold? Firemen watch while a digger moves great shards of concrete from the rubble with its bucket. They are waiting for another corpse to emerge. In the end, they recovered around forty bodies from there. It was a block of flats; it is a mass grave.

Under our guiltless feet, the playground is littered with the bits and bobs of ordinary, extraordinary people, blown two hundred and fifty feet by Russian high explosive: a kid's diary, a prize from the local school for the student, Yulia, for the best mark in a spoken English exam, a note to buy more milk.

Two out of the four blocks of flats were not smashed to bits by the Russian air force. But Russian army looters did their best, ransacking homes for money, jewellery. In one flat, there was a sweet love note from a man to his woman, pinned to a fridge. On the floor someone had laid out a bathrobe and done a shit on it. On another floor, Mike found a flat sealed off because of mines within. Liza picked up a cat, filthy, its face both calm and raging at the unknown horrors it has seen. The Russian Army has scant regard for the rules of war, or civilized behaviour, or common decency. Negotiating a truce with an army that sends missiles against a block of flats, butchering civilians, that rapes defenceless women, that loots people's homes, is not going to be easy.

Has Volodymyr Zelenskiy the chops to sell a peace deal with a killer back to his own people? He is smart. Question? How do you hold a press conference in your capital city when you are Target Number One of the entire Russian cruise missile fleet? Answer: you hold it in a metro station, several hundred feet below the surface where the mobile phones of hundreds of journalists cannot reveal your whereabouts. Dressed in his drab brown T-shirt and trousers, he ambled to a chair placed in front of the world's press in Kyiv, thanked us for being there and doing what we do, and started taking questions. Was he afraid of being killed? He knocked that back. Too many people have died, too many are risking their lives fighting, for him to worry about that.

Every now and then a metro train would idle its way through the press conference, causing Zelenskiy to stop speaking for a bit. His security eyed us all up, wolvishly, but those people always do that. In Sarajevo, in 1993, I watched Susan Sontag's production of *Waiting for Godot* in Serbo-Croat while the city was being hit with shellfire. The Zelenskiy presser was, in its way, even more dramatic, not really for the content of what he said – his voice deep, considered, reassuring – but just the very fact that he did it.

And set down this: during the early part of the war, the hardest thing for me to deal with was good friends in London and New York telling me to get out because I was a known enemy of the Kremlin. Zelenskiy got that, in spades, from Number Ten and the White House, and he replied: 'We need ammunition, not a ride.'

This was – is – his finest hour.

At the presser I had stood for quite a long time, holding up my white piece of paper with 'Jewish Chronicle' on it, and was about to give up on being allowed to ask a question when Liza pushed me into the eye of Zelenskiy's press secretary. I asked for the president's message to the Russian opposition, to the kids who hold anti-war demos and get their teeth smashed in by Moscow police, to the man who got arrested in Red Square for simply holding up a copy of *War and Peace* next to the Kyiv monument, to Navalny. He replied that he was grateful to them: 'Words are just as powerful as bombs.'

Just to knock the point home once again: in Russia I am effectively banned; there are no press conferences; the commander of the Kremlin's private army has SS flashes as tattoos. In 'Nazi' Ukraine, I, working freelance for a Jewish paper, am free to ask the president who is Jewish at a press conference (albeit five hundred feet down) about the good Russians who oppose the war and he thanks them. The philosopher Tim Snyder has invented a phrase to describe this phenomenon of the Kremlin demonizing the Ukrainians as Nazis: 'schizo-fascism' whereby fascists accuse their non-fascist victims of being fascist.

Shortly before I left Kyiv in early May I went for breakfast with journalists and film-makers Oz Katerji and Emile Ghessen. Over three full Ukrainian breakfasts, we three freelancers chewed the fat about what happens next. We all had the same sense that Russia was losing the war and the Ukrainian Army was winning it; that the big guns, the long-range artillery, especially from the Americans, would change the balance of the war against Russia; and that ordinary Ukrainians had lost it, utterly, with Russia and the Russian people, that they had seen or heard, or heard about, too many atrocities for them to accept a negotiated peace with Vladimir Putin's killing machine. More or less, we understood the Ukrainians' position and, more or less, agreed with it. I know my own red line was crossed when a Russian army unit hit Kramatorsk railway station with two Tochka-U cruise missiles when it was jam-packed with refugees.

Firing cruise missiles is akin to golf, endlessly repeating a lesson in Cartesian geometry. It is a very precise sport. Film of women and children packing Kramatorsk station as they fled the fighting in the Donbas was everywhere. The commander would have known that the target was civilian. More than fifty people died. Among the survivors was a mother with her twins. They were photographed on a hospital bed: the daughter had lost both legs, the mother one, the son none at all. The Russian Army was repeating its lesson in Cartesian geometry, in bone.

And then there is Mariupol.

God knows how many civilians have been massacred by the Russian Army in the port city by the Black Sea. There are stories of mobile crematoria vans turning corpses into ash; there are satellite photos of more and yet more mass graves. The chances that the people of Ukraine would agree to a negotiated peace, leaving some of their country permanently under Russian control, is zero or so close to zero as not worth bothering about it. Zelenskiy isn't going to try. The war is not going Russia's way, once again, because the morale of the Russian Army is poor; their logistics are rotten from the head down; their leaders are bad in both senses of the word: bad evil and bad incompetent.

So I believe that sooner rather than later the Russian Army will be defeated and Vladimir Putin will be humiliated.

Will the tsar of all the zombies take his revenge on not just the Ukrainians but us all? Just before I left Ukraine to spend some downtime with my family – I'm heading back in June – I threw a leaving-do party. My final Airbnb in Kyiv was fancy but it had a silly three-way door thingy, so that if you were in the loo or the broom cupboard you couldn't get out if the front door was open. Semyon Gluzman, the psychiatrist, was one of the first guests to arrive. Someone was stuck in the loo so I steered seventy-five-year-old Semyon into the broom cupboard, closed that door, and then a horde of Ukrainian guests bearing presents and British guests demanding alcohol arrived. I headed to the kitchen, poured drinks, and during a lull in the shouting someone said: 'Who is that knocking?'

One of the world's greatest living psychiatrists was locked in my broom cupboard. I let him out and, wry smile on his face, Semyon remarked: 'This place isn't as bad as the punishment cell in the gulag.' What was screamingly funny was that virtually every guest, certainly the British ones, needed to see a shrink. And instead he was the one who got locked up.

At liberty with a drink in his hand, did Semyon still think that Putin was sane? 'Yes. He is a psychopath. But he is sane.'

That's the seriously good news. A rational man, even a rational psychopath, does not blow up the world. The big war in Ukraine has been a catastrophe for so many innocent people, but it has also been dire for the master of the Kremlin. He chose to invade Ukraine with something like 200,000 soldiers under arms. The mathematics of war are simple. If you attack, you need more people than the defenders. One ratio is three to one. The Ukrainians had 200,000 in the army and a further 100,000 in the militarized police, etcetera, making 300,000 in all. So Russia needed 900,000, better still, one million people under arms to succeed. Instead, they invaded with 100,000 fewer soldiers than the Ukrainians had under arms. Putin's expectation was that Ukraine, divided, weak-kneed, enfeebled by gay rights and other Western nonsense, would crumble into dust.

About that, he was entirely wrong.

The Ukrainian spirit, the tractor drivers, the fire behind the mockery, makes me think that the three-to-one ratio is too low and that Putin needed a seven-to-one advantage, more than two million soldiers under arms. He had a tenth of that and he lost the Battle of Kyiv. The Battle of Donbas, at the time of writing this, early June, 2022, is not yet resolved. The Russian Army meat-grinder is making gains. The Russian Army has a massive advantage in artillery. The Ukrainians have lost 10,000 soldiers dead; the Russians 30,000, but Vladimir Putin does not care. He has plenty more fresh meat to throw into the battle. Pieties aside, the West has not yet sent Ukraine enough heavy metal to beat the Russians, so the defenders are slowly, grimly, bleeding to death, losing 100 soldiers a day.

As bad is the Russian Navy blockade of Ukraine's Black Sea ports, the ones they have not yet blown to bits. Ukraine's grain feeds much of the Middle East and Africa. If the blockade goes unchallenged by the West, Putin will win a hunger war.

Vlad Demchenko, the soldier who arrested me on the second day of the war on suspicion of me being a Russian spy, is now a lieutenant in the Ukrainian Army Volunteer Corps. At his battalion's reserve base, while his pals tried to fix a jammed chain-gun of a captured Russian armoured personnel carrier, Vlad explained why many Ukrainians call Russian soldiers 'Orcs': 'It starts from all these Tolkien movies. And Mordor. We have called Russia Mordor because Ukraine is like a green Hobbit land with peaceful people who just want to be dancing and drinking beer and enjoying their lives in the Shire. And there are these creatures who just want violence.'

Vlad believes that Ukraine will win in the end, and I agree with him. When the West finally stops dithering and sends the Ukrainians all the big guns they need, the Russian Army will start to crack. Economically, morally and, fingers crossed, militarily, Vladimir Putin is set to lose the wider war. The West can not afford to let him win.

Russia does not tolerate failure for long. My sense is that Vladimir Putin no longer properly controls the machinery of the Kremlin in the way that he did at the start of 2022. And that the Kremlin machines no longer obey their master as before. He's beginning to look like the Wizard of Oz. All we are waiting for is the little dog to pull aside the curtain, and the shrunken faker bellowing into a loudhailer will be revealed to all.

If Vladimir Putin gives the order to press the nuclear button – something Semyon Gluzman does not think he will do – I do not think that order will be carried out. The Kremlin goon show will carry on making nuclear threats, but it is important to understand that this is ambient noise. We in the West can also point to an uncomfortable geo-political reality for the Kremlin. China is a growing power. One of the future wargames the Pentagon plays features the US Army siding with Russia after China, thirsty for water and oil, invades Siberia. But why should the West help Russia against its big neighbour China, if Russia treats its much smaller neighbour with such unwarranted savagery? For far too long, the West has trembled when Putin has snarled at us. The courage of the Ukrainians has taught us an old lesson that we were in mortal danger of forgetting, that democracy must be defended, that free speech does not come free. After far too long, it feels like the West has got it and that bodes ill for the master of the Kremlin and his proxies.

The last Romanov made the same sort of mistake as Vladimir Putin has done, hopelessly overestimating the might of the Russian Army and the willingness of its serf soldiers to die for a cause no one can explain in a sentence. Nicholas II was shot dead, along with his whole family, in a basement of the Ipatiev House in Yekaterinburg in July 1918.

I predict that Vladimir Putin has not long left for this world. The rouble is being pumped up high by Russian reserves, but when the Western sanctions bite hard the Russian economy will tank and then the Russian people will rise up, again. Or one of his generals may reach for his revolver. Or one of his doctors may see to it that he never wakes up after surgery. Or he may die of a tumour triggered by too many steroids.

That Putin ends up poisoning himself is an ending fit for Shakespeare.

Fortune, turn thy wheel.

Chapter Twenty-One

Metal Fatigue

Kyiv, June 2022

She comes towards me from the thick of the funeral service, her extraordinary beauty disfigured by grief at the loss of her young soldier, killed by the Russian meat-grinder in the battle of Izium in eastern Ukraine. Roman Ratushnyi was just twenty-four, handsome, daring, and famous, before the big war, for protecting 'the mountain' – a strip of ski-runs and woods in the centre of Kyiv – from a predatory property developer close to the Ukrainian oligarch Ihor Kolomoyskyi, himself said to be the power that got Volodymyr Zelenskiy the throne. The image of the weeping beauty captures something hard and bitter about Vladimir Putin's brutal, stupid war, a moment of spiritual exhaustion at the price in Ukrainian blood of fighting the Kremlin's killing machine. But I'm a writer, not a photographer, and I don't have the cold professional steel to take the shot. She walks by me, broken by loss.

Roman's death signals that fortune's wheel seems stuck. Putin may be ill but the signs are that he's still very much alive, his grip on the Kremlin is secure or secure-ish, that the Russian monster keeps chewing up Ukrainian lives, the West is weak, Ukraine is brave but its leadership somehow less noble, and that the war grinds cruelly on.

The big picture remains that Putin is a monstrously corrupt serial killer ruling a nation through fear, whose gang invaded a country at peace in a limited yet murderous way in 2014 and then staged a big invasion in 2022. But that does not make everything in the Ukrainian garden rosy. In 2019 Roman Ratushnyi and his friends had challenged power and money in Kyiv when developers from the Dnipro-based Daytona Group LLC linked to Kolomoyskyi planned to replace the Protasiv Yar 'mountain' ski-run with fancy high-rise apartments, a scheme worth untold millions of dollars. Roman got his first death threat in June when a goon said 'I will find you and break your spine'. In August a lawyer for the developers, Andriy Smyrnov, told him to stop his protests. Roman taped the conversation:

> Smyrnov: The Presidential Administration is on side.
> Ratushnyi: You can't build there. Despite the fact that many people have tried ...
> Smyrnov: ... Roman, you underestimate these Dnipro businessmen. I'm telling you seriously.
> Ratushnyi: On the contrary, I always overestimate because ...
> Smyrnov: They will have 'the mountain' sooner or later. That's the point. Do you understand? And I don't want people shot, I don't want horror stories ... Do you understand?

A few weeks later Smyrnov becomes the deputy head of President Zelenskiy's Office for Administration. Roman goes into hiding. But even on the run, he uses his law degree to keep up the pressure and makes a public appeal to Zelenskiy to discipline Smyrnov, to no avail. But the public and Kyiv's mayor, the former boxer Vitali Klitschko, support Roman's campaign. Klitschko is no angel, but he's a good ally in a fight. Eventually the developer admits defeat, pulls the project, and Roman resurfaces, victorious. He even challenges Zelenskiy about his ominous staffer. Roman's mother, the Ukrainian poet Svitlana Povalyaeva, later tells me that Roman asked Zelenskiy: Why do you still keep Smyrnov on your team, after he threatened me? The president replied that he hired him after the threat. That answer is not good enough for those of us who care passionately about defending Ukraine's democracy. Nor is it good that since martial law was declared at the start of the big war, the country's major TV channels have been welded into one simple continuous stream where opposition MPs don't appear. One opposition MP told me: 'the problem with Zelenskiy is that he is an actor and all actors are insecure. He has a morbid fear of criticism and that's not good for a democratic politician.' Rather too many of my Ukrainian friends worry about the future, that victory might cement Zelenskiy into some kind of Napoleon Bonaparte figure. But, while the war must be won, those voices remain muted. As one wise Ukrainian friend puts it: 'Zelenskiy's shit. But, at least, he's our shit.' While it is right to clock Zelenskiy's failings, he has been a brave and good leader of a democracy defending itself in wartime; Vladimir Putin is a fascist and a war criminal.

In the battles of Kyiv and in the Donbas, Roman fought the Russian Army with the same selflessness with which he fought corruption and power in Kyiv. Like many Ukrainians, the evil of Russia's war darkens his soul. He wrote on Twitter: 'The more Russians we kill right now, the fewer will be left for our children to kill.' In 2021 the United States banned Kolomoyskyi from entering the country, citing the threat to Ukrainian democracy posed by his corruption. One month after Roman is killed, Zelenskiy strips Kolomoyskyi of his Ukrainian citizenship. But the president doesn't show up for Roman's funeral. It is bleak beyond words.

'You didn't build a house, but you formed a community,' says his father, Taras Ratushnyi. Roman is buried in a closed casket, his injuries too severe for the public to see his body.

'You didn't plant a tree, you saved the park,' his father carries on, trying to hold back the tears.

One of his pals, Vakhtang Kipiani, the editor of the *Historical Truth* website, writes: 'Roman Ratushnyi was my personal hope for change in the city and the country. The Russians killed that hope.'

Kharkiv, eastern Ukraine, June 2022

The Russian Army is fifteen miles away, if that. The Russian border is only twenty-five miles distant. It's one o'clock in the morning. I'm hanging out with my pals who have come along for the ride: Max Lenov, the owner of the Buena Vista bar in Kyiv, his friend Vovo, who teaches physics at Kyiv Poly, Matej and Tomas, two journalists from Slovakia. Max has brought along some Scotch and we're counter-attacking the bottle hard when: incoming. They hit the city forty times that night.

In the morning we have breakfast and then go looking for what the Russian Army has destroyed. At the first bombsite, a Russian 'Hurricane' missile has hit a block of flats. The Hurricane is half-shell, half-rocket, punching higher than Mount Everest, then falling to earth with a bang. It clipped the top of one block of flats, before frying dozens of cars in a car park, flipping one onto its back like a turtle, and blasting a hole in the tarmac as deep as an upended coffin. Amazingly, no one is killed.

At a second bombsite, we come across a salon, Beauty Home. On a wall is a picture of a stylized Ukrainian beauty gazing at you, her shoulders bare; behind it the rest of the salon has been blasted to bits. A digger shovels the rubble out of the road. The Ukrainians have a thing about making the place tidy as soon as possible – grace under pressure.

At a third bombsite, the missile plunges into a dirt road, smashing windows, masonry and roofs, digging a hole so deep you could lose a bus in it. The missile hits a water-main which bursts, creating a pond at the end of the lane. Alla, in her sixties, is sleeping in her pretty wooden cottage when the missile blasts the road, much of her front garden and greenhouse to kingdom come. She is saved by the two wooden doors between her and the Kremlin's heavy metal. Her father, Leonid, in his eighties, spent his whole life working in the Soviet rocket industry, so this, he says, is a present from his former work colleagues.

To talk with them, I have to walk over broken glass, splintered wood and blasted herbs. I say that Putin has left them a new fishpond. 'It's not just Putin's fault,' replies Alla. 'Along with him, there are too many other people, other criminals.' Alla's thoughts echo Roman Ratushnyi's. Hatred of all Russians is now a common reaction in Ukraine, that not just Putin but the Russian people too are monsters. This happened during the Second World War in Britain. To begin with people hated Hitler but not the Germans. As the war dragged on and more and more lives were lost, sympathy for the German people started to wither.

I believe, passionately, that there is another Russia. But all the good Russians I know who fought the Kremlin have been poisoned, shot, jailed, fallen from high windows or have fled – so who is left? When Ukrainians – bombed, blasted, their friends and lovers killed – call all Russians monsters, I disagree, but my minority report seems more feeble by the day.

The bleak news is that Russia still trembles under Putin's boot. Bleaker yet, as he spills so much blood in Ukraine, as he generates hatred of all Russians, as the idea of another Russia recedes into the gloom, it feels like he's winning. In Kharkiv, having seen enough civilian targets smashed to bits, we go towards the front line, get blocked at a Ukrainian Army checkpoint, then I call someone who I've only met on social media.

Sarah Ashton-Cirillo is an American reporter and writer who moved to Kharkiv in March 2022 and now lives in Saltivka, the most dangerous suburb of the city, from where she commutes to Zolochiv, a big village only seven miles from the Russian border, where she is a kind of deputy mayor. Simply by filming and writing what she sees every day, she is a hero of our time. Sarah is trans, originally from Las Vegas, and hated by the Kremlin. When the Russian Foreign Ministry spokesman Maria Zakharova slagged her off, saying she was the trans from Las Vegas who hung out with gangsters – meaning the Ukrainian Army – she became a local hero overnight.

My Slovak pals and I pile into Sarah's tiny car and, with Max and Vovo following, we sail through the Ukrainian Army checkpoints out of Kharkiv, keeping the Russian Army to the right. Once again, I am struck by the otherness of war.

In the middle of a wide road lies a van, skewed across the asphalt. Compared to Kyiv, which is almost but not quite back to pre-war normal, Kharkiv is nigh-on empty. You can get killed by a Russian cruise missile anywhere in Ukraine but the odds are pretty remote. Russian artillery is good for fifteen miles to twenty miles, so Putin's killing machine is too close for comfort to Ukraine's second city. A million people have fled. We drive along empty streets, past apartment blocks burnt to a crisp and smashed coffee shops. The big Russian shells produce a pressure wave so great that they flip cars onto their backs like toys. Sarah points out yet another car-turtle, this one having been back-flipped onto the top of a garage.

Living where she does, doing what she does, Sarah is taking serious risks daily. People think I'm crazy, but she's crazy-crazy. She laughs and replies: 'I'm a writer. And sometimes we get caught up in moments that we know will never come again. I came here to write about refugees. I had never experienced war before. And then all of a sudden overnight, I became a war journalist. That's the only way to put it. And I guess my personality, as a student of Hemingway, Orwell, Gellhorn, understood what this meant. And so I just tried to put out of my mind what it is beyond the fact that I'm covering the story. And I am, you know, and I've made it clear to my readers as early as March that they were not going to be getting equal coverage. They were going to be getting the facts. But the facts were already established by that point, I had seen the horror of what Russia had been doing.'

I cut in: 'It's not equal. I'm saying this as a former BBC journalist, there is no duty of impartiality to fascism. This is like 1939–45. And to see it any differently is entirely and utterly wrong. Full stop. These people were at peace. They're not Nazis at all.' Sarah and I then hit the road, driving out of the city towards the rolling countryside, towards the war.

How do Ukrainians deal with the fact that she is trans?

'They don't care,' Sarah says. 'I told the BBC, when they interviewed me, it's better to be trans here than in the United States. We're focused on freedom, democracy and liberty.'

Back in 1988, I tell Sarah, I went undercover to Prague and hung out with the Czech opposition: Vaclav Havel, funny, wry, a chain-smoker with a terrible cough, like Mr Wheezy from *Toy Story*, within a year about to go from disgraced dissident jailbird to president; Jerry Djientsbier, his sidekick and loyal ally; and the writer Ludvik Vaculik, who, with his gorgeous irony, used to annoy the secret police. He wrote: 'Human wisdom is about respect for the beautiful, the unobtainable and simply the different.' That respecting the other – people like Sarah – is what Ukraine is fighting for, along with the other stuff. And Vladimir Putin will never understand this, but the side that looks after the other is never, ever, going to give up.

As we drive, a slow, sad sound comes off the road. Many tanks have been this way and their metal tracks have bit into the asphalt so that when our tyres hit the corrugations they create a song, like whales at sea. I last heard this tank music in former Yugoslavia and start thinking about my dead friend Paul Jenks . . .

The land is a frozen ocean, long rolling waves of black earth breaking in ridges, three miles apart. The first ridge to our right is held by the Ukrainian Army. The next one along is in Russian hands. Occasionally we see a plume of grey smoke rise up, where a shell has started a fire in the cornfields. We stop and plan to walk a little way towards the front line. For the first time in months I put on my flak jacket with punishingly heavy plates, front and back, and carry my helmet, just in case. Max looks up where we are on the map showing the front lines and elects not to go on this particular walk. He kept the Buena Vista open throughout the battle of Kyiv when martial law forbade the sale of alcohol, so he's no coward. Sarah takes us up a muddy track for fifteen minutes. She shows us two Russian armoured personnel carriers and a Russian tank, their heavy metal burnt yellow. The Ukrainians buried two Russian soldiers in a simple grave, marked by a stick. We record a video diary for my Twitter, @johnsweeneyroar, sending Vladimir Putin a simple message: 'Do Fuck Off!' But the melancholy of the little grave stays with us as we walk back to our cars.

In Zolochiv, seven miles from the Russian border, you can feel the weight of the enemy next door. Sarah has used her rock-star status to help the community: 'We've brought thousands of pounds of food, significant quantities of medicine, gas masks, bulletproof vests. We've also worked to get the International Red Cross here.' She shows us the smashed-up remains of the little community hospital. The Russian gunners tried to finish the job but their aiming was off, so they hit a house. She explains: 'Three people died, they were dismembered. They found a head and two different legs.'

Beyond the rubble, a child plays on a swing. Some people are so poor they can't afford the expense of being a refugee, so they stay and live or die. Some are poor and mad. Fifty villagers have been killed. At least one or two people here are telling the Russian gunners their aim is off. That is, there are spies active in the village, telling the Russians where to shoot. Perhaps they are watching us. Here, at the sharp end, you don't feel safe. Because you are not.

We stumble across a puppy and I give it some water. Sarah picks it up and puts it in her helmet. Then its frantic owner appears and a sweet moment when we kind of forgot about the war is snuffed out.

The next day Max, Vovo and I drive across half the country, from the east to the capital. In early evening, as the sun starts to dip, just as we hit Kyiv there is news that a Russian cruise missile has struck a shopping mall in Kremenchuk. Max and I head there: it's five hours by road back the way we had just come. We arrive the next morning.

A jackhammer is smashing into some concrete so rescuers can get at the human remains beneath. A gaggle of firemen are sifting through the wreckage. Flesh and fat vaporize; bones survive the heat. Not everything is destroyed: the remains of a cash machine, some books, paperwork that withstood the fire; a filing cabinet. Pretty much everything else is charred black. They hit the mall with an X-22 missile, chock-full of technology from 1962.

I'm recording for the final episode of my podcast, 'Taking On Putin', and the smoke and pong of death get to me. My eyes close and I say: 'You send a rocket that old here to a city of 200,000 people. It's very likely that you're gonna kill a whole bunch of innocent people and that's what happened. Dear God, God, I'm sorry. I can't find the fucking words.' Psychologically, the problem is I saw something like this before in Chechnya twenty-two years ago, and again in 2014 with the shooting-down of MH17. The bad vibrations of Putin's killing machine get through to you.

There's a line in John Le Carré's great Cold War thriller, *The Spy Who Came in from the Cold*, when Control asks Alec Leamas whether he's tired of spying, 'metal fatigue, I think the term is?' Leamas soldiers on and goes back east. But he has metal fatigue. After almost a year of war, so has Ukraine. So do I . . .

I catch up with my old friend Vlad 'Vova' Demchenko, the soldier who arrested me on Day Two of the war for perhaps being a Russian spy. He's now a sergeant in the Ukrainian Army Volunteer Corps. I ask Vlad for his reaction to a letter from twenty German intellectuals calling for Ukraine pretty much to throw in the towel. He replies: 'I'm tired of these people. It's bizarre. My house was occupied by Russia for a couple of months. So literally, some German idiot is proposing for me to make peace with somebody who took my home away. Fuck you. I'm so angry at this moment.'

I tell him about Alla looking at Putin's fishpond at the end of the lane, saying it's not just Putin, it's the Russians too. Does he agree with her? He does, very much so: 'The Russian opposition are not fighting.' But Vlad is vexed by Western timidity too: 'Western countries already forgot their history. They forgot those times when they fought for their freedoms. They lose connection to reality. We are suffering from fucking murderers, maniacs. There is a war between an autocratic dictatorship and the free world and Ukraine really wants to be a part of this free world. And when I hear from somebody in the free world, telling us that we should give up, I really doubt this free world exists, to be honest.'

The war has changed. Russia lost the battle of Kyiv because it threw too few soldiers at the Ukrainian capital, they lacked a good reason to fight, their logistics were rubbish, their leaders bad, incompetent and evil. But then Putin adapted to reality, pulling his forces out of the north, putting them in the east where the Russian Army's advantages in artillery and manpower paid off. Slowly, pitilessly, the Russian meat-grinder has advanced and far too many good Ukrainians are dying, and that, too, feels like a victory for Putin.

Vlad Demchenko fears that as the price of oil and gas rises, and Russia blockades Ukrainian grain from reaching the developing world, the West will chicken out, a frozen peace will be unjustly enforced on Ukraine and, later, Putin will switch his killing machine back on: 'I'm afraid that my life now, it's the life of the soldier and I don't choose this destiny for myself but I see that what we expect to receive from the Western world is just not enough. So my prognosis is that they will freeze this war at the end of this year, and Vladimir Putin will be winning. Do you know, John, since the 24th of February, more than twenty people I know have been killed? Most of them between twenty and thirty years old, smart people, nice, funny. I don't even count those who were wounded, who lose their legs, who have shrapnel in their bodies.'

The day after this interview one of the guys in Vlad's battalion was killed and it was his duty to inform the family. The metal fatigue in this war is real. So is moral fatigue. There is no sign that the Kremlin's lie factory is shutting up shop and that worries Vlad greatly.

'The worst part of this, John, is actually that Putin is using your strengths against you by paying his puppets.'

Vlad sees more division in the West, encouraged and paid for by the Kremlin. His own future looks grim: 'I have one life here in this world. And why should I spend it fighting some idiots who just don't want me to live how I want? I don't care about Europe, Ukraine, Russia. Just my human feeling of responsibility. I don't feel it's right to let them do this shit, that's all. It wasn't my choice but somehow I read too many romantic books when I was a kid.'

He fears that the West is placing comfort above courage: 'The values of the Western world? Oil and gas and comfort, not freedom and free speech and liberty. It's like, I want to be in warm house.' I share his frustration with those who don't understand the true nature of our common enemy. Putin has gambled, once again, on the West's love of comfort, on our timidity, our greed. The war in Ukraine is a warning, that any attempt to appease Putin is foolish because he will take and take and take again. If the Ukrainians lose, then he will come for us.

The only thing to do is to stop him, dead. Before the metal fatigue breaks us all.

Chapter Twenty-Two

Bad Days at Bakhmut

Donbas, August 2022

Slagheaps and winding gear clunk against the horizon as we drive east, towards Donetsk, Vlad Demchenko riding shotgun, me in the back, the three of us belting out 'This'll be the day that I die' from *American Pie* on Occichone's car stereo, though we're not going 'to the levee in a Chevy' but Bakhmut, a ghost city smack bang on the front line. The land here rises and falls like the Atlantic on a calm day. We stop on a down-wave, see the city about two miles off and listen.

Occichone is a New Yorker, officially cynical, mock crass. He pretends to hate humanity. A photographer who came for a month in 2014 to report on the war, he never left.

During COVID, Vlad hitchhiked from Ukraine to Namibia. After he arrested me for being a Russian spy, we became friends and I suggested he join Twitter and asked my followers to follow him. He now has 70,000 followers. He consumes books, dreams of travelling again and directing films, has the willpower, sense of the absurd, an eye for a shot, and enough charisma to make it to Hollywood. For now, he kills Russian soldiers.

Crump. Crump. Crump. 'Outgoing?' I ask Vlad. 'Incoming.'

He explains that outgoing artillery has a simple coherent sound, a plop, but incoming is longer, stretched out, like a fart. There's ten farts for every plop. Given Russia's massive heft in heavy metal, Bakhmut is not a safe place. We drive on as dusk falls, the electricity dead, the darkness of a city that once held 100,000 people even more intense because of the occasional very loud bang, echoing, re-echoing in the concrete canyons of what was, once, a prosperous Soviet mining city atop coal and gypsum fields. Here and there are a few ironic points of light, signalling the stay-behinds. Bakhmut is creepy with a capital C. The western end of Patrice Lumumba Street is held by the Ukrainians; the eastern end by the Russian Army.

We call it a night and drive back to Kostyantynivka through a few checkpoints where Vlad, as an officer in the Ukrainian Volunteer Corps, reads out the passwords from his cellphone. Our quarters are a gloomy ground-floor flat. There's electricity but no water. Two Ukrainian Army soldiers are already there, Valentin and Vasyl. Their job is to put up CCTV cameras to spy on Russian movements and shelling. The cameras are powered by large solar panels, making them a sitting duck for Russian heavy metal. The cameras give a 24/7 view of the front line.

There's a ban on alcohol at the front. On brand, I've brought a bottle of Italian red and a half-bottle of Jameson's, but I don't open my stash. There's some weed but, as usual, I end up coughing pathetically. Bed is a couch in the room where two computer monitors are set up to look at the CCTV cameras. Every time a Russian shell lands, the monitors flash brilliant white, with the distant heavy bass of shells landing in Bakhmut. During the night, two massive bangs, outgoing. No one stirs.

In the morning I go for a swim in a lake on the other side

of town. Breaststroke to the sound of heavy artillery is quite the thing. We then head to Bakhmut again. War degrades everything – humanity, civilization, personal hygiene – but especially roads. Since the first Russian invasion, the one in 2014, no one worth their asphalt has been down here, so driver Occichone sashays to the other side of the road to skirt deep potholes, all the more scary because he is driving a British Mitsubishi. It's nice to drive on the British side of the road – in Britain. Making a contract with certain death is eased by singing along to Dylan's *Like a Rolling Stone.*

In daylight I can see the damage better, blocks of flats, schools and techs smashed up, mortar splashes on the road, homes burnt black. The wind lifts grit in small dust storms. Bakhmut is not quite empty. The rich and the middle class have fled, leaving the poor, the old, the little bit mad and the disabled.

Although Occichone says he hates people, he's friends with Olena. She is proof of the aristocracy of the human soul. She's been disabled for ages and is wheelchair-bound but feisty and funny. The Russian shells pile in, never too close, never far away. The electricity is off so she can't use her computer to talk to the outside world.

'Why do you stay?' I ask.

'I think the Ukrainian Army will stay strong. Also I cannot leave because too many people need me.'

Occichone takes Olena's picture as I stand with a light trained on her face. I was once all for giving money to Ukrainian charities, but not for weapons. I have changed my mind. Vlad is going to raise some money for Olena and her friends, but now I've seen the front line close-up the best thing to do is to buy the Ukrainians tanks and big guns to chase the Russian killing machine out of artillery range.

We say our goodbyes and take a turn through the city. In the middle of town, a Russian rocket crashed into the central market area creating a vast crater. They knew exactly what they were doing. You want to empty a city of 100,000 people, you smash its heart. Still, there's a kebab shop and a kiosk selling Coke.

We scoot around town and stop outside a technical school smashed to pieces. For my video diaries on Twitter, I bring Vlad in and explain that he and I have a continuing argument. I believe there is another Russia, one without Putin, and that this is Putin's war. Wearing his Ukrainian Army floppy hat and sunnies, Vlad replies: 'Vladimir Putin came and pushed the button and . . .' He points to the great gaping hole in the tech college. He says Russian opinion polls give Putin an 80 per cent approval rating. 'Yeah but,' I reply, 'I don't trust Russian opinion polls.' Still, the rubble makes Vlad's point for him.

The shelling seems to ease off during the day. It's never wholly quiet but its intensity has dropped. The next morning we hear that Alexander Dugin's daughter, Darya, has been blown up by a car bomb in Moscow. Dugin is a fascist who called for Ukrainians to be killed. He is known as 'Putin's brain' and 'Putin's Rasputin', because the master of the Kremlin has adopted his far-right ethno-nationalism as his own. When in 2016 I asked him what the murder of Boris Nemtsov meant for Russian democracy, Dugin riled at my 'completely stupid kind of conversation', ripped off his sound-mike and walked out of the interview. Later, he blogged that I was 'a notorious bastard! An utter cretin . . . globalist swine.'

As a human being I felt sorry for the loss of his daughter. But like her father, Darya was a fascist. She had visited Mariupol and rejoiced at the killing of Ukrainians. Vlad's reaction to the news was harder. He was delighted at the killing and believed the Ukrainians were responsible.

As the story developed, the car bombing became murkier yet. It's entirely possible that the killers were some faction of the Russian secret state. At the funeral Dugin behaved in a very strange way, showing no grief for his daughter. The casket lay open and her face seemed to be untouched by the car bomb. When a bomb goes off, it ignites the oxygen all around. In the small space inside a car, you would expect someone's face to be burnt. As all the truth-tellers in Russia have either been poisoned, shot, fled the country or are in jail, it's hard to know what happened. But it felt odd, heading off to the front line again, that we were all alive and kicking yet Dugin's daughter had been blown up.

We head for Patrice Lumumba Street and take selfies of the three of us with The Art Winery vineyard in the background, partly burnt out. In a gloomy shop on the corner Marina, middle-aged, sweet-faced, laments her losses. She has built up her fortunes from nothing, formerly selling wine to Moscow, making so much money that she has two shops and two homes in Bakhmut. Our conversation is punctuated by crumps of artillery, pounding home her present misfortune. Sure, she hasn't lost family, her sight, a leg or arm, but the sense of a good life of hard work smashed to pieces by an evil she is powerless to stop is saddening. I tell her that I am some kind of professor of smashed-up places, and that my advice is she should get out. She listens, nods, but, as far as I know, has stayed put.

In the afternoon, Vlad suggests we visit a trench. He says to get to it there's a 700-metre walk across open ground that the Russians might shell. I take a deep breath and say yes. We drive south of Bakhmut, along empty potholed roads, crumps landing here and there, and hit the crest of a hill where we hide the car under some trees and find a trench system. From there, 'Lego', a big bearded man with Ukrainian Army camouflage and a skull patch, leads the way downhill. Occichone, Vlad and I wear our helmets and body armour. To make the point that I'm a writer not a fighter, I have blue flowers embroidered onto my flak jacket. It's hot and the walk down the hill is exposed with no proper cover. Occichone tells me to hang back so we are all ten metres apart, lest a shell knocks us out in one go. Spread out, the survivors can help the wounded. My mouth dries up.

As we near the trench system, 'Lego' points out two shallow craters, about ten feet wide, caused by a tank shell the day before. There is also a rocket with tailfin intact, embedded into the scenery, yet another Russian armament that didn't go off.

The trench system is about halfway up the hill, overlooking a lake, woods, a railway line. It's like being in a time machine, dialled to 1917. The formal Russian front line is about five miles away, but one of the soldiers, 'Nightingale', tells me from his lookout position that the Russians have been mucking about in the woods just the other side of the railway line. That's a thousand yards away, less. I make some films for my Twitter followers, someone hands me a cup of tea, and Occichone takes my photograph. Vlad tells me that my cup says in Ukrainian 'Best Grandma', and Occichone says I could be a grandma if I wanted to. It's what the Ukrainians are fighting for.

A lovely old soldier, Botsman, is the trench butler, kind of. He has few teeth but his English is really good. With his knife he opens a British-funded ration pack decorated with a Union Jack. In it are coffee, premium hot dogs, chocolate, drink, cake, nuts and bacon, something to purify the water and a fork. 'God Save The Queen,' I say, and Botsman replies: 'God Shave The Queen.'

As we talk a helicopter flies very low over our trench. 'Ukrainian,' says Botsman. It's on a mission to hit Russian artillery on the backside of the next ridge east, but it misses and comes zooming back so low you can almost touch the blades. The Russian choppers don't bother our friends. In Kostyantynivka, I see four Ukrainian jets and Vlad explains that the Russian fighter jets always stay their side of the line, firing at Ukrainian positions from relative safety. But the five aircraft I saw at the front were Ukrainian and that does not bode well for Putin.

The morale of Lego, Botsman, Nightingale, Vlad, Valentin and Vasyl is extraordinary. They face artillery that fires at them ten times for every shell their side fires back, but their spirit is great, full of humanity and humour. When I read people like former British general Sir Richard Dannatt and the *Mail On Sunday*'s Peter Hitchens calling on the Ukrainians to pack it in, I scratch my head. At the front line, the Ukrainian Army has the best morale I have ever seen in an army. I hereby invite Dannatt and Hitchens to come and see for themselves.

I leave the boys in the trenches lifted by the experience but saddened, too, that something both my grandfathers, Herbert Sweeney and Stephen Owen, thought would never happen again – trench warfare in Europe – is killing people in this century. A line from Wilfred Owen comes to mind: 'I, too, saw God through mud – The mud that cracked on cheeks when wretches smiled.'

August 24th is Ukrainian Independence Day, but it's also Vlad's birthday and the boys make him 'cake' by ramming a candle into a Toblerone packet. Valentin and Vasyl sing Happy Birthday and a Ukrainian shanty. Vlad is thirty-four and has been fighting the Russians for eight years. He blows out the candle on his 'cake' with all the bashful fun of a seven-year-old boy.

Occichone and I head off to Bakhmut one last time, while Vlad stays at the base. The Russian Army is celebrating Ukrainian Independence Day by smashing the city. We see smoke and come to a stop by a wooden cottage on fire after a Russian shell demolished the tin roof. Thankfully, the cottage is empty. The Bakhmut fire brigade are hard at work putting out the fire, but a small knot of people are watching them. A middle-aged man arrives on a bike and joins them. His mother owns the cottage. The people are cold to the firemen, to the Ukrainian soldier with us, to Occichone and me. The soldier is wearing a camouflage jacket with a Union Jack flash on it and they accuse him of buying a British passport. He's very happy with his Ukrainian passport but explains that the people have been brainwashed by Russian propaganda, that they think the Ukrainians may have blown up the cottage.

Polls show that 97 per cent of people are happy that Ukraine got its independence from the Soviet Union. We have just met some of the 3 per cent. It leaves a sour taste in my mouth but perhaps it was just ash from the Russian fire. Vlad says: 'Some locals, mostly people over forty-five, have no reference points in life, except for the myths and legends of the USSR. They live in a past that never existed in reality. But they were young then and life was beautiful. Russia promises to resurrect their childhood together with the corpse of the USSR.'

On his birthday Vlad posts a story on Twitter about Olena asking his followers for money to support her and her wheelchair posse. So far, he's raised $3,000. The difference between the Ukrainian Army and the Russian Army is one of good versus evil.

Chapter Twenty-Three

From Russia Without Love

Kyiv, October 2022

A cruise missile flies low at roughly the speed of a jetliner, around 500 mph, the difference being no one claps when it touches down. On Monday, 10 October, the Russians fire 100 missiles and drones at Ukraine at eight a.m. The swarm attack overwhelms the air-defence system and four cruise missiles hit Kyiv, three in the centre, one at a power station on the outskirts. The Ukrainian capital has not been bombed for months so the city is unprepared. Me, too. While walking to my local café, I see a woman journalist leave her flat wearing a flak jacket and helmet, and I mentally tick her off for being a scaredy-cat. Fool, Sweeney, fool.

In the café I start scrolling through Twitter and see a photo of a missile exploding just by Taras Shevchenko Park, the loveliest little open space in downtown Kyiv. I get an e-scooter and whizz along Yaroslaviv Val, Kyiv's version of the King's Road, and smell the unforgettable pong of burnt fuel, scalded asphalt, fried meat. I recognize that stink from former Yugoslavia, Iraq, Afghanistan. I never expected it in Kyiv. At the start of Vladimir Putin's big war, the Russians got to twelve miles from the centre, but this is the first time the heart of the city has been hammered.

Past Golden Gate, I turn right and get as close to the horror as the police tape allows. The rocket has moon-cratered a crossroads, very central. Three cars had just cleared the traffic lights. The inferno has baked the paint on the cars charcoal. Further back sit a number of cars, unbaked, their metal in ribbons, scissored by shrapnel, doors left open by fleeing passengers. Windows of buildings lining the street, gone, socketless. Underfoot, shards of glass mirror the cold sun. Blankets cover the remains of someone's mother or son.

A second missile lands on the children's playground in the park, pulverizing a carousel, littering great meat-hooks of shrapnel amidst the swings and rope ladders at 500 mph. Fedir Balandin rushes to the scene to rescue kids but, thank God, no one is badly hurt.

A mile away a third rocket crashes into a house just opposite the Samsung Tower, blasting the windows of the skyscraper and a block of flats. In the yard, a graveyard of motor cars, bonnets and boots slashed by shrapnel. A bald young man, Konstantin, vainly tries to open his car's bonnet to see if the battery is salvageable. 'I should have been here in the yard but I was running late . . .' he grins. I tell him that for the rest of his life, if he's late for work, it's OK, and we laugh at the monstrous absurdity of war.

A young mother, Kseniya Kostyuk, disfigured with a great plaster on her chin where she was hit by shrapnel, hurries to pack her kids' toys. Her children are in their new place but she hates being parted from them. They were in bed when the rocket hit but, miraculously, though the windows were blown in, they were unhurt. The next floor up, Natalia

Gegelya, a sweet old lady, shows us her kitchen carpeted with broken glass, a Roman statue smashed to bits, and a monstrous bruise on her shin where she was knocked sideways by the frame of her balcony window blowing in on top of her.

'Do you think Ukraine should cut a peace deal with Russia?' I ask Natalia. 'Are you kidding?' she replies. Every single Ukrainian I ask that day gives the same answer.

Kristina Ratushnaya translates for us. At the end of a long day we interview her mum and dad. They are originally from Mariupol, were bombed out, fled for safety to Zaporizhzhia, were bombed out again, and arrived in Kyiv the night of 9 October, before the missile attacks next morning. Her dad, Sasha, jokes: 'All my friends say, why don't you move to Moscow?'

The big war is not going well for the Russians. They lost the battle of Kyiv in April, Kharkiv Oblast in September, and are losing ground in Kherson in the south and Donbas in the east. But the fear is that Vladimir Putin, humiliated by the Ukrainian Army, may be tempted to use a tactical nuclear weapon. The mood in Kyiv is grim. The joke in the city is that as soon as Putin gives the order to nuke, everyone will go to a hill for the orgy.

Time to hit the road, head to the front line, see the war for myself. I am working with Julia Frances, an Anglo-Ukrainian film-maker, and Dima Kovalchuk, fixer, driver, diplomat. Young people have no taste in music, some say, but after nightfall as we drive through the streets of Kharkiv, Julia puts on *The Sound of Silence* and we drone along to 'Hello darkness my old friend . . .'

There's always a bar somewhere. In Kyiv, the Buena Vista. In Kharkiv, the Irish pub where we bump into my old friends, Matej and Tomas from Slovakia, who filmed me last time in

Kharkiv with Sarah Ashton-Cirillo, the trans woman the Kremlin loves to hate. I order red wine and fish and chips.

Next morning is sunny. Julia's cousin is fighting in an army unit in Vovchansk, close to the Russian border. The boys ask us to buy some sushi for them, so we head due east, into the sun. We stop at a petrol station for fuel and hot dogs. We are commuting to war.

The closer you get to the front line, the more everything degrades. Electricity fails; phone masts don't work, you lose internet connection; the roads have been so cut up by tanks and artillery lorries that you bump, swish, bang along muddy tracks for hours.

Soft crumps in Vovchansk from enemy artillery, but the Russians have retreated to the other side of the border, their heart isn't in it. Or they are running out of ammo to prosecute this heavy-metal artillery war. We listen to the puffs and thumps from the other side, eat sushi on a car bonnet, crack jokes.

'Lang' – Ukrainian soldiers like nicknames – takes us to an abandoned Russian trench. There's a pigsty of rubbish by a checkpoint, a sleeping bag, a zigzag of trenches walled with mud. I had visited a Ukrainian trench in Bakhmut in August. That had wooden panelling for the trenches, well-fortified firing positions, a kitchen, and a concrete bunker for the boys to sleep in. Marks out of ten? Nine for the Ukrainian trench; four for the Russian trench. 'Lang' – an archaeologist before the war – is pessimistic about how long the war will last: 'Maybe two, maybe three years.'

A long drive back to Kharkiv, fish and chips, red wine, sleep. The next morning, petrol, hot dogs, and then the road to Bakhmut, which I had last visited in August. I'm no masochist. Russian social media and their useful idiots in the West insist that the Ukrainian Army is on the backfoot in Bakhmut. For me to go there, report and come back alive is living proof that the Russian claims are pie in the sky.

It's Sunday and we're in luck. The Wagner Army, the private mercenary outfit run by Evgeny Prigozhin, gangster-cum-chef close to Putin, hold the Russian end of the front line due east. Their artillery is having a slow day. Consistent bangs but not frantically so; the heft of firepower directed not at the town centre but at Ukrainian Army positions further east. We don helmets and flak jackets, drive towards a mostly destroyed bridge over the river. We park the car, film civilians edging along a makeshift river crossing of broken concrete. The downed bridge is open to the eastern sky, Russian snipers and artillery spotters, so it's not safe. We scurry back but on the way are hailed by a local woman living on the sixth floor of a block of flats. The lady and I shout to each other while Dima translates and Julia films. 'Everything is good,' she yells in Russian as some bangs come in and some go out. To me, she seems not a little bit mad.

The centre of a city of some 100,000 people is now a theme park to the pitiless inhumanity of the master of the Kremlin and his zombified people. Since my last visit in August, more rubble, broken glass, burnt metal. Artillery rounds snap, crackle and pop. A breeze picks up and broken metal joists clang in the wind. Stray dogs run to and fro. I'm scared but try not to show it.

The electricity is off but a shop is open, lit by candlelight. Julia buys crisps and starts chatting to a local woman in Russian. 'Why don't you leave?' Julia asks. 'I don't want to go to Ukraine,' she replies to Julia's astonishment. Nearly all of the pro-Ukrainian majority have fled to the relative safety of Kyiv or elsewhere. The stay-behinds in Bakhmut are very few, maybe three per cent of the population, but almost all are pro-Russian, middle-aged or elderly, very poor, Soviet-minded.

We film an interview with a soldier and then zoom out of town to live another day. We are stopped at a checkpoint, a *blokpost*, and the Ukrainian cops detain us for a few minutes, saying we should not have entered the war zone without the correct local press office paperwork, stamped. I don't have that. I do have accreditation from the Ukrainian Ministry of Defence but, foolishly, not a hardback copy of this book, *Killer in the Kremlin*, which sometimes helps with tricky *blokposts*.

At Izium, where Roman Ratushnyi was killed in June, we film a beautiful old school, half-intact, half-fried; a broken shopping centre; a coffee shop, shredded with shrapnel; home after home charred, broken.

Back to the Irish pub in Kharkiv for fish and chips, red wine and a surprise. While we were in Bakhmut, we were spotted by Vlad 'Vova' Demchenko and his pal Valentin. They were in town and saw us but had no time to stop. But now, heading somewhere else, they go out of their way to greet us at the Irish pub. We pose for a selfie and yell my catchphrase: 'Vladimir Putin: Do Fuck Off!'

Monday: fuel at the petrol station, hot dogs, groundhog days. Dima phones the local press office, asking for the correct paperwork. They tell us they can't supply it today but we should proceed and try our luck. We drive south-east to Kupiansk, liberated in September. Another bridge is down; homes pock-holed with artillery; the onion dome of a church smashed; the road surface blasted. Onwards, to Dvorichna, a small town on a bluff overlooking the plain eastward. On the other side of yet another blown-up bridge is a big forest where the Russian Army lurks, five miles away, less. In no man's land a grain elevator is on fire, pumping black smoke into the blue sky. The locals say it has been burning for three days but we can't go there.

The war here seems nothing like as intense as in Bakhmut. The countryside is wide open, spacious, the views from the bluff above the town glorious. Big chunks of time pass with no bangs at all; then suddenly you're in trouble. My flak jacket, stuffed with two ceramic plates, and helmet, are cumbersome to wear, but the Russians are closer than we think. Just in front of the eastern-facing town hall, we start filming an interview with Dima Stoyanov, a handsome, steady middle-aged man with strikingly intense eyes. He managed the local bin-collection service when the Russian invasion started. Suddenly a Russian shell lands, 500 metres away, maybe less. 'Get the flak jackets,' I bark and we retreat to the western side of the town hall. Its five stories provide some shelter.

Dima's account is grim. He was a target because he told the Russians what he thought of them: 'Not that fairy tale they were saying about denazification and demilitarization. I told them they are occupiers, that they have invaded our land. They didn't like that.' They didn't bother him at first but then they told him to disband his Ukrainian business and set up a Russian company. He refused, so they threw him out of his own office at gunpoint. After a couple of weeks, in late July, they came to his house, cuffed him, put a bag over his head, and took him to the police station in the nearest big town, Kupiansk. He was there for forty-two days.

'Late at night they took me out of the cell, put a bag on my head again and took me to the interrogation chamber. It wasn't like they were trying to find out something. They were just teaching me a lesson.'

'How did they teach you?'

'Electrode torture. Beating me black and blue. Just for you to understand, the visual evidence of the torture only faded a month later.'

'What did they use on you?'

'I couldn't see because of the bag on my head. They put something on my fingers and dialled the voltage up and down. If they could see that I'm handling the voltage, they would dial it up. They would pour water down my back to make the pain more intense. All the time, they were asking questions.'

'How did you react?'

'It was unpleasant. Put your finger in an electric socket and you will feel it. Shakes, spasms.'

'Where were your hands?'

'They were cuffed behind my back.'

'What is the effect of water?'

'Water increased the power of the electricity, so it was more painful.'

'Where did they beat you?'

'Everywhere. The whole body.'

'How long did the torture last?'

'About three hours every day during the first week.'

'What did you say to them when they were torturing you?'

'The questions were silly.'

'What kind of questions did they ask you?'

'The most revealing question was, "What's your country?" I said, "Ukraine". Then they'd beat me. If they didn't like the answer, they would dial up the voltage.'

Dima explains he was held in the cells in the Kupiansk police station. Normally there would be four prisoners to a cell, but in his there were twenty, about 150 prisoners in all, mostly men, some women. The person who was banged up for longest was the mayor of Dvorichna, Halyna Turbaba, who spent more than eighty days inside; Dima came second.

He continues: 'God knows how long we would have sat there . . . On the 7th of September in the afternoon the jailers disappeared with the Russians. Everyone vanished. There was dead silence. We never heard anything like it. We were confused, like what's going on? They didn't bring us a dinner. But it wasn't for the first time, so we thought, OK, never mind. We went to sleep. Around one o'clock in the morning on the 8th the Ukrainian Army start their counter-attack and we hear that it is close. We start banging on the cell doors, all fourteen cells. No reaction. No one is there. We are locked in. They've abandoned us. The building starts to fill with smoke. Some of our fellow prisoners in another cell smash up some bunks, knock out a window frame, and thank God they succeed. They get out, find the room where all the keys are, and unlock the cells.'

There's a big, big bang, uncomfortably close. 'Ours or theirs?' I ask Dima.

'It's Russian.'

'How far away?'

'Five hundred metres.'

'What is it?'

'Grad. Cassette bombs.'

'Anti-personnel mines?'

'Yes.'

'Fuck them.'

'Let me finish my story of us getting released. So at that moment there were about 150 people in there. If we had stayed there for another two hours, there would have been 150 corpses.'

'Who is gonna win this war?'

'According to the law of justice and to God's law, Ukraine must be the winner.'

'How long will it take?'

'I want it to end today.'

The mayor, Halyna Turbaba, is out of town until five p.m., so we drive back to Kupiansk to film the police station-cum-torture chamber. There's been heavy fighting in the area and the front of the police station is blackened with soot, the windows blown out, a wreck. But inside it's mostly intact, with fourteen cells, as Dima Stoyanov described: beds for four, bedding for twenty; pigsties of uneaten food, half-empty water bottles; a stinking latrine in each cell; feral cats slinking in the gloom; two interrogation chambers, cold and barren. In one cell, a bunk has been smashed up and one entire window frame, bars and all, knocked out. Dima's testimony is accurate in every particular. As we start to leave, a woman tells us that the Russians stole her children from day school and took them to occupied territory. She's been drinking and is unsteady on her feet but I believe her. The agony of the Russians stealing Ukrainian kids is something I fear to investigate. But, down the track, I will.

The sky to the west starts to darken as we drive back down lumpy roads to Dvorichna again. Our luck holds, for a time.

A row of houses has been blasted to kingdom come: rubble, twisted beams, blackened trees. As we film, an old lady, Tatiana, comes by, a shopping bag in her hands. I ask her what happened. 'The Russians bombed this place about a month ago. There's a woman buried here, blown up in her kitchen. Her mother got injured but she was taken to the hospital, but the woman was burnt to death. There was a house there, but now there's a hole. Not even foundation stones left.'

Artillery, incoming.

'Is this normal?' I ask.

'Sometimes, it's louder. I was going out and a shell landed near me.' She points to a big hole in the knee of her trousers.

'When was that?'

'An hour ago. There was a guy walking behind me and he got injured in the neck, so the military took him to the hospital. I was walking along the street and saw rockets flying above my head. I sat down and these soldiers come to me and say, "Why are you sitting? Lie down!" I was coming from a friend's house. Now her house has been destroyed. We go to the council every day and they help us. Free bread, water, some essentials, every day. We are not starving, they are helping us. They even gave me some sacking because I have no windows in my house.'

'Why do you stay here? It's dangerous.'

'I was born here. I learned to walk here. I went to school here. My parents and my husband are over there in the cemetery. My husband and I were in the army for thirty years together. He got injured in Afghanistan. He died five years ago. Where will I go? I was born here.'

'So you don't want to leave this town because . . . ?'

'Well, where will I go? To Kharkiv? There are lots of air-raid sirens there, no gas, sometimes even no lights and water, literally the same as here! Half of Kharkiv has been destroyed. Our village is the best in the whole Kharkiv region. We have an amazing river, amazing countryside. I don't want to go anywhere. It's scary to see what's happening here . . .' She starts to cry. 'This place was so amazing! I don't understand this war. Our guys are bombing but they know where to do that because there is a forest with Russians in it. The Russians are firing their rockets directly at our houses. Houses where people are living in, kids. My neighbour has no roof. He has four girls.'

'Did you ever imagine this would happen to your town?'

'February 24th, four a.m., I got a call from my sister. She told me to take all my stuff and to hide in the basement. My son was here at that moment – he came here because it was my birthday, my 70th. I asked my sister, what happened? She said, war. I asked, with who? She said, with Russia. I said, are you kidding? What do you mean, war with Russia? And after twenty-five minutes the tanks arrived. Lots of armour, so much my house was shaking! Lorries came from Russia, stole our grain, stole lots of it. We didn't think anything like this would happen. They are like fascists, at four a.m.! Just like the Second World War, which started at four a.m.! Why are you killing us? I am Russian, my parents are Russian. I got married and left for here.'

'Who do you blame for this war?'

'I don't know much about politics.'

'What do you think of Vladimir Putin?'

'Fascist! Fascist!' Tatiana spits the words out. 'Why are you killing us? Why? We have buried so many. A woman goes to her garden, her husband follows her. We dig one grave for them both. People were living, working, giving birth to their kids. They even destroyed the school. So many people used to visit us. And what now? Nothing.'

As we finish, two Ukrainian soldiers approach us, asking for local paperwork to show we have permission to be here, at the front line. We don't have that paperwork and no one asked for it on our way here. Our fixer Dima begins to set out our defence. In the confusion, I palm Tatiana a little money. She says she never talked to us for money. I say yes, I know, but take it, and it's from Britain, where we don't have any money left anyway. She laughs, takes it and walks off, another hero of our time.

Andrei is the leader of the Ukrainian Army detachment in Dvorichna this evening. He is alarmed that we don't have the missing paperwork. I find it hard to repress my contempt for the bureaucracy of war. There is no power, no good internet in town, which makes proving our bona fides harder. While our fixer Dima plays diplomat and starts making calls, Julia and I go into the basement of the town hall and film an interview with the mayor, Halyna Turbaba. She is an elegant woman in her mid-fifties, exuding an exhausted civility. She speaks in Ukrainian mostly, but sometimes says something in beautifully enunciated English.

'When were you arrested?'

'On May 11th. I was in my office. They disappeared me. For a long time my relatives didn't know where I was.'

'How many prisoners were there?'

'In our cell the numbers changed all the time. At the start, two to three people. We could hear others. We heard people talking, people being beaten up, people scream.'

'Were you physically tortured yourself?'

'No. Only psychologically. They said if I had been younger, they would rape me. Threats against my family, but no physical torture.'

'You were in a cell for women only?'

'Women only. But we heard men screaming.'

'Who made those threats? Were you able to see your tormentors?'

'Sometimes I could see, sometimes not. They didn't tell their names, nothing about them.'

'Were they local or were they Russian?'

'I don't know.'

'Did they speak with the local or a Russian accent?'

'Both. I heard Russian accents and some people were from Lugansk or Donetsk, counties or oblasts occupied by the Russians since 2014. Some Ukrainians from these counties are with the Russians.'

'How did you cope with the pressure?'

'It's difficult to recollect those days. I didn't know anything about how my relatives were doing.'

Halyna is unmarried and has no children but her mother is eighty-seven, and she has a sister, nieces and nephews: 'They live in Dvorichna. I was scared because I didn't know how they were doing.' That said, Halyna's moral strength shines through: 'I didn't want to work with them, to collaborate. The only thought I had was to survive and come back to work with my people on my land.' She still has nightmares, hearing the screams. She spent eighty days in captivity in two chunks. The food was dire: 'Even my dog doesn't eat food like that.'

'Was there ever a moment when you felt like doing what they wanted you to do?'

'No. Not once.'

A big bang, incoming, scarily close.

'Ours or theirs?'

'I think it's ours. We are tired of it. Everyday.'

'How many people have died in your town?'

'We don't know the exact number of people. Many houses have been ruined, schools, hospitals, roads.'

'Can you ever forgive Russian people for doing this to you?'

'No.'

Time to go because we have to return to Kharkiv before

10 p.m. when curfew makes travelling on roads far more dangerous. Andrei, the soldier, is not happy with who we say we are, so we can't leave for another two hours. Dima then comes up trumps and as we are about to leave Andrei tells me he has looked me up on Google and that I am cool, and can we have a selfie? We do the selfie.

On the road back, we're in a hurry. There's a lot of dust, some mist, and suddenly a great concrete block in the middle of the road. Dima veers sharply and we miss it by an inch, less. Had we hit it, the car would have barrelled, over and again.

Fortunes of war, and all that.

Chapter Twenty-Four

Dead Tsar Walking

An old, mad, blind, despised and dying tsar, Vladimir Putin turned seventy on 7 October 2022, but his brutal war against Ukraine is exploding in his puffy, currants-in-dough, steroid-addled face. Cargo 200s – Sov slang for soldier corpses – are piling up; surviving troops voting with their feet; draftees running for the border; their mothers and wives hitting the streets in protest. You might wager a fiver on Putin making it to seventy-one, I wouldn't bet on it.

How on earth could the man who, on 23 February 2022, stood proud as the ruler of the world's biggest country, armed with the biggest nuclear arsenal, owning immeasurable treasure in oil and gas, whose trophies include Cold War Two victories such as the election of Donald Trump and Brexit, have messed up so badly?

The best, least bad answer is that Putin lives inside a zombie fairy tale, an alternative living-dead fantasy land where the Soviet Union was a great power brought down by Western spies and domestic traitors. His mission is to avenge that reversal, to save the Russian world and return it to its rightful majesty, force ungrateful Ukraine onto its knees, witness the West's timid and corrupt leaders bow before his throne. Putin is losing his grip on power, then, because he has no clear idea how the world, Ukraine, the war he started and his own country and army, work in the twenty-first century.

Russia's tragedy is that Putin has ordered all its truth-tellers to be poisoned, shot, eased out of a window, or tripped down the stairs – or they are in a dungeon or have fled the country. In the early 2000s the brave journalist Anna Politkovskaya warned that Putin was zombifying Russia. She was poisoned, survived, then murdered. He succeeded. There is hardly anyone left in Russia, and no one in the Kremlin, with the courage to tell him that the Soviet zombie fairy doesn't exist and won't return, that (virtually) everyone in Ukraine would rather die than be ruled by the Kremlin, that the West's leaders are not going to bow before him, that his army is rotten at the core, that he's losing his stupid war. That he is a dead tsar walking.

That being said, the grim question is how many more people will die before he falls? A hundred thousand? A million? A billion? All life on earth?

There is no doubt Russia is losing the war. Two great battles have been lost – the first the battle of Kyiv in spring 2022, the second Kharkiv Oblast in the autumn – with a third defeat looming in Kherson in the south. So what does the zombie tsar do when faced with defeat after defeat? He doubles down, drafting the poor but not the rich and threatening the West with the end of times.

In Samarkand, at a meeting of TyrantsRUs on 15 September 2022, Putin, who has been hinting at nuclear Armageddon, accused the West of doing what he's been doing: 'Nuclear blackmail also came into play. We are talking not only about the shelling of the Zaporizhzhia nuclear power plant, encouraged by the West, which threatens a nuclear catastrophe ...'

Yet the Russian Army shelled the power plant. One rocket that didn't go off clearly showed its trajectory from the way its tail-fin had got buried in the earth. It had come from Russian-occupied Ukraine.

'But also,' he continued, 'about the statements of some high-ranking representatives of the leading NATO states about the possibility and admissibility of using weapons of mass destruction, nuclear weapons against Russia.' No Western leader has done or said that.

Is Putin bluffing? Will he or won't he nuke us all? It's not impossible, but it's unlikely, for five reasons: First, Russia is bang next door to Ukraine, so when the wind blows the wrong way he will have irradiated southern Russia too. Second, China needs the West to buy its stuff and a nuke would destroy the European economy; on nukes, China is on our side and Putin fears antagonizing his most powerful ally. Third, Putin is not suicidal. Fourth, if he is, then Russia will be hit with a Western firestorm – conventional weapons, not nukes, but enough to fry the Russian Army in Ukraine and the Russian Navy in the Black Sea. Fifth, if Putin does hit the red button, he'll discover that someone inside the Kremlin has disconnected the machinery of Armageddon. Still, I can't rule out the nuke possibility and I've met people inside Ukrainian intelligence who say it's 'highly likely'. Note this was the official line from the deputy head of Ukrainian military intelligence, who then asked for more weapons in his next breath.

To register his hatred of losing, Putin will do his utmost to make Ukraine as hard to live in as possible. Hence the steady degradation of its power supply, itself a war crime. The latest doom-think is that Putin will blow up the mighty Nova Kakhovka dam near Kherson, unleashing a man-made tsunami. This would further degrade the electricity supply, flood a great area including Kherson, drown thousands, cut the main freshwater supply to Crimea, signalling the Russians' plan to give up their prize annexation from 2014, and strip the Zaporizhzhia nuclear power plant of its water supply to cool the reactor. While I am an optimist about non-use of a nuke, I'm a pessimist on the dam. I think it highly likely he will blow it up, judging that the West will angst but not retaliate. Any non-nuclear degrading of Ukraine's quality of life is very much on the Kremlin's wish-list. The Chinese won't mind. The West won't fight. But the cost in Ukrainian blood and resources will be dire. I hope I'm wrong.

The first draft of Putin's zombie fairy tale was written by Hitler and Stalin in August 1939. They drew up a new map, splitting the eastern half of Europe between them. Putin likes that map and, more or less, wants it back. But with deadly, almost carnal passion, he absolutely wants the map of the Soviet Union of 1989 back, with Ukraine subject to the Kremlin's whims, a vassal region, not a nation.

Putin has never understood why the Soviet Union imploded. It was not stabbed in the back but collapsed because of its own internal contradictions. The Soviet invasion of Afghanistan in 1979 was a disaster for both sides. Roughly 15,000 Russian soldiers died. The Ukrainians believe that 75,000 Russian soldiers have died in the war of 2022. That's five times as many Cargo 200s as Leonid Brezhnev deployed. The 1979 catastrophe happened because, although Brezhnev's generals knew it would be a mistake, no one in the Kremlin dared tell the boss that. Same old, same old. The Soviet Union also collapsed because, despite Gorbachev's attempts at reform, *perestroika*, it could not fund itself. Its economy was broken, incapable of keeping pace with the West let alone overtaking it.

So what we are seeing right now is the last spasms of the Soviet Man, a zombie created by Lenin, Stalin and Brezhnev. Their heir, Putin, doesn't tell the truth about the world or Russia, and its economy can no longer fund his ambition, let alone his war. No one in the Kremlin dare tell him that. But the Ukrainian people are suppling a serious reality check. Outgunned, outnumbered, overrun at the start of Putin's big war in February 2022, the Ukraine, more or less, tells the truth about the world and itself. Its forces withdrew, retreated, waited for the Russian Army to over-extend itself, and then pounced on its too lengthy, too feebly defended supply lines. The Ukrainians are brave and good soldiers. The British, led by Defence Secretary Ben Wallace, got it first, sending loads of NLAWs (New Light Anti-Tank Weapons), which stopped the Russian tanks dead. The Americans, who habitually turn up late for wars, are beginning to supply the Ukrainians with the heavy metal they need to defeat Putin's killing machine.

Wars are lost or won by possession of three keys: morale, logistics, leadership. The Ukrainian fighting spirit is extraordinary. I have been a war reporter since 1988 and I have never seen an army with such a belief in itself as the Ukrainian one. By contrast, the Russian fighting spirit is dire. Some Russian soldiers steal washing machines, or electric kettles without bases, so ignorant are they of modern domestic appliances. Some do unspeakable things, raping Ukrainian women, castrating captured Ukrainian soldiers. Some Russian Army soldiers rape their fellow soldiers. The Ukrainian counter-offensive in the east hoovered up a lot of booty, abandoned by the retreating army, and its paperwork. One grimly fascinating document was a petition from the wives and mothers of soldiers in the 1st Army Corps of the Donetsk People's Republic from Dokuchayevsk, complaining that soldiers loyal to the Chechen quisling Ramzan Kadyrov raped two of their men in Berestovoye. This complete lack of military discipline, never mind common humanity, is not the sign of a winning army. Some abandon their dead, and armies that do that tend to lose. This is partly because most of Putin's cannon fodder doesn't come from Moscow and St Petersburg but from the sticks, Muslims from Chechnya and Dagestan, Buddhists from Buryat in the far east of Siberia. Don't think of a unified army. Think of gangs of mobsters armed with tanks, vaguely allied to each other. They have such little common cause, apart from their semi-feudal overlords' semi-fealty to Putin, that they can't be bothered burying the dead of the other gangs.

True, Ukrainian logistics were poor at the start of the war. Now the Americans are sending the Ukrainians HIMARS, multiple rocket lanchers that have blown up most Russian ammo dumps in occupied Ukraine. Ukrainian soldiers are getting good US intelligence, Australian armoured cars, Dutch self-propelled artillery, fancy French and German guns, British training, Baltic everything. Russia is sending its fresh draft of conscripts into battle with rusty AK-47s manufactured before they were born. Their logistics are dire and getting worse.

Ukraine's top generals are seriously good. This summer they proclaimed they would attack on the Kherson front in the south. They sucked in 20,000 of Russia's best soldiers from the eastern, Kharkiv front, then socked the Russians in the east, reclaiming a vast swathe of territory and abandoned weaponry. Putin is, according to the *New York Times*, personally taking charge of tactical decision-making. Once again, his grip on reality is weak, getting weaker daily. A commander-in-chief who lives inside a palace like a tomb, surrounded by yes-men, believing in a zombie fairy story, cannot be a good military leader. The Ukrainians have all three keys essential for victory; Putin, none.

I have been in the Kremlin once, in 2006 for the BBC's *Panorama*, when I challenged Putin's press officer, Dmitry Peskov, about the poisoning of former KGB spy Alexander Litvinenko by polonium-210. Litvinenko had blogged in 2006 that Putin was a paedophile, after the Russian President had stopped his motorcade and knelt before a small blond five-year-old boy, lifted his T-shirt and kissed his tummy. It was weird and peculiar and it's on YouTube. I asked Peskov whether Putin was a paedophile. He said no and didn't care for the question. But it is beyond doubt that Litvinenko was poisoned by polonium-210 manufactured and delivered by the Russian secret state. About that, Peskov lied unctuously. He then went on to hint, creepily, that Marina Litvinenko had better watch out lest someone in Britain, maybe MI5, maybe Boris Berezovsky – who was still alive back then – might poison her too.

Reflecting now on Peskov's deceit back then, if you sit inside the Kremlin's lie factory, pumping out fabrications daily, how can you know what is true and what is false? At what point do you stop lying and confront reality? The answer is when the Ukrainian Army knocks the Russian Army flat, again and again, such that lying on an industrial scale no longer cuts the mustard. Not tomorrow or the next day, but Putin's downfall moment will happen some day soon.

The other sharks in the sea of tyranny can scent blood. The world's top four autocrats, Vladimir Putin, President Xi of China, President Erdogan of Turkey and Prime Minister Modi of India, hobnobbed in Samarkand. Erdogan was openly contemptuous of Putin's failing war, Modi impatient with the Kremlin, and even Xi reportedly gave Putin short shrift. Chinese and Russian strategic interests are at loggerheads. Putin's goal is to divide and demoralize the West. The Chinese Communist Party hates Western freedom with a passion but wants us to buy their stuff. China wants American and European economies to prosper, not break down; Russia desires the opposite. China may have put up with a short three-day war for Russia to capture Kyiv and decapitate Ukrainian democracy. But a long war? One which a fellow autocrat is losing badly? That was not what the Kremlin had promised.

Putin is, then, a fragile monster. Let's consider the poet Shelley's description of George III, as applied to the Russian leader: old, mad, blind, despised, and dying.

Old? Definitely. Gone are the days when, topless, Putin sat astride a horse, fished for carp or swam the butterfly in a freezing Siberian lake. The funny peculiar homoeroticism of these images produced by the Kremlin's lie factory aside, that was then. Just before the full-scale invasion of Ukraine, Putin couldn't bear to breathe in the same oxygen as the President of France. The Kremlin's serfs set an extraordinarily long table between the two, 'the distance', as Ukraine's great psychiatrist Semyon Gluzman told me, 'between Putin and his death'. As the war began to come unstuck and the Russian killing machine left the battle of Kyiv, tail between its legs, Putin met his defence minister, Sergei Shoigu, once a jobbing builder, never a soldier. What was striking was the death grip Putin used to grasp the table between the two, the hallmark of an old man, afraid of a fall. By contrast, when Putin dropped in on the ayatollahs in Tehran on 19 July, he bounded energetically down the steps of his plane, leading many commentators to wonder aloud whether the man in Iran wasn't the real Putin but a double. I wonder about that too. Elderly dictators are sometimes better than young ones. They tend to spill less blood. Not this one. The many people in the Kremlin and thereabouts who have good reason to hate Putin – the generals mocked for their failure to win an unwinnable war they were never properly consulted about, the oligarchs who have seen billions of dollars go up in smoke, the Russian elites who know they will live in shame for decades to come – note his age. And that is not good news for Putin.

Mad? Putin is not clinically mad, as psychiatrists Semyon Gluzman – who spent ten years in a KGB gulag – and Jim Fallon, professor at the University of California, have told me. He doesn't hear voices or see hallucinations. But mad in the ordinary sense of the word? Well, hell yes. He launched a war against a country at peace, proclaiming a senseless *casus belli*. He was so paranoid about preserving secrecy that many of the serious planners in the Russian Army had no idea the big war was imminent. Without proper planning, there can be no effective co-ordination between infantry, artillery, special forces, air force, air defence and boring old logistics. The Ukrainian Army is now the best in the world at this game; the Russian Army's reputation is sinking daily. But the one person directly responsible for this catastrophic failure of military co-ordination is the commander-in-chief, who, of course, can't be blamed by anyone for anything. That is systemic madness overlaid onto personal madness – again, in the ordinary, layman's understanding of the word.

Blind? Not in the medical sense of course, but as a metaphor for his failure to understand today's world, Putin is blind to reality. I've only met him once, when I challenged him in Siberia about the shooting down of MH17 in 2014. Back then, he was supple and wily and street-smart enough to read the room, to know that the optics of turning his back on a BBC reporter asking tough questions about the killing of 298 people on a passenger jet would look bad. He didn't answer my question but blocked out enough time in Russian, blaming the Ukrainians, appearing to behave like a politician in a democracy.

Since then his carapace has cemented. The suppleness has gone. In its stead is a rigid belief in some kind of imperial Russia, and that anyone who disagrees with him is by definition a Nazi. COVID made everything worse. He lived down the end of a very long decontamination tunnel. So not literally blind, no, but as blind as a creature, a mole or worm, who lives without light, without fresh air.

Despised? Take that as a given in Ukraine. But how is Putin viewed in Russia? I don't take opinion polls seriously in a country where everyone knows that challenging the Kremlin will not be good for you. On 25 September 2022 the Russian performance poet Artem Kamardin appeared in an event in Moscow opposing the draft, with his girlfriend Alexandra Popova. Artem declaimed: 'Glory to Kyivan Rus – Novorossiya can suck it.' Kyivan Rus is the founding civilization of the Slavic world, the point being it was created in Kyiv a millennium ago. Moscow – Novorossiya – was established centuries later. The police arrested Artem and Alexandra. The next day Artem told the Kremlin's patsy media that he was wrong to say what he did. His face was cut and bruised. Alexandra told reporters that the police had pulled her hair so that chunks came out, tried to seal her lips and mouth with superglue while her hands were handcuffed, threatened to rape her, and showed her a video of them raping Artem by shoving a dumbbell up his anus. When Western politicians, journalists and armchair generals suggest the best way to end the crisis is to offer Putin an opportunity to save face, I want to ask them if they would like a dumbbell up their bottom? That said, in Russia, to date, fear of Putin outweighs hate. Yet hatred of the draft is changing that calculation by the second.

Dying? Once again, the absence of truth-tellers – poisoned, shot, fallen from high windows – makes determining the true health of the zombie tsar difficult. But not impossible. People inside the Kremlin know that time is not on Putin's side.

I popped up recently on ITV's *Good Morning Britain* with Ed Balls – Labour's former Shadow Chancellor – as one of the hosts. I said Putin is losing the war, he's a dead man walking. Ed is a gracious human being who left politics to make space for his partner, Yvette Cooper, and started a new career. He asked how Putin could be allowed to 'save face'. I bristled and said there was no way Putin could have a new career hosting a TV show, because 'he has stolen too much money and killed too many people'. I predicted that the only option for him was to leave the Kremlin in a box. Ed looked aggrieved, upset. I get it that he comes from decent parliamentary politics where the be-all and end-all is to resolve arguments through deals and accommodations. But Putin doesn't play that game. Nothing like it.

Ed then worried aloud about the prospect of nuclear war. Again, I don't think Putin is going to go there for the reasons I gave. Secondly, there is a grave downside to the near-universal draft he has called for, six months after launching his big war. The real danger for him is that he will drive his surly, unhappy people from mute acquiescence to open revolt. You don't risk that massive unpopularity if you are going to blow up the planet. Why bother risk losing your grip on power by a nationwide call-up if you are intent on Armageddon?

He's bluffing. His hand is rubbish. As noted, the Ukrainians have three aces: morale, logistics, leadership. The West needs to keep on supplying them with the heavy metal. The good news is that the Americans have just announced they are going to send double the number of HIMARS, multiple rocket launchers, to Ukraine that they have already sent. It's sometimes nice when the CIA agrees with your analysis. I would only add that the agency costs American taxpayers $15 billion a year and the cost of this book is so much cheaper.

Comedy aside, the war is not over. Vladimir Putin's killing machine will harm many thousands of innocent lives before the job is done. But one day, soon, Putin will exit the Kremlin.

In a box.

Acknowledgements

This book has been twenty-two years in the making so there are a ton of people who helped me understand Vladimir Putin who may not find their names here. But thank you.

Back in 2000 I went undercover to Chechnya for my old paper *The Observer* and Channel 4's Dispatches with the late James Miller and Carla Garapedian, while David Henshaw of Hard Cash Productions held the fort back in London. I must thank our Chechen team anonymously and all the brave Chechens who spoke to me for our film and my later BBC radio documentary about the Russian Army's use of torture.

I gravitated to the BBC, where I worked on a series of radio and TV documentary films about Russia, many for Panorama and Newsnight. At the same time, the Russian secret state used proxies to try and shut honest reporters up. Good people, some of them politicians, sat up and took notice. And then there were brave Russians and others who dared to speak out on the BBC and on my crowdfunded podcast, 'Taking On Putin', and especially for this book. In alphabetical order: Roman Badanin, Darius Barzagan, Chris Baughen, Catherine Belton, Roman Borisovich, Oliver Bullough, Tom Burgis, Liam Byrne MP, Jonathan Coffey, David Davis MP, Professor Norman Dombey,

Arthur Doohan, Professor Jim Fallon, Tom Giles, Steve Grandison, Professor Ashley Grossman, Andrew Head, Paul Joyal, Peter Jukes, Dan Kaszeta, Sergei Lebedev, Marina Litvinenko, Jenny Klochko, Seamas McCracken, the late Boris Nemtsov, Tomiko Newson, Nataliya Pelevina, the late Anna Politkovskaya, Professor Donald Rayfield, the Dean and staff of Salisbury Cathedral, Bob Seely MP, Arthur Snell, Nick Sturdee, Ceri Thomas, Tom Tugendhat MP, Zarina Zabrisky. At Chalk & Blade, thanks to the wonderful Laura Sheeter, Ruth Barnes and Jason Phipps.

Thanks to Jeremy and Margaret and Alessio and Jason for looking after Bertie.

The opening chapter of this book contains writing which originally appeared in the *Jewish Chronicle, New Lines Magazine* and *Index on Censorship.* Thanks to Ben Felsenburg and Martin Bright. I paid some of my way by TV and radio spots on Good Morning Britain, BBC Scotland, Wales and Northern Ireland and LBC. Thanks to all there.

When I arrived in Kyiv I had no backers and then two sweet things happened. I started up a Patreon thingy and I now have two thousand patrons. Thanks to one and all. Secondly, I crowdfunded my 'Taking On Putin' podcast, so thanks to everyone who has supported that too.

In Kyiv and Ukraine the following cheered me up in the dark times: the world's greatest fixer, Yevhenii 'Eugene' Yermolenko, and Vladyslav Shvets who, in his dodgy Skoda, got me inside the bombed Kyiv TV Tower complex before the pack, stand out for their humour under fire. I went to Kyiv in mid-February with the great Oz Katerji, got a ride on the back of Emile Ghessen's scooter just before curfew, drank with Iain Burns, Johnny Mercer MP and Lev Wood and danced on the tables of the Buena Vista, watched over by Maks Lenov and Dasha. Mariana Shostak at Bassano is the best war zone cook, in the whole world. Rost Belinskyi showed me the blood on the snow after the Kyiv TV Tower missile strike. When the war is over, I'm going up in his hot-air balloon. For their courage and humour, thanks to Lyudmila Buymister MP, Paul Conroy, Tomas Davidov, James Gregson, Liam Kennedy, Kristina Ratushnaya, the staff, clown and patients at Kyiv Children's Hospital, the staff and elephant at Kyiv Zoo, Vaughan Smith, Matej Šulc. In Bucha, thanks to Alex Kazletsky, Giuseppe Attard and Neil Camilleri. In Borodyanka and from New York, thanks to Michael Weiss.

Humfrey Hunter, my agent, Henry Vines, my publisher, and Jack Beattie, my audiobook producer, have been indefatigable.

My family, Sam, Lou, Shilah, Molly, tolerated my foolishness with love.

I must thank the ordinary, extraordinary people of Ukraine, but three in particular stand out. Vlad Demchenko arrested me as a Russian spy on day two of the war. Once we sorted that out we became friends and I salute his courage for fighting for his country and the free world. Semyon Gluzman, President of the Ukrainian Psychiatric Association, is endlessly wise and fascinating about the KGB mindset and, once again, I apologize for locking him up in the broom cupboard.

Lastly, I must thank Liza Kozlenko, journalist, producer, axe-wielder. Vladimir Putin's war is stupid and cruel but it proves the old truth, that the worst of times brings out the best in people.

Notes on Sources

Chapter One: The Killing Machine

Some of the writing in this chapter originally appeared in the *Jewish Chronicle*, London, *Index on Censorship*, London, and *New Lines Magazine*, Washington DC.

Chapter Two: Rat Boy

Bastard

https://www.zeit.de/feature/vladimir-putin-mother https://www.telegraph.co.uk/news/worldnews/europe/russia/3568891/Could-this-woman-be-Vladimir-Putins-real-mother.html

Yuri Felshtinsky and Vladimir Pribylovsky, *The Age of Assassins: The Rise and Rise of Vladimir Putin*, Gibson Square Books, London 2008, pp. 116–21

Donald Rayfield, 'Taking On Putin' podcast

Vera Dmitrievna Gurevich, schoolteacher

First Person: An Astonishingly Frank Self-Portrait by Russia's President, Public Affairs, 2000

Rat hunting

First Person, ibid.

Chapter Three: Once and Future Spy

Dresden
https://www.washingtonpost.com/wp-srv/inatl/longterm/russiagov/putin.htm
https://www.dw.com/en/who-is-nord-streams-matthias-warnig-putins-friend-from-east-germany/a-56328159

St Petersburg
Masha Gessen, *The Man without a Face: The Unlikely Rise of Vladimir Putin,* New York, 2012

Kremlin corruption
https://www.theguardian.com/world/2000/jan/28/russia.iantraynor

Skuratov
https://bylinetimes.com/2022/03/15/lebedev-the-kgb-spy-who-helped-put-putin-in-the-kremlin

Lebedevs
Jacopo Iacoboni and Gianluca Paolucci, *Oligarchi*, Rome, 2012.

Chapter Four: A Bomb Made of Sugar

Ryazan
John Sweeney, *The Observer*, 12 March 2000 https://www.theguardian.com/world/2000/mar/12/chechnya.johnsweeney
John Sweeney, Cryptome, 24 November 2000
https://cryptome.org/putin-bomb5.htm

Chapter Five: War Without Pity

Blowing Up Russia
Alexander Litvinenko and Yuri Felshtinsky, *Blowing Up Russia: Terror from Within*, London 2002
David Satter, *Darkness at Dawn: The Rise of the Russian Criminal State*, New Haven, 2004

David Satter, *The Less You Know, The Better You Sleep: Russia's Road to Terror and Dictatorship under Yeltsin and Putin*, New Haven, 2016.

Chechnya

Astolphe de Custine, *Empire of the Czar: A Journey Through Eternal Russia*, New York, 1989

John Sweeney, https://www.theguardian.com/world/2000/mar/05/russia.chechnya

'Dying for the President', *Dispatches*, Hard Cash, March 2000

John Sweeney, *Victims of the Torture Train*, BBC Radio 5, 2000

Chapter Six: The Poisonings Begin

Sobchak

Gabriel Gatehouse, BBC, 'The Day Putin Cried':

https://www.bbc.com/news/stories-43260651

Arkady Vaksberg, *Toxic Politics: The Secret History of the Kremlin's Poison Laboratory from the Special Cabinet to the Death of Litvinenko*

Moscow Theatre Siege

Alexander Goldfarb and Marina Litvinenko, *Death of a Dissident: The Poisoning of Alexander Litvinenko and the Return of the KGB*, Santa Barbara, 2011

Radio Free Europe: https://www.rferl.org/a/1342330.html

Shchekochikhin

'Taking On Putin' podcast

Vaksberg, ibid.

Chapter Seven: A Death of No Significance

Politkovskaya in Chechnya

Anna Politkovskaya, *A Small Corner of Hell: Dispatches from Chechnya*, Chicago, 2007

Beslan
https://www.theguardian.com/world/2004/sep/09/russia.media
David Satter, https://www.hudson.org/research/4306-the-aftermath-of-beslan

Putin
Anna Politkovskaya, *Putin's Russia: Am I Afraid*, New York, 2004

Chapter Eight: One Lump or Two?

Litvinenko
Sir Robert Owen's report into Litvinenko's death: https://assets.publishing.service.gov.uk/government/uploads/system/uploads/attachment_data/file/493860/The-Litvinenko-Inquiry-H-C-695-web.pdf
Alexander Goldfarb and Marina Litvinenko, *Death of a Dissident: The Poisoning of Alexander Litvinenko and the Return of the KGB*, London, 2012
Norman Dombey, *London Review of Books*, 'Poison and The Bomb', https://www.lrb.co.uk/the-paper/v40/n24/norman-dombey/poison-and-the-bomb
BBC Panorama, 'How to Poison a Spy' http://news.bbc.co.uk/2/hi/programmes/panorama/6294771.stm

Chapter Nine: Russia's Greatest Love Machine

Putin's private life, cult of personality
'Taking On Putin' podcast
Proekt investigative website, https://www.proekt.media/en/home
'I want a man like Vladimir Putin' song, https://www.youtube.com/watch?v=zk_VszbZa_s
https://www.wsj.com/articles/u-s-withholds-sanctions-on-a-very-close-putin-associate-his-alleged-girlfriend-11650816894?mod=e2tw

Chapter Ten: Mr Pleonexia

Khodorkovsky

https://www.vanityfair.com/news/politics/2012/04/vladimir-putin-mikhail-khodorkovsky-russia

https://khodorkovsky.com/ten-years-ago-today-khodorkovsky-dared-to-challenge-putin-on-corruption

https://www.dailymail.co.uk/news/article-5495003/British-boss-oil-firm-killed-Russians-friend-claims.html

Deripaska

https://www.youtube.com/watch?v=48Kk7kobMQY

Masha Gessen: *The Man without a Face: The Unlikely Rise of Vladimir Putin*, London, 2012

https://www.youtube.com/watch?v=ziKUzn-5UcU

https://edition.cnn.com/videos/politics/2017/11/10/deripaska-fake-news-chance-sot.cnn

Chapter Eleven: 'So, sir, do you regret the killings in Ukraine, sir?'

BBC Panorama, 'Putin's Gamble' https://www.youtube.com/watch?v=kOk1OGbECyo

Chapter Twelve: The Leader of the Opposition Has Been Shot

Nemtsov

https://www.lrb.co.uk/the-paper/v37/n06/keith-gessen/remembering-boris-nemtsov https://www.independent.co.uk/news/world/europe/winter-olympics-2014-welcome-to-sochi-a-city-where-there-are-no-gay-people-9086424.html

Dugin

BBC Panorama, 'The Kremlin's Candidate?': It is no longer up on the BBC website, but you can find it here: https://eastbook.eu/2017/02/06/aleksander-dugin-eurazjatycki-glos-w-twoim-domu

Chapter Thirteen: Taking On Putin

BBC Panorama, 'Taking On Putin'
https://www.reddit.com/r/Documentaries/comments/84jpqq/bbc_panorama_taking_on_putin_what_life_is_like

Chapter Fourteen: The View from the Spire

Poisoners
https://www.youtube.com/watch?v=Ku8OQNyI2i0
https://www.thesun.co.uk/news/7268509/salisbury-russia-poisoning-drugs-sex-prostitutes-london
https://www.rferl.org/a/novichok-suspects-gay-or-not-russian-state-media-bashirov/29490426.html

Putin's reaction
https://www.youtube.com/watch?v=Wvbc4vG7Ppw

Russian disinformation
https://www.kcl.ac.uk/policy-institute/assets/weaponising-news.pdf

Bellingcat
https://www.bellingcat.com/resources/podcasts/2020/06/16/bellingchat-episode-3-hunting-the-the-salisbury-poisonings-suspects
https://www.bellingcat.com/news/uk-and-europe/2020/09/04/gebrev-survives-poisonings-post-mortem

Chapter Fifteen: A War We Don't Know We Are Fighting

Chris Donnelly
'Taking On Putin' podcast

Chapter Sixteen: The Kremlin Candidate?

Donald Trump
https://www.youtube.com/watch?v=-k3B-tw2sB0

https://www.bbc.co.uk/news/uk-23152829
https://www.nytimes.com/2018/11/29/us/politics/trump-russia-felix-sater-michael-cohen.html
Russian embassy statement on 'Trump: The Kremlin Candidate?'
https://rusemb.org.uk/fnapr/5941

Mifsud
https://www.bbc.co.uk/news/world-us-canada-43488581

Chapter Seventeen: Useful Idiots

Vanessa Redgrave
https://www.theguardian.com/uk/2000/apr/09/johnsweeney.theobserver

Seumas Milne
https://www.newstatesman.com/politics/2016/04/the-thin-controller

Evgeny and Alexander Lebedev
https://www.bbc.co.uk/news/world-europe-20030346
https://bylinetimes.com/2020/08/20/sweeney-investigates-what-changed-to-make-evgeny-lebedev-no-longer-a-security-risk
https://bylinetimes.com/2022/03/15/lebedev-the-kgb-spy-who-helped-put-putin-in-the-kremlin

Boris Johnson
https://www.opendemocracy.net/en/opendemocracyuk/revealed-boris-russian-oligarch-and-page-3-model

Nigel Farage
https://www.telegraph.co.uk/news/2017/09/19/bbcs-slur-has-caused-family-misery/
https://www.youtube.com/watch?v=x8CSVCAIayc

Arron Banks
https://www.dailymail.co.uk/news/article-6374471/Arron-Banks-Russian-wife-entranced-husband-getting-rub-BUTTER-her.html
https://www.bbc.co.uk/news/uk-41740237
https://www.bbc.co.uk/news/uk-46460194

Chapter Eighteen: The Underpants Poisoner

https://www.bellingcat.com/news/uk-and-europe/2020/12/14/fsb-team-of-chemical-weapon-experts-implicated-in-alexey-navalny-novichok-poisoning
https://www.youtube.com/watch?v=T_tFSWZXKN0
https://www.bbc.co.uk/programmes/m0016txs

Chapter Nineteen: The Kremlin Patient

https://newlinesmag.com/reportage/is-putin-sick-or-are-we-meant-to-think-he-is

Chapter Twenty: This Ends in Blood

https://www.newyorker.com/news/annals-of-communications/inside-putins-propaganda-machine
https://www.proekt.media/en/investigation-en/putin-health

Chapter Twenty-One: Metal Fatigue

Roman Ratushnyi
https://www.ft.com/content/fe988de0-c2a0-4731-811d-7ec822434f21
https://glavcom.ua/kyiv/news/oprilyudneno-zapis-pogroz-zastupnika-golovi-ofisu-prezidenta-zahisniku-protasovogo-yaru-639201.html?1573482767

About the Author

John Sweeney is a writer and journalist who, while working for the BBC, has challenged dictators, despots, cult leaders, con artists and crooked businessmen for many years. As a reporter, first for the *Observer* and then for the BBC, Sweeney has covered wars and chaos in more than eighty countries and been undercover to a number of tyrannies, including Chechnya, North Korea and Zimbabwe. Over the course of his career, John has won an Emmy, two Royal Television Society Awards, a Sony Gold Award, a What the Papers Say Journalist of the Year Award, an Amnesty International Award and the Paul Foot Award.